Chapter 1

It was Friday 14th March 2014. Luke Inigo Trevelyan decided to get up very early that morning, and went into work before anyone had turned up. His architectural office, which he had only been with for a month-and-a-half, was situated in a leafy small town called Dorridge. He noticed as he entered the office that a lone umbrella, with what seemed to Luke like a particularly sharp tipped skewer, was resting ominously by the office main entrance door. He had never noticed this ordinary everyday object before in this location. Feeling decidedly tense and sweaty, Luke had the definite belief that someone in the office was intent on seeing him dead.

Within the last week, he had been mulling over why Benjamin, a handsome black man, had started to work at the office within such a short space of time of Luke commencing his post there. Benjamin had a powerful physique and a long standing relationship with one of the martial arts. He had recently been doing a lot of training in that field. Luke was sure Benjamin could do a lot of damage to someone, if he was threatened or if he was instructed to do so. A train of thought started to emerge in Luke's head that Benjamin had been recruited by MI5 to kill Luke off. He had confided in Luke that he had almost killed someone when working as a bouncer in Birmingham, after that individual had said he specifically wanted a fight with Benjamin.

Luke pondered over why the authorities saw him as such a threat, and he realised that his views were a little hostile to the Western mind-set's over-emphasis on materialism and consumption, as a path of progress. This Western culture's ideology, which had now become a global way of thinking, was based primarily on greed and the delusion that real happiness and peace can be found in external objects and things, rather than developing internally the workings of the mind and the heart.

Luke believed that the authorities could see he was a very able and capable individual, who had all the hallmarks of an inspiring and gifted leader. What also occurred to Luke was that he had released a video on youtube, about half a year previously, in which he had made a very bold and radical statement, suggesting that once he had transformed himself spiritually he would then transform the world out of compassion for all beings. These ideas circled around in Luke's mind like vultures around fresh carcasses, and started acquiring a new validity and power.

Once his computer was on and ready to use, Luke spontaneously looked up anything to do with Superman, to provide himself with some heroic inspiration for what was becoming a febrile, burgeoning imagination. With his heart thumping, and realising the enormous danger that he might be in, he clicked on a trailer for the most recent Superman film. It started with stirring classical music that immediately hooked Luke's emotions. There followed a scene with a number of noteworthy military officials all assembled in a very large hall in a secretive location. They sat in a large oval seating configuration, accompanied by a multitude of video and television display units. They all seemed to concur on the fundamental point that Superman posed a real and genuine threat to democracy and to their notion of peace in this world. According to them, his march of progress must be curtailed or else, in their collective view, there could be an Armageddon. Then followed some clips of Superman performing various heroic acts, and trying to save humanity as much as he could from the evil forces around him. They were just snapshot images, but they were enough to get Luke sucked in and enthralled by this tremendous vision. He felt he was in a similar position, and that a large proportion of the population would forever regard him with suspicion and extreme caution.

He looked at his clock: it was nearly 8:30am. He knew he had to leave as soon as possible, before meeting his boss or any of his other work colleagues that morning, otherwise his plan to 'abandon ship' might be scuppered and thrown into tatters. He thought he heard the sound of a car rolling up in the forecourt, and his heart started to pound faster than before. It could, however, be the other company's employer next to Brian Levison's office - he said this to himself as an act of mollification. He just required a little luck to be on his side today, but his nerves would not recede from their delicate state. Five minutes later, he was out the door. Luckily for Luke, the car in question had indeed been the one belonging to the neighbouring office.

As he strode purposefully along the high street to his car - parked at the other end of Dorridge – he felt a little exhilarated but also apprehensive of this new departure opening up in his life. However, a sense of liberation from the shackles of office life was slowly but gradually lifting his spirits to new heights. Experiencing a light breeze on his face, he appreciated the dappled light beneath the trees, where the sunlight was partially streaming through. Feeling now wonderfully alive - things appeared fresh to him. His nerves were beginning to find a natural equilibrium again, and his heart beat was also slowing down steadily. Fortune and luck were on his side, as he passed no-one on the street familiar to him. On his way back home, Luke did not predominantly drive at a reckless speed, as he was prone to do in the last few weeks, but every now and then, while he was listening to a few passionate rock tunes, he accelerated and drove with racing driver pretensions, tempered with an awareness of other motorists and pedestrians around him.

While on his drive back home, Luke received a call from his father asking how he was. In the back of his mind he was desperately hoping that his father would not ask the question about whether Luke was going to work because he seriously believed that he would find it too difficult to lie. Luke momentarily prayed that because he had answered the call in his car, it would not raise any suspicions or concerns with his father. Fortunately for Luke the call was a practical call, and they discontinued their conversation quickly.

Luke now felt more empowered by the trailer he had watched in the office that morning, and a thought had formed that he should make an immediate trip to the centre of London, where all the significant powers in politics and culture converged. For this brief foray into the thriving metropolis, he would dress up in the most flamboyant attire that he had in his possession. About a year and a half earlier he had bought some purple trousers at a well-known department store, and he had, on a number of occasions afterwards, paraded around town in them. He knew they were striking to people, as purple was not a colour men were normally comfortable wearing in public. He secretly felt that it caught the admiration of many a female passer-by. After making this purchase, he felt that a waistcoat would also be a good accessory. This article of clothing had been, in part, inspired by the sartorial presentation of a well-known comedian turned political activist, who Luke admired because of the comedian's audacity and some of the views he espoused.

Luke had found a wonderfully eccentric, light blue suede waistcoat in the large department store in Leamington, which was fast becoming his store of choice for any clothes. Although it was a very expensive garment he knew he had to possess it, otherwise he would regret it for a long time. When he had bought it he was aware of how perfectly it would go with his purple trousers and a stylish white shirt, which he had also recently purchased. Finally, there were the shoes. He realised that this item would either complete the visual spectacle or mar the beauty of the colourful ensemble. He found that expensive shoes from exclusive brands in his collection were very uncomfortable, as he had quite slender and flat feet. He had always appreciated the practical attributes of one of the more traditional high street brands. Some of the shoes in this store were becoming ever trendier in appearance. On a recent occasion, a couple of months previously, he had visited one of these stores with the intention to buy some light brown shoes. He spotted some sleek lightly tanned brown shoes with a lightweight but robust under-sole. They had a wonderful quality to them in that, when worn with most long trousers in his possession, the laces would not be visible and a large expanse of the front of the shoe with a rounded pointy front would be delightfully on show. Upon arrival at his flat, he wasted no time in undressing from his somewhat boring office attire, to don his piece de resistance in exuberant garb. Luke felt very safe and protected in his basement flat. First of all, he had some kind and courteous neighbours, whom he found friendly and amenable. The road, the flat was on, was quiet especially at night, and normally had very little passing traffic on it. The students who lived there in term-time were never any bother to him, and the station was conveniently only five minutes' walk away, but was far enough that Luke would rarely hear the sound of the trains shuttling across the tracks. He left his flat about ten minutes after he had arrived, and boarded the train bound for London.

As the train was pulling into Marylebone Station, Luke had gotten up out of his seat, before any of the other passengers had done so. He felt emboldened to be setting a precedent for others to follow his lead. Once through the ticket barriers he went straight for the Bakerloo line on the Underground.

Something curious happened to Luke, while standing in the tube on the Bakerloo line. He encountered a short black man, dressed in a smart suit. His snappy attire looked incongruous with his unshaven face. He came over to part of the carriage where Luke was standing, and started staring in short bursts at Luke. As a few more people entered the carriage from the Baker Street stop, Luke overheard him say in a relatively loud voice to a gentleman in a suit, who had just joined the tube:

"Someone needs to take out that cab driver. It has got to be only a matter of time." Feeling distinctly that this malignant wish was directed at him, due to interpreting the reference to the cab driver, as that of the psychopath from the well-known film 'Taxi driver', and thinking that the black man was basing his assumption about Luke on what he had seen on satellite television. After an initial jab to his guts from this incidence, the notion began to fester inside him, but he also felt certain that he would not be beaten. He was sure it would be only a matter of time before he was able to conquer many of his fears, and to transform them into a calmness and stillness.

Disembarking at Tottenham Court Road tube station, he ascended the staircase leading to the junction at the start of a busy Oxford Street and Tottenham Court Road. As he arrived at the top of the flight of stairs, he stopped for a good half-minute, and slowly surveyed all around him in a 360 degree arc. As everyone seemed to be in a hurry to get places, he tried to slow all his physical processes down, to go counter to the general hustle and bustle around him. He had started to let go of the black man's affront to him, and was slowly experiencing a glimmer of joy peeking through his hefty emotional disposition.

Earlier that day, while driving back from work, Luke had formed the plan to go to the British Museum, as he wanted to go to a part of London, which he was familiar with. On a number of other separate occasions, accompanied by a friend he had known at University, he had gone to the museum not only to get a flavour of the various exhibits on display, but also to appreciate both the historic and contemporary architecture that the museum had morphed into. There was one particular section that Luke was drawn to - and that was the Buddhist statuary.

On approaching the gates to the museum, he walked slowly and deliberately up to the monumentally sized colonnade at the museum entrance, and wasted no time in delaying his view of the Buddhist art, within the vast and beautiful splendour of this magnificent institution. It had been a while since he had last paid a visit to the museum, and he could not remember in which part of the building the statuary was situated. Somehow he was mysteriously drawn to the correct part of the museum, without having to study a map of the area. It was as if there was a magical force emanating from the room, which was delicately but assuredly pulling him in, on an unconscious level. It was as if a gossamer thread linked Luke to the Buddhas, who were lovingly reeling him in. His more sombre mood was now lifting to be supplanted by a joy and relish.

Amongst the sculptures on view, there were also some Hindu depictions of their gods, but at this juncture Luke had no time for the Hindu art, and he focussed primarily on the statues he had set his sights on. One figure really caught his eye. There was a slender but strong quality in its physique, combined with a refinement and beauty of the Buddha's expression, which grabbed his attention most. It was the figure Avolakiteshvara – the Lord of Compassion.

Finding a stone slab seat directly opposite, he sat down and gazed lovingly and intently at the beauty of this particular exhibit. For what seemed like ten minutes, Luke was rapt in the overall exquisiteness of this frozen triumphant display. What peace and contentment he was presently feeling. He knew that by the very action of remaining totally absorbed in this spectacle, he was causing heads to turn. He could not be sure of this, but he got an intuitive sense that this might be the case.

After his deep reverie and entrancement with the Buddha figure, he rose from his seat and sauntered fluidly around the rest of the Buddhist exhibits in the space. None of the others quite seized his attention as much. He then ventured out of the ornate, high ceilinged room to the main concourse area at the hub of the building, with its high tech glass vaulted canopy, which he knew was a design by a celebrated star-architect. At the time of its build, it was a stupendous engineering feat. Luke always marvelled at how some constructions managed to be built at all, with their complexity and their death defying motionless acrobatics. These amazing edifices were all predominantly a team effort, but the public would always associate the construction or building with the lead architect only. It was, however, so much more than that one individual, but people were always prone to label and categorise. Life was always simpler if people and objects could be pinpointed and defined, so as to obviate the need to delve deep into the complexity and wonder of things and beings.

Luke glided across the light buff coloured, stone flooring towards the exit. He then spotted an inviting stone seating slab near the exit to the museum, and nestled himself between a mother with her young baby boy and a medium-sized group of young girls, of what sounded like Italian nationality – (undoubtedly on a school trip!) From this commanding vantage point, he slowly took in the people around him. He had a niggling sense that some of the people in this vast internal space were not quite genuine. It seemed to him that the middle aged man on his own about five metres to the right of him looked suspicious. He kept darting glances in Luke's direction yet nevertheless discreetly. A few minutes later that individual greeted another man, of a similar age, with what Luke felt like was a fake welcoming greeting. The smiles, and what Luke could hear of their verbal exchange just did not seem authentic to his perceptive ear.

He then spotted a couple of older distinguished looking gentlemen in the middle of the concourse space, talking to each other. There was also something unnatural about their interaction, as they were intent to mill about in the same spot, and then, every now and then, they would shoot him furtive looks. He felt their deception to be real and palpable. For the period he was sitting on the slab, he experienced an overwhelming tightening of fear, which was compounded by his view that he was secretly known by so many people, and why the black man on the tube had made the comment he did. Although Luke had a deep primal fear that was now gripping his body, he reflected on what the Buddha had suggested in tackling the emotion of fear. The Buddha had said that one should just sit with the fear and try not to run from it, and continue with whatever one is currently doing – be it sitting, standing or walking. The fear will eventually pass and be transformed into calmness, stillness and joy. Luke possessed an underlying strength and resilience in the face of this nameless fear, and the Buddha's experience and wisdom provided him with a bone-deep solace.

While Luke scanned the concourse area, he spotted a woman, who struck him as being a highly competent type of worker, directly opposite him. It was not so much what she was wearing - namely a mustard-yellow shirt, not tucked into her trousers, and a pair of formal grey suit trousers – but her imperious look that led him to believe of her superior intelligence. She was looking around the space, until she clapped eyes on Luke, and looked at him with a serious and concerned expression etched on her face. This woman, he was convinced, was also part of the secret service world.

The party of school girls, who had been talking in fairly quiet tones, left, vacating their seats. This left Luke's right side exposed. He took this as a natural cue for him to exit the museum. The fear was still with him, and his nerves were really being put to the test, but he knew he just had to be patient, and all would be well.

As he descended the grand staircase and made a slow path towards the main gates, he decided to pause yet again, and rested his body against the stone walls demarcating the grass lawn at the front of the grounds from the museum's main outdoor thoroughfare. He waited in this location for a short while. Luke was intent on taking his time milling in this spot, and observing the large assortment of mutedly dressed bodies with dashes of bold and eccentric colour. Once he felt comfortable he went straight for a well-known coffee house, conveniently situated directly opposite the main gates to the museum.

Once Luke had ordered a flat white, he parked himself on a stool at one end of the countertop, by a plate glass window overlooking the hurly burly of traffic and people. There were hordes of people in this part of London, but it was hardly surprising being a Friday. Although fear was still pulsing through his whole body, Luke was progressively feeling more together and composed, and he knew he just needed to sit with this fear for longer, until it would eventually transform.

He realised that with all the Buddhist teachings that he had imbibed over the last twenty-one years the fruits of his spiritual labour were now beginning to blossom in this momentous period of his life. He knew he was categorically following in the heroic footsteps of the Buddha, trodden some two and a half thousand years ago. What the Buddha ultimately achieved - Luke was sure - he would also realise for himself as well.

Luke sat motionless on the bar stool, and just let the frenetic activity wash over his psyche. Behind him he could hear two well-spoken and apparently well-educated men. One seemed like the boss and the other was a junior colleague; Luke guessed the younger man to be in his thirties, and he had a shock of ginger hair. He was trying to pitch some elaborate idea to the older gentleman. Not taking much notice of the content of their conversation, Luke spied, in the corner of his eye, the older gentleman swivelling his head towards Luke anxiously. It mildly amused Luke that they might also be spies, trying to get a handle on this enigmatic figure.

Luke's gaze was also drawn to a group of girls giggling intermittently, sat at a metal table just outside from where he was parked. They were cradling their coffee cups with both hands, as if the act of clasping them could in some way keep them warm on this cold but sunny day. There was a moment when he caught the eye of the blond-haired girl amongst the group. She was wearing a black, hip leather jacket. He gave her a warm smile. In that brief instant, his fear transformed fully into a deep stillness and what Luke could only describe as a blissful, expansive state of awareness. She looked away quickly with a quiver of anxiety and embarrassment, but reasserted the confident manner she had been evincing moments before.

As he gazed out of the coffee shop his attention was drawn again to a man and woman couple walking very slowly by the coffee shop frontage. The man in particular fascinated him. He was of a tall build, but with a warm, brown complexion, and sported a grey stubble. Initially estimating his age to be in his mid-forties, Luke then thought that he could have been a young-looking fifty something man. His attire was of a military persuasion, with his khaki-coloured and long faded overcoat. He reminded Luke of a distinguished actor. A wire was dangling down from an earpiece, nestled tightly in his left ear. This suggested to Luke that he was someone who needed to be in continual contact with the intelligence services. The man looked directly at Luke, and then quickly but naturally and effortlessly turned his attention to the woman to the side of him. With a short sharp jolt to Luke's guts, this look of his immediately resurrected the fear in him. The man's speed had slowed right down, and, along with his female colleague, they were currently inching forwards.

They suddenly stopped in their tracks just a little beyond the coffee house, and angled their bodies towards the museum. His overall appearance and demeanour seemed to suggest to Luke that he was an American, due to his overt self-assurance and calmness. Were they working closely with the British government? He, along with others, would take any necessary preventative action against Luke, who was at the centre of this vortex of their paranoia.

Luke tilted his head back, and poured the last remnants of the coffee down his gullet. The time was now right to leave the coffee shop. Once he had been to the toilet, he made his way to the exit, and, standing about a metre outside the store, he paused to check both directions. The man with the khaki-coloured overcoat and his accomplice had disappeared from view. Luke did not register anything peculiar about the people hurriedly making their way past him, or the groups milling about the entrance to the museum.

He put his hood up on his Paddington Bear style duffel-coat, which, as one of his friends had remarked, made him look like some kind of Jedi knight when the hood was up. This idea appealed to Luke's sci-fi and cosmic interests and leanings. Luke made a point of not looking over his shoulder, but instead directed his focus straight ahead, at whatever was in his immediate field of vision. The fear was now lingering in him, after having seen the military man and it had begun to possess his psyche once more. Luke decided to play with the idea that the universe is just flow repeatedly, while walking slowly and mindfully back to Marylebone station. The words that sweetly and gently resounded in his inner ear were 'Just Flow', which began to relax his fear into a more profound sense of peace and comfort.

During his walk back to Oxford Circus tube station, he saw some construction workers suddenly stop the build activities they were engaged in. As he motioned past them, they seemed to express a deep curiosity and interest in this thin, shadowy figure. Luke could also sense quite a few people keeping at his pace behind him. Were any of these people behind him special agents? Could some of them be carrying weapons with silencers, to discreetly put away this human inconvenience to their cherished ideals of power, status and wealth? As well as the two words that Luke played as a continuous loop in his mind, he also reflected on how he had utter faith in the gods and their protection of him, using their higher power, namely magic, to help those beings who strive for goodness and purity.

The mass of people around him started to swell to congested numbers, as he joined Oxford Street from one of the narrower side streets. He was conscious of how slow the walk had now become, and he could hear someone behind him talking in a concerned voice on his mobile phone. Keeping his attention glued to the people in front of him, either going his way, or passing him by, the fear was being slowly and gradually transmuted into stillness and calm again. This expansive state of mind seemed to accentuate the slow and deliberate nature of his physical movements, lending him even more an air of mystery.

Once back at Marylebone station he boarded the train, and sat by the aisle of a two-seater, calmly pondering the earlier events of the day. The idea that raised its head again was of being like the character Truman, from the film, 'The Truman Show'. This felt plausible and real to Luke. Over the last day or so, it had established greater and greater currency in his mind, due to many people's inquisitive reaction to him as they passed him on the streets in the last week or so. Relying on his intuition primarily, he would also back it up with a keen intellect and reason.

On the journey back the train came to a complete stop, and it was announced to all the carriages that the train staff were busily trying to remove timber debris that had accidentally fallen on the railway lines – in front of its path. This announcement seemed very mysterious to Luke, and it seemed to confirm to him the influence of the gods on his own life trajectory. He started to think that they were in some way softening the blow of what was awaiting him at his destination. Knowing he could not be sure about this notion that, to most people's minds, would appear like an incredulous assertion, it seemed to him that this falling detritus was not an accident. As he sat there very still and composed he was aware of the very quiet, hushed tones behind him, of a young couple in their mid to late twenties. Luke could feel their quiet yet curious observance of his actions and movements boring into the side of him, but he resisted the urge to turn around and sneak-a-peek. Luke sat in the seat not moving a muscle, and felt both energised and calm simultaneously.

As they came to a halt at the Leamington station platform, Luke alighted with a little trepidation. This manifested as a more unsteady gait with heightened senses. What would be awaiting him on the route back to his flat? Had the incident on his train journey in some way disrupted the secret service's original plans? As Luke arrived back at his flat's outer entrance, and opened his low black metal gate, he paused to look if anyone had been following him from the station. With a mixture of surprise and relief, he spotted that no-one had been trailing him. Closing the front door and turning the key in the lock, Luke took a few seconds to pause, breathe and relax. Inwardly, he reassured himself by saying, "I am now safe," and then let out an involuntary sigh.

Chapter 2

It was the very beginning of 2014. First one distant explosion, then, a split-second later, a riot of muffled yet quite clearly audible bangs were heard coming from outside the space Luke was in, while he sat quietly amongst the other retreatants. Luke could feel himself inwardly seething due to the retreat leader, who was still continuing with the devotional mantras. Could she not see that she had overrun the ushering in of the New Year and that the timing of the evening was not how it had been carried out on previous occasions in this retreat space? It felt wrong to Luke for this lack of correct timing, but he realised this particular moment was a teaching and a practice for him - this being the practice of patience. He then took another angle and questioned the need to be on time with the firework display. Did it really matter at all? Was he not just making a mountain out of a molehill with his foolish desires and attachments? He surveyed the room and noticed that no-one else seemed to be bothered like what he was experiencing.

Although these qualifying and soothing thoughts were necessary, he could not subdue the strong anger inside, and he was finding it difficult to let go. This was the moment to embrace and wish everyone a prosperous New Year, and she had not even acknowledged the time to properly celebrate the turning of the New Year.

What seemed to make matters worse, in Luke's mind, was that once the mantras had been chanted she took the drum she had brought for the occasion, and started to bang it solidly and with deliberate determination. She invited everyone in the space to follow her outside. Even though she had extended the mantras beyond the New Year, Luke felt that once they had completed them, she could at least then allow the retreatants to wish each other a prosperous New Year.

Luke felt an urge to bypass this delay and decided to take it upon himself to wish the man to his left a Happy New Year, as they all still sat in the confines of the cylindrical shrine room building. They were located in the Suffolk countryside, with very few dwellings near-by. The man appeared slightly confused by Luke's desperate need to do it differently to the retreat leader. Luke felt a little embarrassed by his unusual impulsiveness, and reluctantly withdrew into himself again.

Once they all had made their way out of the shrine building, and were congregating outside in the grounds, the organisers and two leaders were desperately trying to light their unexpectedly large size firework in the middle of the large wet grounds. Luke could hear his harsh, critical voice saying to himself, "I told you so! That's what happens, when the rituals aren't timed well."

Suddenly, a mild wave of sympathy arose in him, and he started thinking that they were all just trying to do their best, but fumbling precariously in the process. However, traces of resentment still continued to linger in the background of his mind. Once the fireworks were ignited and the bright and loud display had passed, Luke could not contain his disappointment with the proceedings anymore. After wishing everyone a Happy New Year, he began to vocalise his frustration to a certain individual - a young tall man in his early twenties, named Andrew, who worked as a photographer in London. Dressed with a hip, black leather jacket and blue jeans, he was definitely someone he had warmed to on the last few days out in the country.

"I tell you I was getting really incensed in the shrine room that the retreat leader wasn't ushering in the New Year in a timely fashion. I could feel my temper getting worse when she started banging the drum she had, which seemed to just compound my anger. I've been coming to these retreats for the last four or five years, and it has never been delayed as badly as this!" Luke shared with Andrew.

"Personally, I didn't really mind, and I just think go with the flow," This attitude immediately defused some of the anger that had been latent in Luke, and Luke replied,

"I think you're absolutely right. I was just making a fuss about nothing. Thanks for shifting my attitude so suddenly. It makes me feel a lot better,"

"Don't get me wrong. Although I just said to you that I didn't really mind, there was still a small part of me that slightly resented the delay. I can see where you're coming from, and I just think I managed to prevent my indignation from coming to the fore, slightly better than you were able to. I just thought you should be made aware that I'm not perfect or enlightened, and I succumb to desires and ill-will like anyone else."

"That's good to know! I was initially thinking deep down that it seemed slightly unusual that you didn't seem to mind at all. I think just by talking about it, and hearing your balanced viewpoint, just puts it into context. It gives me a chance to let go of my frustration and resentment. All a worthwhile practice and teaching!" said Luke.

"You betcha! Anyway let's go inside to the warm sitting room, and join the others. I fancy a bit of New Year revelry, without the alcohol, of course!"

"Too right! This is normally the best part of the retreat, from what I remember of previous years," stated Luke. Admittedly, once he had sat down in the cosy living room, he felt that this New Year was ending on a bit of a low, and he could not get engaged. Soon after he retreated to his bedroom to go to sleep.

One of the women on the retreat continued, as she had been doing over the past four days, to give him a cold shoulder and frosty looks, and he reluctantly wished her a Happy New Year. Why was she such an ice maiden with him? He had hardly spoken to her, but right from the outset, at the start of the retreat, she had just ignored him. She struck Luke as a feisty individual, which contrasted with her delicate pale features and slim frame. He had overheard her on one occasion saying she was Canadian and not American! She liked to laugh and giggle a lot with others. Whenever Luke got close to her; she turned into a woman of steel. Luke did not understand why this was, and was sure he came across, more often than not, as a friendly, good-natured type. He was befuddled by her demeanour towards him over the course of the four days. There was a young man on the retreat with whom she was good friends, who did not ignore Luke, but seemed to treat him with disdain and condescension - or so Luke interpreted from his body language, facial expressions and occasional outbursts of mirth.

Luke could not work out what this all meant. It was as if they knew something of his life, and they were collectively judging him harshly and severely. Perhaps they had seen the youtube video he had brought out about half a year ago. But would she not have been more amused than what the thunderstruck expression she constantly wore with Luke suggested? This was all very bizarre to him, but it would begin to make more sense to Luke in the ensuing months of 2014.

Chapter 3

It was Monday 17th February and Luke found it a strain to shift himself from the comforts of his warm duvet and sumptuous grey bed cover, in order to go to work. He had eked out as much time in bed as was feasibly possible, but he was so enjoying being cocooned in its cosiness.

Luke was a very professional employee, and he quite often presented himself with what he would describe as boring attire from the waist up. The main reason this happened was due to his reluctance to iron shirts. If he could get away with it, he would prefer to wear non-ironed shirts that would have no deliberate creases, but were however more plain in appearance. Not unlike others in the world, he suffered from a modicum of vanity and he would not dare parade in an office, or in a town, with a smart cotton shirt that was un-ironed. He would normally have respect for his colleagues, wherever he worked, and he had a strong feeling of empathy and connection with many of those he encountered. This was brought about mainly through his Buddhist practice, but also his very balanced upbringing and his rounded educational schooling at one very prestigious boarding school in the heart of Warwickshire. This was contrasted by time subsequently spent in an unpretentious and down-to-earth yet successful University in Scotland.

It was a cold but bright morning in the middle of February 2014, and only half-a-month since Luke had left the Estates Office department at the University of Warwick to work in an architect's office once again. At the university he had been more heavily involved in Project Management, which had latterly become a source of general unease and discomfort in his life. He felt there were greater demands being placed on him as Project Manager and as an architect, due to being put on a higher pay grade, in-line with managers. The weight of responsibility did take its toll on his mental wellbeing. At the time, he thought he required a fresh outlook and a world that was more familiar to him – namely, working in an architectural office.

Luke had a secret that he disclosed to very few people, and was only willing to share with those friends who were very close to him. This linked to a couple of experiences in his early university life.

The first was at the start of his second academic year at his Scottish University, where his mind went into meltdown after a couple of months of intense, wilful application in his Buddhist practice and meditation. This resulted in a very serious mental breakdown. The symptoms that manifested themselves then were firstly a need to eliminate himself from the planet, and also a manic hyperactivity and partial psychosis which meant not seeing things clearly and rationally.

The second breakdown came about while he was working in his sandwich year, between his two degrees in a firm in Glasgow. This time Luke had the wherewithal and insight, before it got to be really serious, to know that he definitely needed help and medication. Fortunately he was living with his parents at the time in Glasgow, and this happened to be a good safety net. Both his parents could see something was out of sorts with Luke. As swiftly as possible, he extricated himself from the architectural firm despite only having been there for a mere three to four months.

At the time, Luke had been diagnosed with schizophrenia. He was prescribed largactyl after his first breakdown, and after a year of being on the drug he managed to come off it slowly and gradually. After experiencing his second breakdown, Luke had developed the awareness to know when he needed treatment, or when the drug was not having the desired effect. Trying a few drugs after his second breakdown with no consistent success, he was then put on a drug called 'Depixol', its technical name being flupentixol decanoate. This became the medication that kept him healthy and stable.

This regular course of medication consisted of an injection administered fortnightly at a local doctor's surgery. It was a small dose, and Luke had been on this little dosage up until the latter part of 2013. This was when Luke had begun to suffer a greater degree of mild paranoia, primarily brought on by greater stress at work. Agreeing with the doctor, and also a firm but gentle pressure from his parents, he had his dosage increased slightly. Luke noticed that the glutinous & globular drug consistently had a beneficial effect on his wellbeing. One of the side effects of the drug was that he felt noticeably more tired at the end of the first and at the beginning of the second week. After this brief two to three day period he would slowly start to recover his energy levels - without ever exhibiting any accompanying mania or psychosis.

One of the main overriding symptoms he noticed, with a lack of the drug, was an increase in his heartbeat. He knew something was up with his medication, when his sleep patterns were affected detrimentally. However in his long period of being on this medication he had successfully achieved two degrees, and he had then gone onto holding down a number of jobs, and then passed his Part 3 Architecture diploma alongside working in an office, which, by all accounts, was no mean feat. His father had so often praised him about these achievements, being slightly in awe of his commitment and dedication to work and further education at the time, despite his condition.

When the dose was correct, Depixol was the wonder drug that worked every time, to stabilise the chemical imbalance in his brain. Also, for Luke, it had no side effects that he was aware of, other than the soporific effects for two or so days in the fortnightly cycle. His uncle Terry, who had been on the same treatment until he passed away in 2013, joked that the drug had a reputation for being termed 'Dead-dicks-ol' – referring to a depression in one's sexual appetite. This never seemed to bear itself out with Luke. Perhaps if Luke was not on the drug then his sex drive would be rampant, but who can tell if that would have been the reality, or if he was just trying to massage his own ego with this very palatable idea.

It was near the middle of this first week of medication, when he made what seemed like a monumental effort to stir himself and rise from his warm and cosy double bed to get ready for work. He followed his usual ritual of breakfast and then ablutions. There was one addition to this routine, which would always enhance his day if he could fit it in, but on days like these the inertia was too strong - and that was the joy of meditation. He knew that the power of the drug would not allow him to succeed in creating a daily morning mindfulness meditation routine, and so he had to sometimes make-do with early evening sits instead. He really understood the benefits that it could give him, as long as it was kept at moderate levels – particularly for him. Above all else, he really enjoyed the quietude and space it afforded him.

As Luke drove to work along undulating country lanes slowly waking up to the bright morning sunlight, he skipped between Radio 2, a Classical station and a Rock station. The Rock station would quite often play some enjoyably, gritty and dark songs. Occasionally, he would listen to Radio 4. Normally, it was all about the music with Luke, and what appealed to his emotions or general mood at the time. Generally he would hop, like a grasshopper, between stations to find the most appropriate tune.

That morning he arrived at the very picturesque little town of Dorridge, where the office of Mr. Brian Levison was based. Luke would always park a little out of the town, and make a brisk walk to the offices at the heart of the village. He was the second person to enter the firm, and was satisfied that in his first two weeks he was establishing a good impression with timeliness and with what he also felt was the volume of work that he was producing. This knowledge gave him a spring in his step, and made him feel happy and valued. Unsurprisingly Brian was the first person to have arrived that morning, and was concentrating hard at his screen when Luke entered the space that he and Brian and two others shared.

Brian's practice was the first company Luke had gone to for an interview, because his urge to leave Warwick had been stronger than the potential downsides that were intimated by his website and the projects they were working on. In Brian's offices there was not much communication at the start of the day, other than saying "Good morning" to each other. The previous Friday Brian had set Luke an assignment with respect to a large factory complex in Brazil that his company were at the initial stages of undertaking, so unless there were any questions to be asked they would both leave each other alone.

Luke had quite an interesting desk in the office, overlooking the main high street, which meant that when people passed by they would often look in inquisitively. Consequently, Luke could often not resist the temptation to meet their gaze, and have a direct visual encounter, which at first was exciting to see if he got noticed, but then slowly, overtime, changed into one of tedium. Above all, it was a distraction from work. He did have the ability, if he wanted, to zone out from the pedestrian footfall - but in his first couple of weeks he, more often than not, got carried away by the impulse to see if there was any attractive woman walking past - and looking with interest in his direction. This would naturally be a way to bolster his ego and be pulled away from his work by desirable sense pleasures.

Through his Buddhist practice Luke had begun to grow weary of searching for a partner or his soul mate, and he had resigned himself to a life of quiet solitude and healthy friendships with people who shared his values and ideals. Good wholesome friends, normally of the same sex, were what mattered to him. They were what gave him psychological and spiritual nourishment. He had also begun very much to enjoy his own company and would relish indulging in a good film at the weekend. The latest film, with which he had been enamoured by, was of Italian origins, and had come out in the cinemas recently. It was a sumptuous, dazzling film, full of leanings towards the creative life of a one-time successful writer. It was also a poignant tale of the death of a woman he had had a romantic fling with in his youth, but who still pulled his heart strings of connection and love. It was above all a tale of the brevity of life and especially his impending mortality.

Next to him in the office, Luke could perceive a high degree of architectural ability of a black man, named Benjamin. Benjamin was always dressed with snappy elegance. Occasionally he would recount to Luke how at the weekends he would go to London to mix with celebrity types. Lots of women desired his cheeky sense of humour and powerful physique, and he got lots of solicitations from keen female admirers. He did however have a steady girlfriend towards whom he maintained his loyalty and devotion. Benjamin also had two daughters, whom he loved and doted on - often finding it difficult not to spoil them with gifts. There were times when Luke looked carefully at his private work, and admired how he carefully suffused the drawing with detail and colour, to give the drawings life and credibility. Often Benjamin would gloat that a lot of people in his area came to him for the quality of his architectural submissions, which he produced for the planning stage. Luke could really believe the authenticity of this claim.

This particular morning Benjamin was quite subdued as he had spent a lot of the previous evening burning the midnight oil on a particular commission. His computer was at right angles to Luke's desk, and at times this could be a touch disconcerting, as Luke would not be sure if Benjamin was looking at him or at his own monitor. In the past in previous offices this desk arrangement would have bothered Luke a whole lot more, but now it felt only like a minor inconvenience that not much heed was paid to.

Luke was particularly pleased about having experienced, and come to terms with a large open plan office at Warwick University. Starting his time at that office he was very self-conscious while speaking on the phone, but gradually he had grown in confidence. In the last few years of his time at Warwick, he no longer had any qualms about speaking on the telephone to people. Luke had a particularly loud and commanding voice, and sometimes he had no idea that he could be heard from the other end of the office. Even when this fact of Luke's loud and penetrating speech had been pointed out to him by a certain individual, who sat close by, it had not subsequently deterred him from still engaging warmly and confidently with anyone he spoke to on the telephone.

Luke turned to Benjamin and asked,

"You look very tired. How late did you work till, last night?"

"I think it was about 3 o'clock, when I eventually headed to bed. It's interesting, but I've been working on a planning submission for a couple who are having a few issues with neighbours. You wouldn't believe it, but the neighbours had caught wind that this couple want to build an extension onto their house, and they've been threatening them, saying that if they go ahead they'll make their lives a misery," Benjamin expressed incredulously.

"That sounds positively wicked, in the pejorative sense that is!" Luke countered.

"Another thing I couldn't quite believe is that the neighbours, who are making the threats, are not in their 30's or 40's, but they are retired pensioners - of all people!" Benjamin said shaking his head in utter disbelief.

"Just because their pensioners, doesn't mean that they are going to act any more ethically than younger people. Wisdom doesn't necessarily come with age, I'm afraid," Luke said sagely.

"I guess I've always had it in my head that older people are harmless and wiser, and would never resort to violent means, due to their more frail years. How wrong I am," replied Benjamin.

"I think part of the problem with older people – not all mind you - is they very much get stuck in their habits and emotional tendencies, and find it much more difficult to break out of those constricting modes of behaviour. It's as though, through their lives, they have been forming deeper and deeper ruts or grooves of their habits, so they become mired and entrenched, and find it very difficult to let go. When something comes up to upset their equilibrium, they can become very reactive and aggressive, due to being so trapped in their habitual way of operating. Just thought I'd share that with you, as a snippet on the psychology of aging," Luke added pithily yet emitting an involuntary exhalation of air through his mouth.

Life at Brian's office was a great deal more parochial than the time he had spent at the University. This difference of size and diversity only seemed to confirm to Luke that his time at this office might be limited.

Luke was managing a few projects other than the factory in Brazil, and he appreciated these smaller schemes as a complement to the larger more unwieldy assignment, especially when the cost of the works of the Brazil project were continuously being reduced due to financial pressures by the client. The client was a large manufacturer and supplier of detergents making inroads into the Brazilian market. It was becoming a bleaker prospect to produce something with architectural finesse of the offices to the factory, due to the continual tightening of purse strings.

Brian kept banging the drum, to get the client to commission a proper topographical and underground survey of the site. A survey had been commissioned, and it was what the people in the office were working to, but it had been described in the office as being woefully inadequate, with all sorts of ambiguities and inaccuracies dotted on the CAD drawing. Knowing that this plan was all he had to go on, Brian slowly, over time, resigned himself to this fact, yet he would often be very vocal with his disappointment.

While parked in front of his monitor at the office in Dorridge, a slightly sinking feeling of not being happy and fulfilled in the world of architecture was looming ever larger in Luke's life. Over time, it had started to grate a little. He then thought about a eulogy he had given about a week previously to a fellow Buddhist friend who was embarking on a four month long retreat in the mountains of Spain. A few people had commented afterwards on what he had read out to the assembled gathering, remarking on the clarity of the prose, and they asked if he wrote in his spare time. He began to wonder if he could make a living out of writing. It was definitely food for thought, and something he would give serious consideration to in the following weeks and months ahead.

Chapter 4

It was about a week-and-a-half later, on Friday 28th February, when Luke noticed how his mind was slowly becoming a little more excited, and how, there had been a string of past evenings where he was not getting good night sleeps. At the time he did not question his state of mind, as he had made a visit to the nurse at a new doctor's surgery in Leamington. He had placed complete trust in her, as he had done with all the other nurses and doctors, at previous surgeries.

That weekend Luke did something completely out of character compared to his normal weekend activities. It was a Saturday evening, and, after checking the inbox with his e-mails, he found a seductive thought rearing its horny head, tempting him to check his junk box, knowing full well that there would be messages from porn sites and links to them. Was this going to end up a seedier evening than the innocuous nature it started off with?

Luke found himself drawn into the world of pornographic web-chats. He found an ostensibly reputable site where a constellation of prospective women flaunted their physical beauty. Luke had only one thing to go on and of course it was skin deep. He was particularly drawn to the eastern European types, who had a slight air of mystery about them, with their penetrating and twinkling eyes.

On that Saturday evening one woman stood out for him from the vast selection of women from what seemed like most countries of the world. She was from Latvia, and had a fiery, sultry look, and a tantalizing display of cleavage. Her eyes were bewitching and spellbinding. Luke thought, "What have I got to lose?" and decided to log on to her site. The camera was stationed in front of her, and she was planted behind an angled computer with again a very flattering low V-line top accentuating her exquisite bosom. There was a colourful, contemporary painting hanging on the wall behind her - the wall being in a bold red colour. He was immediately hooked by her look and screen presence, and decided to communicate a very short message, yet with a degree of trepidation.

"Hello, you look good", he typed with not much hope that she would respond to him out of all the other men who frequented this website.

Luke watched her type and then messages would appear on the screen. To begin with she was answering other men and then after two or three, she answered him with,

"Hello Luke! How are you on this fine Saturday evening?" which she sealed with a smiley face. His first thought after reading some responses to him and other men was what a good grasp of the English language she had. Her writing was indeed very skilled. There was a feeling of exhilaration with getting her attention. It seemed, by the fact that she was responding more quickly to his messages that she was starting to show greater interest in him, seeing as he was also extolling her patently wonderful physical attributes.

Noticing that with the press of a red button he could start a private web viewing, he let the conversation develop a little more before he decided to embark on a private one-to-one exchange. It could potentially cost a lot of money. Slowly but surely, Luke was getting sucked into her fascinating world, and thoroughly enjoying it. He had not felt this good in years - in what he thought was them both flirting as their texts were peppered with emojis and kisses, and they were both lavishing praise on each other. Cognizant of the fact that she could not see him, but he could see her, he was nevertheless stimulated and intrigued by their bona-fide dialogue.

Beginning to feel reckless, he said to himself 'Let's throw caution to the wind!' He pressed the private viewing button. Here it would just be him and her in a scintillating, gorgeous exchange. Normally in these private viewings the woman would undress and bare all, but she, however, was determined to keep sitting behind her monitor, and keep typing. Luke was also keen to do the same. What interested Luke most was to flirt with and flatter this beauty queen!

"Has anyone ever said that you look a lot like the original wonder woman from the seventies TV series? You could be a dead ringer for her." Luke messaged her, but he was also speaking from the heart.

"I've never come across the word 'dead ringer' before. That's a new one to me. You do mean that I look identical with her. A few people have commented on my look being similar, but none have been as obvious and gracious as you have been, sweetie" she wrote delightedly and smiling radiantly on-screen.

Finding no desire to halt this display of vicarious courtship he gradually became more and more locked into her world. He mused to himself that 'Over time, the internet will develop so you will be able to smell each other's fragrances through an olfactory sense in the computer.'

He proceeded to tell her about his grandfather, who he had a very close relationship with, and wrote,

"My grandfather was German and also a very small part Swiss Italian. He was a very successful doctor in the region, and he had a particularly gifted touch in healing people. This might have been partly dependent on his own father being an eminent GP in the area as well. My grandfather loved big German cars, and in the sixties he had a large black vehicle, which was one of a number of very desirable cars in those days. He once showed me a photo of it, and it looked identical to a car the mafia would have driven. He definitely was a man with fine tastes, and funnily enough he would still drive very fast on the German autobahn, up until his last remaining

year of his life. Personally, I drive a small sporty car, and that suits my needs perfectly. Do you drive?" Luke was pleased that he had painted a rosy picture of his grandfather leading the high life, and this would be one more story to hook her emotions, and reel her heart in towards his sizzling interest of her.

"Yes, I do drive, but nothing fancy yet. I hope to also purchase a German engineered car, as they're nearly always well-built and have a good and quick performance. Tell me more about your relationship with your grandfather. What was his name?"

"His name was Berndt, and he was a really lovely man to get to know. He was confident but also sensitive to a wide range of people, and when I used to walk with him in the streets so many of the public knew him, and acted in a friendly way towards him – normally by engaging him in joyful conversation. He would always stop for everyone, even if he was under pressure to get somewhere. Nearly always did he have time, and he would exude empathy and compassion. His other two notable qualities that he possessed were a great sense of humour and a distinct charm that seeped from his pores," reminisced Luke with the fond memories of time spent being with him in Germany.

"He sounds wonderful! What a lovely relationship you must have had. I'm sure you have a very positive view of your childhood and growing up."

"Yes you're right there, yet school was a little more difficult though, especially my secondary school or boarding school that I was at. So, it was not all plain sailing, but is life ever like that anyway," stated Luke sagely.

"You're right. Life is always bittersweet, but it would be nice if it always ran smoothly though," she replied wistfully, but with resilience.

She played current songs, the whole time she was live on the webcam. One of the songs that caught Luke's attention had lyrics in it about shining bright like a diamond. Mentioning that he particularly liked that song, he asked her to play it on a couple more occasions. Later on that evening he went so far as to say it was their song. Scrutinizing her reaction from this remark, whereby she remained quite impassive at this suggestion, he sensed that it was probably more his song than hers. This did not prevent her from obediently playing his request, seeing as he was paying for their conversation. He had heard the tune being played on other occasions before that evening, and had been immediately captivated by the gravitas of its melody.

Quite often that night Luke would write messages without letting spelling or any internal anxiety hinder the fluency of his typing exchange. The rush of adrenaline in his system was contagious. As soon as he felt the message was complete, he would hit the return button with a flourish, exulting in the confidence he was exhibiting. During their repartee, he was glad how he had found someone on these sites who preferred a civilised yet scintillating conversation, was drop-dead gorgeous, but was not willing to bare all - except for a pleasing display of cleavage.

What Luke was experiencing in himself was truly revelatory, and he could not stop the conversation with the kick he was getting. Two-and-a-half hours passed with little time for respite from tapping on the keyboard. It had reached 2am in England. Seeing as she normally finished at this time, she said she was starting to feel exhausted, due to commencing her shift at 9pm Latvian time. Luke respected her wishes, but still felt a slight pull to just continue the conversation a little longer - eking out as much emotional gratification from the evening as possible.

Eventually Luke knew he had pushed the evening as far as it could go, but ended with suggesting she play their song to conclude the exchange. They just sat silently and motionlessly, except for the dramatic chords of the music playing; Luke mesmerised and entranced by her overall voluptuousness and charming personality that manifested itself through her writing and on-screen aura. He wondered if, while she was reclining in her high backed leather armchair, she was imagining what sort of man Luke might look like. He had tried to paint a fairly honest but ever so slightly exaggerated picture of himself; likening his jaw to that of Superman's; indicating that he was a perfect height, and that he had greyish-blue eyes - all desirable features he thought, which would draw her into his world as much as he had been sucked into hers.

That night in bed Luke found he could not sleep. Endlessly playing the song in his head with a mixture of joy, but also one of very mild frustration and annoyance due to not being able to unwind properly, he felt the song was now indelibly linked to her. He skipped through the thoughts of what he had written and the delight and thrill she and Luke had expressed. This feeling of euphoria was beautiful as there was no nudity, just mutual appreciation and attraction, at least on his part. Anticipating a hefty credit card bill, he had no idea how much it would cost, but Luke would not normally let money get in the way of unadulterated pleasure. Being an architect he was sure that, for one night, he could bear the cost.

The following Monday after Luke had taken himself off to bed, he let temptation get the better of him, and decided to see whether the Latvian beauty was working that evening. Knowing he had work the following day, he felt impelled to just communicate with her again. He thought it would just be for a short while, nothing more.

However that night he got drawn into a two-and-a-half hour conversation with the seductive bombshell. After he indulged in lots of frivolous and jocular repartee, he thought he would bite the bullet, and ask her,

"Would you like to come to London for the weekend, and we could sample a few of the many delights that London has to offer?"

"That sounds like a great idea! I would definitely be up for that. Do you have any ideas where you and I could stay?"

"I have a few hotels in mind near the centre of London, by places like Soho and Mayfair. I would pay for your own room, and all the

food and drinks we consumed. All you would need to do is pay for the flight to the Big Smoke." Luke was letting himself be free and uninhibited by his gestures of generosity, even though it was still very notional at this stage. He felt that he wanted to pull out all the stops to make it a very memorable and romantic weekend for the both of them.

"Don't worry, I would not expect you to pay for everything, but it is a very generous offer. You're a charmer you know that don't you!"

"I try my best, and especially as I get a good vibe from you. What do you think you would wear out on your visit, or more to the point, what sort of clothes do you like wearing?" he asked.

"It depends on where we go into town, but I would probably wear some tight fitting blue jeans with a shirt that hugged my bosom, and just for you I would have quite a few of my shirt buttons undone, to get you wild with excitement. What would you wear?" she said with a coquettish stance in her bodily posture that had the depths of Luke's heart fizzling with sexual thrill.

"For the evening, I would wear some colourful trousers, a white shirt, a blue suede waistcoat, and then some appropriate shoes. Unlike you of course I would only undo the first couple of buttons to give a hint of my moderately hairy chest, which is the way I like it. In the day time I would probably wear some comfortable jeans with an understated T-shirt with no flashy logo emblazoned on it. I find that in the clothes department, simplicity is normally my preferred option, but with a varying degree of colour, either bold, muted or a combination of both."

"I'm also a fan of tracksuit bottoms and a jogging top, to be worn in the daytime for leisurely strolls in the city or park," once she had sent this message, Luke could feel his psyche inwardly reeling at the inappropriateness of the attire especially in the city, and quickly changed it to the subject of hotels. Knowing it was undoubtedly his class snobbery rearing its ugly, misshapen head again, stemming from his former boarding school conditioning.

When Luke was speaking about his clothes, he was aware that he needed to keep the descriptions succinct and sparing, so he could keep a semblance of mystery intact. He believed, from what he had read in magazines, that women were drawn to the mysterious, but then again Luke believed that this quality also appealed to men, but unlike women not quite as intensely. Men normally smothered that faculty of wonder with more mundane interests. Most of his Buddhist friends shared an interest in the mystery, magic and wonder of people and the universe, but none of them could surpass Luke's passion in this domain.

Chapter 5

It was Saturday 8ᵗʰ March. In the last week or so Luke had been driving particularly fast, to the point of displaying a high degree of recklessness. His dangerous yet skilled driving, which he put down to quick reaction times, had been fuelled by listening to rock music on the radio. Some of the songs ignited his passions and his mind. He was still experiencing a degree of restlessness; and added to this he was still getting very little sleep, which was affecting his ability to concentrate at work. On this particular day he did not, on this occasion, feel the need to show off, or drive at any hostile speed.

Luke was going to a meditation class that morning, and later he would be meeting a Buddhist friend, named Daire, for lunch, who had been ordained into the movement he was affiliated with. The thought of getting ordained was becoming a priority in Luke's life, as he had managed to build up a very steady spiritual practice. About a year ago he had asked his friend if he would like to be his private preceptor, or spiritual mentor in more layman's terms. There were hints that Daire might formally accept his wish of becoming a private preceptor very soon.

One of the thoughts bothering Luke while driving to Birmingham was the belief that after accessing the porn-site he was somehow being watched, and his every movement was being scrutinized by the Intelligence Services. Seriously believing that this might have been going on for a very long time; his mind started to develop wild imaginings. One arresting idea he came up with was that through the art of deciphering symbols and scrutinizing predictions, GCHQ, who possessed some of the smartest minds of our time, were trying to track down someone who they thought would be the devil on this earth, and they had been doing this for years, even before Luke was born. The belief that consolidated in his mind was that the authorities were convinced that he embodied all the characteristics of what they presumed a devil would masquerade as: namely an individual who could be charismatic, intelligent, in their minds would feign kindness, would defiantly disbelieve in the existence of a creator God, and, at times, would be a radical individual.

Luke believed his life might be in mortal danger were it not for his strong faith in the gods from other world systems, who especially afforded him protection because he was sincerely treading the path to enlightenment. These gods were just as near as they were far, and magic was their exalted form of power. They could perform miracles over distant galaxies, as some of the higher, more elevated gods had intimate, experiential access to each living being on this planet and innumerable others in different world systems. With time, Luke would grow to become more confident in exposed public areas because of the love and compassion of these numberless gods.

Over the last two-and-a-half years, Luke had been involved with the leading and supporting of meditation classes in Birmingham, and prior to this Saturday he had asked Christopher, one of his friends, if he could lead the meditation class that day, as he did not feel emotionally stable. This was a wise move, as they were in a room called the Garden Shrine Room, which was a relatively small space, and the numbers had swelled that day to about sixteen people. This would have been really unsettling for Luke's state of mind if he had been leading the class. He could now sit back, relax and just listen.

A ritual for people on the team was, an hour before the class started, they would chant refuges and precepts, and then tune-in to the group with any issues that were current and live for them.

When it came to Luke's turn he said tentatively,

"I have to say, but I'm not feeling all that well today. I'm sure you can probably tell." Luke wavered slightly feeling the enormity of what he was about to express to the group. He then decided to take the plunge, and began to articulate,

"I strongly believe that the British government and governments around the world want to eliminate me, due to their misguided belief that I am the devil or the anti-Christ. However hard they try, their attempts will always be thwarted by the intervention of the gods. I think that the real truth is that I'm destined to become Maitreya, the future Buddha, but a Buddha not in this lifetime, but in hundreds of lifetimes to come."

Christopher, who was leading the class, became seriously disturbed by Luke's disclosure to the group, and said very little in response to him. Luke noticed his visible agitation, while Luke was enunciating the words. A similar reaction from the others was not perceived by Luke, and he pondered whether the other two were keeping their emotions in check, to keep the mood as calm as possible, and to tenuously hold a semblance of harmony in the group.

Very few, if any, of his Buddhist friends, (even those closest to him - he would come to realise) - would share these sentiments about the presence of gods in their human lives.

Luke finished the class, and was relieved that he had not had to teach. Daire was waiting in the small but inviting reception area to the Buddhist Centre, as Luke came striding towards him from the back of the building. They warmly embraced each other, and then without any extended delay, they left the building for a charming French restaurant in the centre of Moseley.

Daire had a slow, deliberate gait, whereas Luke preferred a brisker pace, but was happy to compromise his habitual responses to a gentler motion. Luke always tried to work 'with' people and not against them, endeavouring to work at their level, allowing him to develop a degree of humility towards those he met.

The desire not to share the story of his little outburst that morning with Daire in the restaurant was strong. He suggested to Daire that they retreat to the residential community that Daire belonged to, and then he would spill the beans of his current views.

After polishing off lunch and then walking back to Daire's abode, Luke got settled into a slightly tatty but comfortable armchair in the community's small but adequate living room, and waited for his friend, who was making tea for both of them. Daire entered the room and carefully placed one of the mugs on a silver coaster by Luke, whilst grasping the other with his powerful right hand. He then slowly sat down opposite him. Although Luke was tall, Daire was even taller and he had a broad frame, which magnified his imposing stature. When he spoke, his words were thoughtfully chosen and enunciated deliberately and at a slow pace, yet suffused with warmth.

"It's good that we're in a nice quiet space here, so we won't be overheard, as some of what I'm about to tell you is very personal", Luke opened with (although at the back of his mind he had a niggling thought that he was being eavesdropped by GCHQ and the spy world). He thought for the sake of this particular discussion, he would not qualify his opening gambit.

"Yes, it's a nice cosy space in here. I agree with you we were a little exposed in the restaurant, sitting behind that large party of slightly rowdy couples, who I could sense you were feeling uneasy about. So tell me more...what has been troubling you, and how are you feeling?" Daire gently eased in the question.

Daire was a kind man, who listened carefully and especially to Luke, who was communicating some of his deeply held views, which to lots of ears would sound bizarre and strange due to their more radical nature. These views consisted of gods, who were keeping him from harm, and then GCHQ, the secret service and the government, who were trying to employ covert ways of ending his life. After delivering a quite lengthy monologue, and feeling that most of what was necessary had been said - he watched as

Daire carefully deliberated and then replied,

"I can see why it was bothering you, and why you wanted to wait until we were in the privacy of our own space - here in the community." A short pause ensued, where he collected his thoughts and then continued,

"Do you really think that the intelligence services would be interested in you? Don't you think that they would be more concerned with catching terrorists and spying on them, than knowing what you're doing? You're not a terrorist or someone with grievances to bear, are you?" he said looking quizzically at Luke.

"No, I'm definitely not!" said Luke defiantly.

Luke had explained that the trigger had come about from the exchange with a gorgeous looking Latvian woman. Gradually, he had pondered the significance of that communication, after which he thought he might be being monitored by the intelligence services for it being such a random and out of character act. Doing a lot of reflection in his life he had thought for a long time that he was a particularly special individual. He had mentioned in his lengthy speech to Daire that the security services had a misguided belief in him being a devil or anti-Christ. Hairs on the back of his neck rose, when Luke broached this particular subject, but he knew that divulging this thought was for the best to try and deepen his friendship - by being completely open and honest.

Once Luke had finished sharing with Daire some deep-seated views, he watched as he calmly took this all in - pausing for a few seconds, before answering,

"I really don't think you need to worry yourself." He said with a soft, consoling tone, and continued,

"Have you spoken to your doctor about your medication recently?"

"I really don't think I need to see my doctor about my medication", Luke said with a degree of restrained composure, yet feeling just the faintest hint of resentment at this suggestion made by Daire. Luke carried on by saying,

"Although, having said that, I do feel as if I've not been sleeping well in the last week or so. I can't explain it, because the medication should have kicked in by now. It could be that having had the webcam exchange has effectively excited my mind, yet I hadn't been sleeping well before that. However, it might be possible that the nurses, at the new doctor's surgery that I go to, could have administered the wrong drug, or instead deviously and knowingly didn't give me the correct medication."

Over the last week Luke had mulled over that it was a bit strange that when the nurse called him in to her treatment room, she already had the syringe loaded and ready to go. Why did she feel that he should not be party to the opening of the ampoule and loading up of the syringe? He could, after all, have a friendly dialogue with her, and get to know her a bit better! The more he ruminated about that particular situation, the more uneasy he felt. He recalled how the nurse seemed rather distant and aloof, while also acting very seriously towards him. Later on that day, when he had finished saying a warm goodbye to his Buddhist friend, Luke thought to himself that he would still give the surgery the benefit of the doubt – for now at least.

Daire ended their conversation by asking Luke about the webcam lady,

"How much did you pay to speak to her? I'm sure you're aware that those web-chats are really expensive. I think you said that you'd been communicating with her for over two hours, on two separate occasions. Just be careful what you're getting yourself in to."

"They are expensive, I know, and I think I should probably refrain from continuing my exchange with her. Although, she is so gorgeous. I'm positive I've already run up a hefty bill. You're right - I should probably sever that link before it gets out of hand, but I do love our communication...."

"You don't even know if she really likes you, and she is probably just seeing you as a way of making money. She can't even see what you look like!" Daire said imploringly with an increased volume in his voice.

After they said their goodbyes with a big, hearty embrace, Luke had decided earlier that week that he would spend the whole day in Birmingham both with Daire and then a friend called Aslan. He had arranged to meet Aslan at about 4:30pm for a walk and an evening meal afterwards.

Aslan was a particularly inspiring individual. Not only was he a very gifted teacher of Buddhism and meditation, but he was kind to others, and really worked hard on improving his mental and emotional states. Being a playful man, he liked to tease Luke in a loving and gentle way, which Luke appreciated and responded to with an equal lightness of touch. One physical characteristic of his was that he did not bother with a clean cut look. His hair would normally be dishevelled, and he would normally be sporting a ragged looking beard. His dress sense always had an eye for colour and tones in an unfussy and uncomplicated way. Luke definitely loved being in his company. One particular quality that united them both, which Luke had expressed to him on a number of different occasions, was their mutual idealism and commitment to the goal of enlightenment.

Luke had gone for a short walk in Canon Hill Park to kill time between his two meet-ups, and was slowly sauntering back from the Midlands Arts Centre. He loved the beauty of the park and being around so many wise and ancient trees. Anyone with any sensitivity and empathy had to be amazed by such magnificent beings, so solid, immovable and majestic. The sky was blue and free from clouds, except for some wispy stragglers skirting languidly across the firmament.

Luke had exited the park, and was gradually approaching the zebra crossing on the way to Aslan's community building, when he noticed a couple of large, expensive and angular looking black cars with blacked out windows, one behind the other, driving towards the crossing. In the past Luke had tended to feel he had the right of way, so would boldly enter the crossing and raise a hand towards the driver as a mark of acknowledgement and gratitude, but also with a degree of presumption and foolhardiness.

However today he felt there was something slightly sinister with these two cars, and something in him said, 'you need to wait and let them go.' Strangely enough, as he approached the crossing, he waited for a brief second and both the cars just shot straight over the crossing. The next car in line, a rather small and dainty vehicle, stopped to let him traverse the road. Luke was particularly struck by the kind expression on the woman's face, as she smiled sweetly at him. Her warmth was further accentuated by her juxtaposition with the previous two masculine looking vehicles. This sparked in Luke's mind, the lightly held thought that these faceless drivers had strategically planned this apparently random occurrence, seeing as he had his mobile phone on him, whose signal could be tracked. Of course, he could not be sure, but some inner voice was hinting that this suggestion might in fact be correct. Luke managed to shelve this view, and calmly continued walking.

Luke pressed the buzzer on the door of the community, having arrived five minutes early. He wondered whether he would be greeted with Aslan's friendly face or someone else.

There were, in total, six people who lived in this large, early Victorian house, which was quite a common build-type in Moseley. They all lived in harmony, based around common shared values and commitments to a relatively simple Buddhist lifestyle.

The door to the house opened very slowly, and Aslan had one eyebrow raised in a mock-serious expression.

"Hello, can I help you", Aslan said in a very croaky voice, as if he was some wizened old man, with his head squeezed between the leaf and the jamb of the door.

"I have come to meet the legendary man called Aslan. Doesn't he reside here?" Luke responded in an equally affected accent - stifling a rising and escalating mirth, whilst speaking.

"Yes he does. That is I. I have arranged to meet a man called Luke. Is that you I wonder?"

It was then too much to keep up the pretence, and they both started to dissolve into laughter. After a brief moment inside, they went for a long walk together into Canon Hill Park and the adjoining Highgate Park.

Despite Aslan's sweet and gentle side, he was a courageous man and very capable. While they walked briskly, Luke felt a great sense of appreciation for his straightforwardness and bravery. He remembered one particular occasion in one of his classes, when Aslan mentioned to the assembled group a wise aphorism. This was, 'bravery was feeling the fear and doing it anyway'. Since he had come into Buddhism in his first year at University, Luke had experienced fearful situations, yet was always on the look-out for new scary challenges – predominantly in the realm of communication.

After their bracing and invigorating walk, they were walking around the centre of Moseley, trying to decide which restaurant they should go to. Aslan mentioned that he had been to the Indian restaurant on the high street, one too many times, and suggested they try somewhere else. Being always flexible in his preferences, this would never stop Luke from taking the initiative and making a considered suggestion. The main body of restaurants were on one side of the high street, and they noticed a new one had opened up, which was a new Italian restaurant. Standing outside, they looked intently at the interior, assessing its merits. Agreeing that it appeared very smart and elegant, they then concurred that they would try it out.

A pretty and friendly looking young woman, with what seemed like a Polish accent, walked slowly towards them, as they entered. After an initial greeting she offered a table for two just by the entrance and directly adjacent to a large window overlooking the high street. Luke purposefully chose the chair with its back to the window facing towards the interior of the restaurant with a commanding view of the tables and chairs. They had arrived particularly early for dinner with only one other couple parked midway into the space against the wall, discreetly within their own booth.

For some reason, Luke had not ventured to explain to Aslan his weird and wonderful views during the walk, as he wanted to get a bit of time to process his thoughts, between his first meet-up and this one. Luke had really appreciated being able to clear his head, during a reflective movement through the two parks. Obviously they did talk on their walk, but they stayed clear of weighty topics, and entertained themselves with short bursts of comparative small talk.

Somehow in the restaurant that evening, Luke possessed a great command of the English language, and felt a strong surge of confidence and strength. It rarely came his way, but that evening it was as if he was on fire with his eloquence and verbal dexterity. Reflecting later on in the car back home, he thought that this might have resulted from his voracious reading habits and his regular teaching practice at the Buddhist Centre, which gradually helped him overcome some of his psychological demons.

During the main course, Luke began expressing his theories to Aslan on gods, the devil and the state of affairs for our current humanity, in more depth than he had previously articulated to anyone else, and watched how he was progressively taking them in, all very calmly and impassively.

"The first thing I want to mention to you, Aslan, is how the gods arise. These gods had, at one time, been humans living a very similar pattern of existence to us, with their world revolving around an emphasis on material wealth and consumption. They had been part of the population that wanted to grow and develop spiritually, through leading a more ethical life, and using meditation as a tool for transforming their minds to greater levels of awareness and consciousness, whilst also becoming wiser beings. They were also those humans, who were just looking for something more meaningful in their lives, than the common one of materialism and consumerism."

The space was filling up with people. It was almost as if the whole restaurant was becoming his audience, and he was addressing them too. Luke's emotions were completely galvanized, and they definitely supported the ideas he was trying to define and bring clarity to. Sometimes he was unaware of how much his voice carried, and, as such, he was probably being overheard by most of the diners. Luke continued his explanation with Aslan murmuring from time to time to suggest that he had not stopped listening.

"Hate and negative energy had been gradually growing in their world, and there was a devil that was feeding off this gross negative and unhelpful energy, and was consequently becoming more and more powerful. He existed on an alternative plane of existence to the one, humans or gods were on." Luke continued with his views without allowing Aslan to interject.

"I want to explain to you how a devil arises in the cosmos. There have been innumerable devils in the past in numberless world systems. The story of the arising of a devil figure is not too dissimilar to the story in Milton's Paradise Lost. It started with a being, who had advanced himself in the spiritual world of the god realm to such a degree that he was almost on the brink of realising supreme enlightenment, which is a truly mighty and awe-inspiring state of mind. This path of continual spiritual progress and development lasted for an unfathomably long period of time, culminating in a final stage, which could only be described as a state of complete universal consciousness or supreme enlightenment. He was suddenly thwarted by a huge upsurge of extreme pride that was none other than Mara, the Buddhist name for one's own spiritual devil – assailing and gripping him in feverish intensity. Each individual in the cosmos possesses a spiritual devil, and he or she is always being tempted, seduced, belittled or whatever evil we could think, say or do. This Mara is always in opposition to our Buddha-nature, a gentle and compassionate yet heroic and powerful force and energy that is also a part of us. The side of us that succeeds is the one that we feed. To undertake goodness and purity takes effort and goes very much against the grain of Mara and his or her army of psychological demons, which prefers the easy option or a lazy acceptance.

The supremely developed being died instantly, and was then reborn in a hell realm, where he suffered great mental and physical pain and torture. While as a god he had developed all sorts of magical powers, and one of those powers was the ability to see into his numberless previous lives. He was still in possession of these many magical abilities, while he traversed through the depths of hell. Over time, he conquered his fears and also physical and emotional pain, but he could also see where he had originated from, and who he had been before in countless previous lives. Over time he amassed more and more hate and negative power, which, over a vast expanse of time in the hell realm, became greater than the monumental love he had built up in the god realm.

Once the hate became greater than the love, he transformed into a negative power and force-field. He then had the ability to extricate himself from the hell realm, which he was residing in, and emerged on another completely unique transcendental plane. The devil then coursed through the cosmos, and finding a suitable world system - latched onto it.

Each innumerable world systems in the cosmos either have or will have their own distinct devil, and our own specific devil has been feeding off the negative energy of this world for thousands of years, and in the process has been getting ever stronger and more powerful." Luke was curious to see if Aslan was registering all of this with an open mind, but Luke inwardly felt that it was a case of information falling on deaf ears. He nevertheless continued with expounding his deep-seated views.

"The devil was very close to descending onto this earth. This would be accompanied by a terrifying display of thunder and lightning bolts, in which he will fashion himself into a humungous incandescent behemoth, and a highly intelligent one with no regard for the sanctity of anyone's life.

The people in this world, who are in search of some higher, spiritual and more liberating goal will be plucked from this earth, and transported by gods in their spaceships to their heaven worlds. The gods will descend just before the devil strikes to whisk those beings away to earths like ours, but how ours was about a million or so years ago - that is beautiful, heavenly paradises.

As you and I know nothing is permanent in existence, and although these gods live in these heaven realms for an extremely long time, it is nonetheless limited. There are also a multiplicity of levels of bliss and happiness, corresponding to their different spiritual attainments. I think we can see distinct evidence of the gods' presence through the numerous reports of UFO sightings, where they are trying to make contact, either indirectly or directly, with humans whose minds are open to higher dimensions of consciousness. As I'm sure you're well aware of, there is more and more hatred and fear manifesting itself in this globe and change is now rife. I think, for some, life is too much of a struggle, and something has to give.

The beings who'll be left on this planet will be immersed in increasingly evil ways, becoming demonic in appearance, as well as strong and powerful by conquering both their fears and physical and emotional pain. Eventually, all in this hell realm will possess total disregard for life, and they will pounce ferociously on the expression of any miniscule sign of weakness displayed by the living. The world will escalate in temperature to unimaginable proportions, to which the demons would be impervious and concerned with just one thing – their own twisted souls.

One quality that both the gods and the demons share is a sense of freedom. The god realm is considered a place where beings work together in harmony, and they are always seeking the welfare of each other in a place of beauty and outer and inner peace. I would term this a constructive or positive anarchy. In the realm of the demons nothing is sacrosanct, and nothing is off-limits, with destruction being waged not only on life but property and possessions as well. This I would term destructive or negative anarchy.

There is a third category of being living in this present day world that I need to explain to you. There are those in the world of finance, politics, business and the skilled professions, who are very intelligent and able individuals. They have surmounted variously sized obstacles, along their way of working life. They are now extremely successful individuals in their respective fields, and they are all extremely competitive. They're all concerned with their own personal gain and quasi-enlightenment. The sexes polarise themselves, so the males are generally aggressive, butch men but with a high degree of intelligence. The women have great intelligence and also a voluptuousness and charm that ensnares the men in their web of entrapment and control. This type or class of being will also be transported away from this earth just before the devil arrives, by what Buddhists term, jealous gods or titans. Their environment is mostly stationed in their spaceships, and they endlessly course through the depths of space, visiting and passing by all sorts of different worlds. They have always been in continual internecine warfare with the heavenly gods, by forever attempting to capture the tree of abundance and magic - a wish fulfilling tree that is only accessible to the heavenly gods.

The jealous gods will never succeed in gaining access to the wish-fulfilling tree, and their attempts have and will always be thwarted from time immemorial into the unceasing future.

I thought I would also tell you about the female counterpart to the devil. Before both of their descents from the pinnacle of spiritual evolution, they were soul mates to each other, and they lived together in blissful union. They were spiritually androgynous beings, which meant that they possessed male and female characteristics in equal measure, and were completely content and complete in themselves, without needing to be fulfilled by the other gender's distinct qualities. This goddess also lived for an eternity in utter bliss, and, like the god, who had become the devil, was seized by a substantial pride just before she was about to realize supreme enlightenment. However, the goddess lacked the substantial drive and courage that the male god possessed, and she formed into the planet earth as we know it today. You always hear talk about Mother Earth bandied about in New Age circles, but I believe that this concept is completely real and true. This world is alive just like the trees, plants, animals, and so called inanimate objects that inhabit this globe."

Luke sought to round off the informal speech, and reassure Aslan by saying,

"We have all been so many people and types of being, right from the most powerful in conditioned existence to the most miniscule. This has always come into being due to an infinite network of conditions at play in the universe, both arising, playing itself out and ending. A revered Vietnamese monk, who had been a non-violent activist alongside Martin Luther King, stated that the effects of a few claps of ones hands, has an effect into faraway galaxies. A good friend also once told me that science posits the theory that each atom with their corresponding electrons are inextricably linked to all the other infinite amount of atoms in the universe, and if one atom is affected either positively or negatively then that will have either a positive or negative effect on all others.

It's so important now in the world we're living in, to try and perform as many acts of kindness and love to each other and the environment, to counteract the negative energy that is steadily accumulating on this planet. The essence of existence boils down to a cosmic battle between the forces of good and evil. However, goodness and purity will ultimately always triumph over evil."

Finally, Luke thought he had explained enough about his views, in as much detail as he could muster. The restaurant was nearly full with customers, except for a couple of empty two person tables in the middle of the space. A lot of eyes had orientated themselves towards him, and although he had been aware of customers trickling in throughout his speaking, he had been lost in a kind of heady vocal trance.

Later on that year, Aslan confided to him about his impressions of the evening. He said how Luke had left him very little room to speak, and he had seemed totally self-absorbed to the point of there not being any dialogue, and instead just a very lengthy monologue. It was not surprising after their meet-up on that eventful evening that Aslan appeared emotionally drained by being extraordinarily withdrawn and taciturn. On the other hand, Luke had felt totally engaged and energised by, what he thought, was his eloquent discourse. There were some moments in Luke's life, when his powers of explanation and speech were inspired. On that evening, he loved the sound of his own voice. It was a thrill, but not one to be repeated for the sake of forming deeper connections with friends.

Earlier Luke had mentioned about the Latvian lady who he was besotted with, and he explained to Aslan how he was entertaining the idea of meeting up with her in London. As they walked back to the community Luke raised the issue again, expressing his fondness for her even though they had never met in the flesh.

"I really felt we had something special between us and that we were being drawn together," said Luke in an impassioned way.

"I can assure you that it won't lead to anything, and you'll have spent a great deal of money communicating with her in vain. After all, she's making a business for herself and is probably preying on people like you, who will fall for her." Aslan said in a gentle and kind manner, being respectful of Luke's obvious infatuation.

"Okay, you know what – I'll now make a vow to you. I will never communicate with her again, and I will also not go on that website or any like it again. I want you to be my witness." Luke said this with a deep and heartfelt conviction. He understood that a vow in the Buddhist tradition was a serious undertaking, and once made should never be broken. It could potentially have grave repercussions, if it were to be breached.

"I hear and witness your vow brother. Do you think you'll be able to honour it?" Aslan enquired delicately.

"I realise the importance and weight of a vow and I believe I have it in my power to accomplish it. I'll now rescind my involvement with her, and that you can be sure of." Luke had no doubt in his mind that the vow could be accomplished, and he went home that evening satisfied that something truly positive had come out of their meet-up - an exchange he could be quietly proud of.

Chapter 6

One of Luke's routines at the weekend would be to while away some of his leisure time in coffee shops in the centre of Leamington. It did not bother him that one of the coffee houses he frequented on a regular basis was a mainstream establishment. He appreciated the friendliness of the staff that worked there, and the décor was simple, uncluttered and unpretentious. It was also a light and airy space which he liked.

It was a cold but bright Sunday morning. Sauntering past boutique shops, with a somersaulting joy within his heart, along Regent's Court Parade, he entered the unfussy and relaxed setting of the coffee domain. He ordered his beloved coffee, which was a Flat White – a choice he very rarely deviated from.

As he sat down on one of the timber chairs and planted his book, which was a meditation handbook, onto the veneered circular table in front of him - he became aware of the woman sitting opposite him, neatly ensconced in a corner, with a view out of the window. She was an attractive older woman with fine features and a good figure, who he had seen on quite a number of occasions, over the last couple of years - nearly always sat in the same location. As she arrived more often than not before him and others, she would quite regularly get her pick of the seats. No-one would ever accompany her on her visits to the coffee house, and she appeared to be a very self-contained woman, rarely expressing emotional colour – at least not to Luke.

She would always be reading one of the broadsheet papers, which was a Sunday ritual that Luke used to continually entertain in his University days and for quite a few years after studying - during his working life.

On this particular day she was wearing black jeans, a black fleece and a black beret. She would quite often wear black, carrying an austere demeanour, and she would very rarely meet his gaze. When she did, it would normally be with a fearsome expression. Luke imagined that she could pass for an assassin - trained to kill - and be able to leave a scene of death and destruction without a shadow of remorse at the enormity of her crime.

Luke questioned why an attractive woman, with what seemed like a rich dollop of class should always be in this coffee house. Would she not be more suited to an independent coffee establishment? Or did she appreciate this shop for the same reasons that he did? She definitely seemed intriguing, but someone who he was not willing to get to know.

His imaginings about this woman spiralled outwards. Could this woman, normally clad in black, be working for MI5, and the only reason she came to this coffee house was because of Luke? All it needed was Luke to go off to the bathroom, and she would then be able to slip some poison into his coffee. She would then make her way back to her seat, calmly sit down, and immerse herself in the Sunday papers again.

Licking his lips, with a satisfied look adorning his face, and believing that this woman posed little threat to his life, he tried to get the attention of the female staff to say his goodbyes. He always tried to be courteous and pleasant with those he met, but he had developed a particular fondness for the staff. On this occasion, they were busily attending to a couple of different customers, and he thought it was futile to interrupt their flow, so he left in silence. Luke had at times, a wonderful timbre to his voice. It would occasionally be a very harmonious pitch. Though, the degree to which this occurred would fluctuate greatly, depending on his moods. At his peak his voice was unrivalled in quality and texture, lending itself to clear and articulate formal presentations and public speeches. In the past, Luke's parent's had mentioned to him about the clarity and beauty of his voice. He was convinced that they were not lying, but it was indeed a genuine sentiment of theirs.

Ambling leisurely towards his next Coffee shop - another well-known outlet, he loved studying the architectural details when meandering through towns and cities, but especially when the buildings were modern and contemporary. Often he would walk along the pavements looking up to study some quirky detail about the architectural design, and notice the interface of other disciplines. He had read once about how Antonio Gaudi, a famous Catalan architect had met his demise by being run over by a tram in the centre of Barcelona. He could really empathise and understand how that would be possible - especially as an architect. He shuddered at the thought of actually living in a city with trams, and on a couple of occasions he had experienced close calls with them, when visiting some German cities. Admittedly, the problem in those instances was that he did not look the right way, and was just a little impulsive with crossing the street.

Entering the other coffee house, he loved the interaction with one particular member of staff, who was a bright, intelligent and good looking blond woman. She was very welcoming to him, as her eyes appeared subtly wider and more lustrous on seeing him enter. Luke wallowed in this frisson of pleasure, and would normally delight in their short exchange.

"Hello, how are you?" Luke dutifully enquired.

"Quite well, thank you. How are you?" She responded with a warm smile that he later savoured, while he drank his coffee.

"Pretty good, thanks," he replied.

"What's the book you're reading?" she enquired.

"Oh, it's a book on meditation," sounding a little embarrassed.

"I tried meditation recently, but I didn't think I had the patience for it, and I got very frustrated. I don't think I'm really able to do it." She proffered.

"I believe everyone is able, if they put their mind to it, to be mindful, which is primarily the quality one is trying to cultivate. Even you can do it, I'm sure. Just persevere - if you wish that is. There are no shoulds or musts in Buddhism, thankfully, only guidelines and advice to be accepted or rejected."

"So now then onto more important matters, what would you like to drink? Let me think…could it possibly be a regular Latte?" she teased out of him, while screwing up her eyes in mock concentration.

"How did you guess….Can you read my mind I wonder? I guess you'll be predicting where I will sit as well", Luke ventured.

"Just there on that comfy armchair," as she extended her left arm, and pointed near the window at the front of the shop.

"In fact yes, that's where I had in mind. You're a terrific mind reader." Luke thought of adding, 'next you will be telling me what colour underwear I'm wearing', but he stopped short of expressing this, for fear of sounding too risqué, and also because there were other customers waiting in the queue.

"Here we go - one perfectly formed latte", she placed the coffee on the ledge in front of him,

"You've even given it a heart shaped froth…how romantic." he enthused. Now experiencing a degree of sexual arousal, he reluctantly acknowledged the other customers waiting to be served, and prised himself from the conversation.

As Luke sat down in the predicted seat, he opened his book, and began to read. He tended to sift through the text quite slowly, in order to try and absorb the concepts and ideas more readily, but also to experience joy on occasions when the author had beautifully phrased sentences, or had used delightful metaphors and similes to explain ideas. Luke would also have moments where he would pause from his book, sit still, and try and reflect on the topics. At other times, he would just get distracted by the array of different personalities that entered the coffee shop. As T.S Eliot once said, 'we are distracted from distraction by distraction.' On this particular Sunday morning, he noticed something slightly odd about the couple who had entered the coffee shop after him, while he was comfortably positioned in the light brown leather armchair. Both of them had severe problems with their legs, and they were using crutches to get around. The woman who was elegantly attired, almost as if she had just been to church, looked over to Luke, and gave him a warm smile. The man, who Luke presumed to be her partner, had a very serious look on him, and was wearing black tinted glasses. The quality that struck Luke the most was their stoical and uncomplaining nature. They both had severe disabilities, but they were resilient in the face of them.

He started thinking how they might have got their serious injuries, yet remaining so stoical. He had watched a series about CIA spies recently, and the thought of agents being in the field came to him. The initially tenuous view emerged that they had once been acting as special agents located in a volatile region of the world. They had both got injured in the line of duty, and now they were working for GCHQ, which seemed to Luke to be a plausible idea, which started gathering ground and momentum. Had they come to spy on him, or even check him out at close quarters, to assess how much of a genuine threat he posed to the authorities and the establishment?

The more Luke churned this circular story over in his mind, the more he realised that he would only go to that coffee store for one reason only, and that would be to talk and flirt with that blonde member of staff. Otherwise there would be no pull or draw to enter that premises for him.

Luke came to suspect that there was something up in his world, and it seemed he was only starting to scratch the tip of the iceberg of this web of entanglement and intrigue that up until recently he had been blind to. Luke's initial emotional response was one of being chilled, and he experienced a momentary fear engulfing him, but just as quickly as it had surfaced, did it then dissipate. He thought whether he could be a number one target for all the governments around the world. Could this be true or was this just a symptom of his schizophrenia condition, and his consequently creative, yet at times, fanciful imagination. Out of the two of them, the woman was more overt in her interest towards Luke, and on a number of occasions continued to give Luke heart-warming smiles that he willingly reciprocated. What he also observed was their stillness and serenity, where they did not feel the pressure to indulge in idle chit-chat, but instead just savoured their coffee and their environment intently with a few exchanges of necessary but hushed and tender words between them.

Luke was also conscious with the book he happened to be reading, which was called 'The Heart' written by a person from his Buddhist movement. The book explicated a universal loving kindness meditation with a wonderful depth and clarity. It was in a resplendent red colour, which was emblazoned all over. He noticed himself thinking whether they thought this was a book Luke was particularly drawn to because of its colour - due to connotations of devilish passions. This is not how Luke saw it at all. Instead, it was a colour that symbolized love and compassion – embodied predominantly in the Buddha Amitabha – a red coloured archetypal Buddha figure that existed in Buddhist teachings. More than anyone else he knew, he responded very favourably to this loving kindness meditation practice. He profoundly resonated with the idea of metta or universal loving kindness that the Buddha had encouraged in all his followers - all those years ago. A lot of people, who had grown to know Luke, picked up on this quality of friendliness and kindness from him, which normally manifested as warm, connecting smiles, and helpfulness to nearly all he encountered in conversation.

Once Luke had left the coffee shop, with the peculiar occurrences still playing on his mind, he ventured back to his spacious one-bed basement flat. He was starting to feel a little emotionally unsteady with these two coffee shop incidences. Walking slowly but deliberately through the local park near the centre of town - named Jephson Park, he loved the variety of trees that were assembled there, and he would commonly stop and sit on one of the many benches that were available. On this particular Sunday, there were quite a lot of people making their way very leisurely through the picturesque grounds. Quite a few of the benches had been snapped up, but Luke managed to spot one bench, which seemed to be basking in the sunlight. He parked himself on it, and just quietly and mindfully absorbed the sounds and visual delights of that wonderful resource - for a brief fifteen minute spell.

Luke sometimes thought that these grounds acted like his own substitute garden. Although he had a garden at the back of his flat, he spent very little time using it, partly due to its small but bijou parameters, partly due to the fact that it was directly overlooked by both of the neighbours' kitchen and bedrooms, and partly due to him possessing a tired, old timber table and chairs, which were all slowly falling apart. He felt all three of these conditions lent themselves to a sense of claustrophobia in his back-garden, and where he basically preferred the resource of the wonderful open space of the park instead.

Chapter 7

The following week at work, Luke started to act differently. Being aware that he was probably on show to at least the government and intelligence services; he made a point of dressing more flamboyantly. His mood was becoming more hyper and manic – the by-product of an increased heart rate, and his mind was beginning to buzz more with mental activity.

On Monday 10th March, he wore a cuff-linked white shirt with a single breasted blue blazer jacket with gold buttons and stylish, smart grey trousers from a fashionable clothing outlet. To complete the look, he had his newly purchased polished black shoes, which would make a strong sound on the ground, while he walked - due to his tendency to drop his feet first on his heels, and then the rest of his feet.

Luke would always park at the edge of Dorridge town, by a wooded area. This backdrop gave him a little cause for concern, due to the potential for someone to lurk and ambush him, while Luke would be getting into or out of his car. Luke knew he just had to trust that he was being completely protected by unseen forces at play in the universe.

It was a sunny day, and there was a completely clear blue sky that morning. Both with the weather and his attire, it gave Luke a spring in his step to work, but one which was partially tainted by an inner restlessness. Although it was quite a cold day his blazer jacket, which was a figure hugging tight fit, kept him sufficiently warm not to need an overcoat. The desired look would have been spoiled if he had to don a thick overcoat on top of what he was already wearing.

As Luke entered the office domain, Elaine, the PA to the director Brian, had already arrived, and had an ordered pile of papers in front of her that she was carefully and meticulously sifting through.

"Morning, Elaine", Luke uttered in a very strident, almost military tone that was very reminiscent of his boarding school days. There was a genuine clarity and musicality to his voice today, and it pleased Luke to hear himself in this way.

"Morning, Luke." She was quite a pretty girl but not very self-assured. She had told him on a couple of occasions that she did not really enjoy her job, and Luke pondered whether this was the cause of her low self-esteem. At times she could be quite nervous around Luke. This was nowhere more evident than when Luke was making himself coffee or tea, and was standing silently in the back kitchenette area - waiting for the kettle to boil - in a moment of mindful contemplation. She would appear at the entrance door, and get a short, sharp jolt of fear - triggered by his quiet presence.

"You're in early today? What possessed you to come into the office at this hour?" said Luke cheerily towards her on that particular morning.

"The admin was getting on top of me, so I felt I needed to grab the bull by the proverbial horns and do something about it. I wouldn't normally come in so early though. It's a little unusual for me." She replied with the side of her mouth curling upwards in amusement.

"I think that's commendable of you. It's healthy to have some dedication to your work, at times at least!" said Luke emphatically, with a part smile also emerging.

Sitting at his computer, after about an hour and a half of half-hearted work – many thoughts, ideas and images scurried around in his consciousness. This time, more than usual, he observed the various passers-by filing past his window. On various sporadic instances Luke would start to smile to no-one in particular, except to himself, due to thoughts that he would not be beaten by the authorities. To him it was a like a game of giant unwieldy cat and nimble mouse between them. At other times he would try his best to muffle outbursts of laughter. He would then instinctively look over to his right, to see if Benjamin was clocking his peculiar uncontrolled behaviour. Seeing that Benjamin appeared not to be taking any notice, Luke was unconvinced by his seemingly taciturn behaviour.

One woman, who walked by outside the office, stood out for him. She was an older lady wearing a cream coloured mackintosh, all buttoned up, and she carried a long, thin black umbrella in one hand and in the other hand, what looked to Luke like an attaché case. She just did not seem to fit the mould of the country folk in this small town. She appeared as if she was someone who could easily be working for Scotland Yard or MI5 in her general dress sense and in her purposeful physical movements. What also struck Luke as different was that she looked directly at Luke - then as he looked at her, she hesitated - looked in the direction she had come from, and then looked ahead of her, and walked briskly on as if to suggest she was unfamiliar with the town, but also that she was firing a warning shot across the bows. From this brief instance, Luke thought that the jaws of the undercover world were slowly starting to lock onto this shadowy figure named Luke, and slowly try and grind him down until he was gasping his last remaining breath.

There was a back exit from the office through the car park, and was the shortest route to a local supermarket that Luke would sometimes use to buy his lunch. There were places for people to hide behind pillars and cars, but Luke seized the opportunity to face his demons and fears. At lunchtime, he went through this back alleyway, pushing through the internal obstacles he was facing, and went to purchase a well-known brand of flavoured rice, a packet of crisps and a chocolate bar at the supermarket. A suspicious thought popped up in his head, while standing before the aisle where the rice packets were located. The scurrilous thought he had, hinted that the first packet of rice on display might have been tampered with by the intelligence services. He believed that they definitely knew that piece of information about him, since while he had been at the office; he had always picked the vegetarian option of that brand of rice. He then reached right to the back of the selection of packets, and he felt emboldened in the belief that he was now, in some way, managing to outsmart the authorities. After consuming his lunch back at the office, in a small relaxing seating area, he had the intention of making his regular routine of a fast-paced walk around the town. Although, on this Monday, it had started to cloud over from the morning being so bright and clear - now rain clouds were looming. He decided he would still give it a go, and started to make his clockwise route around the small town, which would normally last for about twenty minutes. As he approached the end of the first leg of his customary lunch-time route, and with him still on the edge of the high street; it started spitting light drops of rain. Luke took this as a sign not to continue his walk around town, and did an immediate about-turn. He then proceeded to head straight back to the office.

As soon as he had done this sudden change of direction, he saw two quite muscular men look at him very intently, while passing him by on the high street. They could only have been about five metres behind him, before he made this abrupt change of course. During the brief walk back to the office, the thought surfaced that the two men might have been seriously intent on doing him extreme bodily harm, but the weather had altered just at the right time for his continued safety.

Having about twenty minutes to spare before his lunch break was over, and whilst sat back in the office, he decided to access his e-mail account. Very assuredly he typed in his password and pressed enter.

"Incorrect password - please try again," came the response back on the screen in red. He was sure he had typed the correct password, but thought he must have been mistaken, and promptly went through the same procedure again. Like before the same response flashed up on his screen. Instantaneously, a surge of panic gripped his body tightly. The intelligence services were now playing a game with him, and they were enjoying themselves. He could feel himself blushing, thinking they were all having a good, old laugh at his expense. He believed that they were now flexing their mighty muscles against this lone, vulnerable man. At other times, before this event, he thought he had control over his life. Now he pondered on how he could ever be any match for such an enormous machine as the government.

Ultimately, Luke did not want to harm anyone, but he did feel deeply that the authorities were intent on terminating his life because they saw him as an insidious threat to their hallowed view of democracy - ultimately one built around selfish interests and motivations.

The following day the weather was overcast, but Luke was not put off by the seemingly stealth actions against his life, and made a brisk walk on his lunch break around town again. Not taking his normal route, he instead opted for the route through the park. He was wearing his duffel-coat and he had the hood up. At one point, near where he started his walk through the park, he slightly hesitated, thinking he would go back the way he came, and continue the remaining stretch on more secure territory. Deciding against this, he strode through the park, battling his demons. He defiantly said to himself that they were not going to get the better of him.

The part of the park he was walking through was a fairly open area with a few spindly immature trees, evenly spaced to loosely define the tarmacked pedestrian route. Approaching the last stretch of park, where he had to go through a small car park; he saw two refuse collectors from the council. They were busily emptying the contents of one of the bins into a big green polythene sack. He was no stranger to the antics of MI5, in feigning to be workers in order to make a raid. He had watched the spy programmes on television, and although it was not all factually correct, quite a lot was probably based on reality.

One of the operatives shifted his head from his task to meet Luke's gaze, and he seemed to wear an expression of bafflement yet curiosity. The other operative was focussed on the bin, and was also carrying out more of the strenuous lifting, so was not paying Luke any attention. Luke's heartbeat started to quicken to a rapid-fire procession, as he came towards them. As he passed close by, he maintained a fixed focus on the way ahead, and after about four or five metres past them, he could hear them whispering to themselves and then both of them emitted a hearty exchange of laughter. This prompted Luke to relax a little, thinking they were probably genuine workers from the council and not MI5 agents in disguise. They were probably finding hilarity and amusement in the sheer peculiarity and absurdity of what had just transpired.

That week on the Thursday evening, Luke had gone to bed early with the intention to get up in the middle of the night and do various things, like wash the dishes, meditate and read a book. He had grown accustomed to this singular habit over the last couple of years, and it seemed to work well for him. It was not a habit he indulged in regularly, but every now and then, when he felt tired early in the evening, he would take himself off to bed – sleep for about two to three hours - rise from his slumber - and busy himself with activity for about two to three hours, before going back to sleep again.

He rose from his brief, early evening sleep, went to glug down some tap water in a glass, and then proceeded to brush his teeth. Setting himself up for meditation in front of his shrine, with a beautifully detailed small copper statue of the Buddha that acted as the centrepiece and a few postcards embellished with a few different Buddhas - both archetypal and historical - he saluted the shrine with a verse common in the Buddhist tradition, and then knelt on his yoga mat, whilst sitting on his meditation stool. He found that regular meditation just seemed to calm him down, and allow him to be a little less restless and agitated. If anything it evened the pace of his heartbeat to a gentle but nevertheless faintly punching rhythm.

About halfway during the fifty minute sit that he had scheduled to be on his stool for; Luke felt, what he thought, was a moment of clarity and insight open up to him. What if the intelligence services were not the only people, who were viewing his life? Could it not be beyond the realm of possibility that governments had opened up a channel on satellite stations, devoted to this peculiar and curious individual, and his every movement was being filmed, whether outdoors or inside buildings? They would have the most cutting edge and sophisticated technology at their disposal. Through very advanced thermodynamic and satellite systems, they could effectively spy on any individual in the world, showing a complete clarity of picture resolution to a wider global audience. Could this be why the girl at the last New Year's celebrations on retreat displayed such a hostile reaction towards him? Could it also be why members of the public displayed a deep curiosity with him, when he passed them by on the streets? He harked back to their sense of fascination with him, that at the time he had not been aware of, or thought that is how they look with everyone. Luke wondered how long he had been like a Truman show protagonist.

After his fifty minute meditation, Luke was nervous and slightly overwhelmed by the prospect of being on show to perhaps millions if not billions of people around the world – all judging him in their own way, and him thereby being either praised or criticised in equal measure. The world's scrutiny would be into every area of his life – seeing him with all his foibles and idiosyncrasies, as well as his more flattering attributes, which in Luke's mind seemed to pale against the murkier aspects of his character and habitual tendencies.

He remembered his father, Jeremy, relating to him what the registrar of the University of Warwick had said to his father on one occasion. Jeremy, a tall handsome man, was doing part-time work in a senior role and capacity at the University. Jeremy had said that the registrar had commented about Luke that he was like an onion, in that whenever you thought you knew his character, or habits, another layer of the onion would be peeled away, to show a deeper and more complex side to him. The registrar had said to Jeremy that he found Luke to be a very complex and interesting individual, and he was not always able to predict his behaviour. Where did this view come from? It was almost as if the registrar had first-hand experience from making this assessment of him. Luke had only spoken to the registrar on one particular occasion, and although it was friendly - it was nevertheless brief. It could be that the registrar had been fed information and anecdotes about Luke from other senior people in the University hierarchy, but Luke was sure that the registrar and others were viewing his life, like a Big Brother spectacle.

Luke walked into his kitchen after his sit, and saw the stack of dishes piled high in front of him. Immediately, he had a strong aversion to clean them all. He had left it a number of days, but realised if he did not wash them clean tonight, then he would have to resort to take-outs. Fortunately, he very rarely let it get that bad, and whenever he left them to breaking point, he would nearly always step up to the mark and do the necessary household duty.

Before he tackled the dishes, he was drawn to the idea of playing some music to accompany his domestic activity. Standing in front of his relatively large collection of CDs, he opted for an album by one of the most successful female singers ever. He loved her music, and she would always reinvent herself with new musical styles, in a chameleon-like way. Whilst engaged in the washing-up, he felt a lot of energy welling up and let go in a free dance expression to the sounds of her mature voice. He paid particular attention to the lyrics of one of the songs, with its psychedelic soundtrack and its words talking about the universe spinning out of control and being in a trance. This song just ignited in him an unadulterated joy, which he expressed as an exuberant display of wild and free dance abandon. This was enhanced by the strong belief that he was a televisual spectacle in the on-going drama that was his life. After the dishes were done, he went to his bed and sat up half under the sheets and spoke to a perceived global audience.

"Hello," he opened in a kind, jovial tone.

"I know you're all watching my every move. I guess you thought from my usual serious expression that I was a man with evil intent or possibly malice. This could not be further from the truth. I've always loved humanity, and I believe very much in helping those who are in need. I believe in kindness and honesty especially," he paused for a moment of deliberation, feeling a weight of emotional pressure and nerves bearing down on him, and then continued,

"I must make a point of talking to you more often, rather than keeping my thoughts to myself and secret! I'll have to make myself more transparent in future. It's time for me to go to sleep, so goodnight to you all." Luke ended there, and then tried to get some shut-eye.

The following day on the Friday 14th March, he left his office in Dorridge, because of the perceived threat to his existence by Ben, his work colleague, and made his excursion into London to challenge his shadow side.

Chapter 8

Holding his phone in his hand – poised - Luke felt very worried about what he was about to do. Over the course of last Friday, when he had left his job, and had embarked on his excursion to the centre of London, and through to the Sunday; his thoughts proliferated around the subject of spies, and that his every action might well be televised to many people around the world was fast becoming an ever expanding mental whirlwind. Luke had by now started to believe that even his father might be in on the act of deceit, as he had worked for the Ministry of Defence a few years back, and he had on one particular occasion told the family that he had interviewed special agents and the Chief of Military Intelligence. He imagined it would not be too much beyond the realm of possibility, to think that his father had been briefed about his son, and then they had enlisted his cooperation against his son. He was sat on his sofa with the landline phone resting in the palm of his hand, for what seemed like an age. Beads of sweat were slowly building on his palms and forming on his brow, before he managed to build up the nerve to ring his parent's home and speak to his father, Jeremy. His father was the first to come on the phone. Immediately, Jeremy asked in a very positive and upbeat tone in his voice, which he was prone to do,

"Hi Luke. How are things going?"

"I want to ask you something Dad, and I want you to tell me the truth!" Luke uttered with a stern and solemn voice. Immediately his father switched to becoming very concerned, and the agitation in his voice was distinctly palpable, which made Luke feel physically uncomfortable, and not to say a little queasy.

"Oh no! What's wrong?!? What's happened?!?" said Jeremy.

"Are you a spy Dad?" Luke came straight out with the question that was on his mind - without mincing his weighted words.

"What do you mean a spy? I worked for the Ministry of Defence but", Luke felt he was evading the question, and was very suspect with his answer - so very forcefully interrupted him, by repeating the question and then following it up with,

"Just answer yes or no Dad!" Again his father prevaricated and tried to avoid replying categorically yes or no, which increased the concern and worry in both him and his father's voices.

Finally, after Luke pursued this quite rigid line of approach in a confrontational manner, his father suggested to Luke saying,

"I think Luke you should come over to ours straight away and speak to us face to face about all the concerns and issues you might be having."

He sensed that his father was deeply affected by this apparent accusation. Luke agreed that this would be a good idea, and as soon as he had put the phone down and had collected his thoughts, he left his flat for the village that they lived in, called Crick. It was quite large in size and it boasted a small supermarket store, two pubs, a gastro-pub and a restaurant on the outskirts.

Luke drove carefully and considerately to his parent's home, with a very smooth and easy journey that was made stiller, by not playing the radio. However, the closer Luke got to his parent's residence, the more the anxiety and expectations, of what would await him, swelled. Might mum be in floods of tears and how would his father be towards him, after what could be conceived as a thinly veiled accusation?

He parked the car on the gravel driveway, and saw in the corner of his eye his father making his way from the side entrance to the entrance gates, in order to close them.Jeremy had been a very successful person in business, and he had risen up the ranks from the bottom, to become managing director and later chairman of a few companies. In terms of worldly life he had been very accomplished, and that gave him an assurance that occasionally teetered on the edge of smugness. Luke was indeed very impressed with his achievements, especially the ability to overcome himself and his foibles with grit and determination, and not be worried about what other people thought of him. He was definitely his own man, and this particular heroic streak ran through Luke as well, which Luke had particularly nurtured once he had left school.

Jeremy opened with a trivial but relatively comforting question to Luke, but which ominously anticipated the more serious and weighty conversation to come,

"How was your journey over here?"

"Good thanks", Luke replied with a bitter and nauseous feeling squirming in his gut. "Let's go in and speak to Mum as well, and raise your concerns. By the way Luke, I've been shaking quite violently with what you've said, and it has definitely moved me to the core. You must realise that both me and mum love you very dearly, and have only your best interests at heart. We only want you to succeed in life."

After Luke hugged and kissed his mother, who was sat in the study area where they habitually watched television; Luke sat down at one end of the room, in a low lying brown tanned leather armchair, while his mother was seated on the opposite side of the room in the matching leather three-person sofa. His father, who had been trailing behind Luke, now nestled into his favourite high-backed, bold-striped, upholstered armchair, which he would often park himself in to watch television.

Before anything was uttered, Luke had a profound sense that they had a very much larger audience than themselves, to this ensuing conversation and discussion, with the audience being also of a celestial nature.

"How are you Luke? We were really concerned about you when you called, but we are glad that you decided to come and see us, and not wilfully and dogmatically stay in Leamington." Louise, his mother eased in the question and statement tactfully, and with a mother's sensitivity.

"I really haven't been sleeping well, for the past two to three weeks, and I suspect that the nurse at the new surgery in Leamington has either willingly or out of sheer incompetence not given me the correct medication." Luke proffered.

"I knew it was a bad idea for you to change surgeries especially as you were changing jobs, and there was a lot of upheaval in your life," said Luke's mum with muted anguish in her face.

"What's done is done, and we cannot change the past, but perhaps you might be right Luke, as it seems so out of character for you - not to be well. Hasn't it been almost two months that you've been with this new surgery?" Jeremy enquired.

"I think it's about six weeks. As long as I am getting my medication, I should be healthy and sleeping well, but it hasn't been happening."

Luke felt a deep reassurance and safety being with his parents. This feeling of comfort and ease was amplified by the warm ambient lighting in the room, and the temperature being at an optimum heat; making Luke feel very much loved and held by his parents in their homely environment. He had always appreciated what a loving and stable family environment he had grown up in, and he really did feel that, at least, his mother had always had his best interests at heart, steadfastly trying to encourage and nurture his talents, but not in a pushy over-domineering way.

"One of the things the nurse did strangely, at the new surgery, was to have the syringe fully loaded and prepared before I entered her treatment room. There wasn't much in the way of dialogue, and she didn't seem to be particularly interested in me as a person," Luke added."Jeremy what do you think? That doesn't sound genuine, and it does appear to be a little suspect with the practice's procedures. Have you seen the doctor who is meant to be referred to you yet?" Louise asked inquisitively.

Luke's mother was a beautiful woman, and had kept herself

trim throughout her life. She had had exquisite eyes in ...
but they had slightly lost their lustre with the inevitable ageing,
passing of years. Luke noticed this particularly when a few years
back he saw a photo of her, after she had got married to Jeremy. Luke
was particularly drawn to the utter beauty of her eyes, and her skin
also had a very healthy glow to it. She was also an extremely strong
willed woman, who definitely ruled the Trevelyan household with
an iron fist, but one which had a soft gooey core to the shell of her
defiant exterior. This was probably due to her Germanic origins.
She was definitely a considerate woman to her family and friends,
and at times, Luke would be aware of her compassionate side, and
he would occasionally watch her response to people's suffering on
the television, and quite often she would be moved to tears.

"No, I haven't and that is also something very odd about the
practice's state of affairs," replied Luke.

"And also irresponsible for that surgery not to demand it,
considering they were bound to have realised that you have been
on medication for a long period of time, and considering you had
filled out a registration form, when you joined," Louise added.

"Luke, on the phone you were suggesting from the sounds of
it, as if you thought I was a spy, working for the government, in
order to keep tabs on you. What makes you think that I would ever
do that to my own son?" Jeremy tried to say it calmly, but his voice
belied the undercurrent of anguish with this specific question.

"Well Dad, you did work for the Ministry of Defence, and you
did say you had interviewed the Chief of Military Intelligence in
a Whitehall underground bunker. You then mentioned how you
had spies in the secure room as well that you were interrogating
or asking pertinent questions to - obviously related to your area
of National Security. It didn't seem to me like too much of a
stretch of the imagination, to think that they had roped you into
their world of subterfuge and espionage. I really don't think that
mum in any way has a clue about your involvement, and she is
completely innocent."

e, I did interview those people as you
.s never interested with what went on in the
16. I was obviously aware of their departments,
ʋs worked in the space next to them. Quite
just intent on doing a good job for the MoD, and
Jeremy said with what seemed to Luke like genuine
whʋ ʋedness.

Luʋe inwardly paused, and he suddenly felt convinced that what his Dad had just said was true and accurate. If he had been recruited by MI5 or MI6, to spy on his own dear son, he would be inwardly torn and frustrated at his despicable deception. He had always been such a loving and dear father to Luke that he believed Jeremy would never be able to undertake such a massive betrayal of trust. Luke also reckoned in that instant, that the secret services knew about this real tenderness that overflowed from his father towards his offspring, and therefore they would never ask Jeremy to carry out such a reprehensible act, which the authorities would assume he could not properly execute.

"Dad, it has just come to me that I now truly believe you're innocent, and I really believe that you and mum are genuine in this overall game of subterfuge. I do think that I'm like the character out of the Truman show, with my every action being televised around the country and possibly the world as well. Isn't it too much of a coincidence that I've a passing resemblance to the main protagonist of that film?!?" Luke said.

"I'm glad you now believe your parents would never do something as awful as spy on their own first-born son. We've only wanted to see you succeed in your life, and be the best you can be. Anyway, what makes you so special that MI5 or MI6 should want to know your whereabouts and that you should be a continuous television spectacle to the world?" his mother now asked with a strained control to her voice.

"I believe that governments around the world have a real concern about the threat from a possible radical lone individual, who could rise up and dismantle this present world order. They mistakenly think that this individual is me. Having said that I think I will become a Buddha in future lives and I believe I am destined for spiritual greatness in this life to come. It was prophesied by the Buddha that someone will emerge in this world, and will be called Maitreya, and I believe that someone is me!" said Luke.

"You're not going to be a Buddha. You're so unlike what a Buddha would manifest as!" Jeremy replied indignantly and a little mockingly.

"How do you know Dad?" Luke collected himself before he continued to proceed.

"You really do not know the qualities I have developed over my life that resemble that of the Buddha's. Before he became the Buddha, it is stated in the scriptures and biographies that he had an almost super-abundance of talents at his command. As you know I've got many aptitudes and talents. When I read the accounts of his early life, he also had an abundance of material wealth. He was very handsome, not too dissimilar to me, and he was part of the warrior caste in Indian society. I too am an inheritor of a lot of material wealth in this family, and it is interesting to note that our family stems from the landed gentry with our motto being 'Moriens sed invictus' – 'Dying but Unconquered'. This implies bravery, courage and valour; like that of the warrior caste of the Buddha's time. The other name that Maitreya goes under is Ajita, which literally means Unconquered. I think this synonym of Maitreya's and its link to our family motto is more than a coincidence, don't you?"

"Still Luke, you're not going to be a Buddha. There are many more people in this world, who would be a candidate for that title or mantle!" His father said with a disparaging tone.

"I'm not going to be able to convince you both, but I believe it to be true", Luke wearily stated to his parents. Louise then suggested to Luke,

"I really think you must change surgeries to back here in Crick. The surgery in Crick has always been so good to you, and you really liked the staff there."

"I definitely agree. I'll ring the surgeries up tomorrow or sometime this coming week."

The realisation sprung on him with a short, sharp kick to the guts that they did not know that he had left his job last Friday and that he was adamant in not going back. He did not want to divulge this crucial piece of information for fear of the presumed backlash that would ensue, and the possible vitriol that this would engender towards him, while he was dwelling in a tender and fragile state. In his mind he was thinking that he would give it a few more days until he told them. He would then feel more comfortable to withstand their anger and anxiety; which he perceived would be the natural corollary of the bold decision he had made.

With a little more bandying of ideas about and discussing the way forward, Luke said to his parents that he would retire to their small sitting room, and read one of the latest issues of an interior design magazine that his mother religiously bought every month. He loved looking at other people's homes, but with no desire to possess any, or do up his own place in those styles, but just for the sheer pleasure of savouring and enjoying the designs and elegance of the interiors, and also seeing the grandeur of some of the many homes or flats that people lived in. He also appreciated the articles that had been written, and he would occasionally read some of the issues from cover to cover - intensely wallowing in the overall delight of the publication. In some ways, he preferred this magazine to the multifarious architectural publications, which largely focused on the architectural shell and exterior form. Luke pondered on this for a moment, and thought that he might have been a more accomplished interior designer than architect, as he had a genuine aptitude for colours and textures, but also possessing a gift in draughtsmanship. The overall form and spaces that could be achieved seemed less interesting to him now than the quality of their interiors, and what could be achieved within a defined building shell.

Chapter 9

The following week on Monday 17th March, he arranged an appointment with his doctor at the Leamington surgery, to explain matters and his concerns. He had arranged it for Wednesday 26th March, the day before his next fortnightly appointment on that Thursday. Rather than contacting the Crick surgery, he would wait until he had this scheduled meeting, before taking any steps to go back to the surgery at his parent's home. There was still no reprieve in Luke getting a proper, decent sleep, and his meditation was the only way to salvage some glimmer of peace and cope with a slowly mounting restlessness, but one which was still partially contained.

On the Wednesday 19th March, he had a very strong idea pop into his head, which would not let go, but seemed to acquire snowballing momentum. Luke started to ruminate over the possibility of going to London early in the afternoon, with his meditation stool, some warm clothing and some food provisions, all contained in a relatively small rucksack, and venture off into one of London's main parks. He would then find a majestic tree to sit under, and meditate well into the night just as the Buddha had done before his enlightenment, all those years ago. He felt on this occasion he was very much following in the noble footsteps of a great spiritual warrior, and trying to overcome some of his fears in a very exposed location. Also it would be the middle of the night where darkness would completely surround and envelop him.

That morning he rose from his warm, sumptuous bed; and before he had breakfast he did his morning ritual of meditation.

In a surprise turn, this particular morning he decided to indulge himself, in order to give himself as much strength for the ordeal he would be facing that evening. Normally, he would have a shower in his roll top bath, but this time he felt the strong desire to use the bath as it had been originally intended and allowed hot water to pour from a thin cylindrical stainless steel post. He then found some bath liquid to create a luxuriant foamy surface to magnify the pampering indulgence. This felt really good to Luke, and he was relishing this intense satisfaction, with his physical movements taking on a slower and more deliberate nature.

He filled the bath as much as he could, before his conscience started hinting that he might now be a little excessive in the quantity of water he was using. Luke had a strong ethical sense that had been developed and nurtured over twenty one years of Buddhist practice. Luke had filled the bath up to a generous measure, and delighted in the hot liquid embrace of this early morning experience. All he needed in this instance would be to have a few scented candles to light the bathroom, without the comparatively harsh light that he was more accustomed to. Definitely being drawn to the feminine and sensual qualities and experiences his sister and female colleagues at work shared with him - and what gave them unalloyed joy - he really resonated with their simple pleasures that gave them sweet delight.In the afternoon just before Luke was going to set off for his adventurous and momentous trip to London; he was sitting in his comfortable wickerwork armchair, situated in his bedroom, when his landline phone started ringing. Rather than thinking that it might be a cold caller, and not answer; something impelled him to reach for the phone, and find out who was on the other end of the line.

"Hi Luke", his sister Rebecca said in a solemn voice. "What are you doing?" she enquired with a soft and low sternness. Luke immediately thought: how could she possibly know to ring just before he was to embark on a serious adventure, unless she was also party to the televisual display of his life. If she was not involved in this big conspiracy against his brother, then why did she ring when she must have known that her brother would probably be at the office?

"Hi Rebecca, I'm okay thanks."

"Why aren't you at work Luke?" asked Rebecca in a tone that suggested she was trying desperately to keep herself measured and a calm, responsible presence on the other end of the line.

"Well, I've decided to give up work for a while, as I felt I wasn't safe in that office environment. I really feared for my life and I felt the only sensible thing to do, would be to completely remove myself from there, and then live a little with the savings and the inheritance that we might be getting."

"Don't you think that it isn't very sensible giving up your work like that? I also think that it's very unlikely that you were in danger of losing your life in the office. It just seems to me to be unbelievable and completely far-fetched and fanciful!" his sister said with worry that bristled through the phone receiver.

While his sister was speaking, Luke hoped that she would not ask what he would be doing that evening, as he could only be truthful, and the disclosure would be reported straight back to his parents, which would cause loud alarm bells to go off in all of their minds.

"I just think I need a break from working for the time being, and my leaving the office has been the trigger for that."

"Have you taken your medication recently?" Rebecca enquired.

"It's interesting you should mention that as I was with Mum and Dad last Sunday and I told them there was something fishy about the surgery in Leamington - both mum, dad and me think it would be better to go back to the surgery in Crick, because they had always been really good to me. As Dad said to me, 'They cared for patients rather than processed patients, which is a quality that's becoming more unusual in this day and age." Luke said this with hope in his heart that this would go some way to comforting and relaxing the concerns of his sister.

"Oh well. That's a good step at any rate. Wouldn't you like to come and see me today?" she asked. Inwardly Luke felt the panic assault him with a violent blow to his innards, thinking his cover would be blown, and that she would discover what could only be called his mission for the unfolding afternoon and night ahead.

"I can't come to see you today, as I'm doing other things but some other time might be better," he prevaricated, trying to desperately suppress the tension in his body and mind. "It would be really good to see you, though."

"Really not today, but definitely some other time, Becks." Luke was now just willing the conversation to end due to his extreme awkwardness, and also as he had a train to catch, which would be leaving in about ten minutes.

"Okay whatever Luke. It's your life and I can't tell you what to do or what not to do. Just take it easy and hopefully speak to you soon."

"Will do siss… Thanks for your concern. Speak to you soon then. Bye," and with that he hung up straight after the first mention of the word bye.

He quickly grabbed the rucksack that he had earlier in the morning filled with the necessary provisions; got his warm navy blue duffel coat, locked the flat, and lightly jogged towards the train station. Nothing would now prevent him from changing his course of action, and he deliberately did not take his mobile phone with him. There were two reasons for this decision. Firstly, he did not want his parents or sister to have the possibility of contacting him during a momentous night, and then spoiling his heroic undertaking in the blackness of one of London's parks. The other reason was that he did not want his movements to be so explicitly tracked by the intelligence services. He wanted their potential efforts in locating his whereabouts to be made that little bit harder, rather than it being given to them on a plate.

Luke was definitely walking into the deep unknown: the mysterious, exhilarating yet frightening void, but nonetheless felt surprisingly calm about what might await him.

On the train journey there he found himself deciding that he would pick Hyde Park as a venue for his meditation sit. He had been there before quite recently, and he appreciated the proximity to Oxford Street, Soho, Mayfair and also Marylebone station, where the train arrived at its end destination. He was convinced that he would find the ideal tree to sit under for his late night meditation after a spot of perambulation around Hyde Park in the bright sunshine.

The journey to London was nondescript, with everything running efficiently and smoothly, and the carriage he was sitting in being quiet and fairly empty. This helped in giving him space to think clearly about how to structure his evening, with a vaguely coherent plan of attack. Luke had decided to wear warm, practical items of clothing, and nothing flashy or extrovert, like his previous visit to the capital.

For this day near the end of March it was particularly sunny and warm, which was a relief to Luke if he was going to be out in the open air - for most of the night. After having walked very briskly from Marylebone station to Oxford street, he continued to head straight for the interior of the park, and have a good look for that elusive timber giant that was unaware it was going to be selected as a haven of tranquillity.

Coming across quite a number of people in various locations, sitting in huddled groups, or lying as couples stretched out on the ground, in order to catch some much needed rays; he sauntered past these groups, who were in the large grassy open area of the park. Luke was keen to find somewhere more secluded and in a slightly denser, woodier part of the grounds.

Then as Luke was walking into a more tree-covered and partially overgrown area, at least on one side of the path; he spied a tree that a young couple were under. Very little could be heard from them, as they were talking quietly. They were about a good twenty-five metres away from where Luke had stopped in his tracks. Behind them there was another row of trees, and he noticed a very majestic oak tree, which had no-one under it. It felt suddenly like a strong force was impelling him to choose this being out of all others. It was its close proximity to the path that Luke was standing on and its location, grandeur and energy, which seemed to be completely in accordance with his aesthetical sensibilities and intuition.

Luke pulled the fold-away meditation stool out of his new rucksack. The rucksack was purchased just for the occasion. Laying out a warm blanket on the ground in front of him, he planted the meditation stool on top. He began to sit in a meditation posture for all who passed by to visibly become aware of. The tree was a good twenty metres away from the tarmac path that snaked alongside the undergrowth. As a relaxing and comforting thought, he mused that there must be many eccentric people pass through this park all year round, and Luke was just upholding a long-standing tradition of this park. Anyway, what was so big a deal about meditating in public, in a quiet setting like this - he pondered to himself. At the beginning of his sit, he was overwhelmed with jangling nerves, which meant his closed eyelids fluttered vigorously – albeit to him at least. Their quivering nature did slowly subside, but an echo still lingered for the duration of his time on the stool.

Luke knew that he was nowhere near the development of that of Siddhartha Gautama, before he became the Buddha, and about twenty minutes into his sit, he could feel himself getting a little restless and feeling a desire to explore the city. The realisation slowly crept up on him, like an advancing shadow that he should now do what his heart desired, which was to venture into the thriving metropolis. He knew he had found the most appropriate tree, and he could now go wandering as if he were some lone, predatory animal, and find somewhere to have a meal, so as to keep him sustained for the evening's surprise instalment. As he was aware that the nocturnal drama was fast approaching, this made him slightly less calm than he was earlier on in the train, and the stark reality was steadily dawning on him.

Date 19/5/16   LOOKSWAY   No. 6 2

Received from DRAZ

RECEIVED WITH THANKS (repeated watermark) 0-75/6/3554513

the sum of

£

Carefully packing all the contents away back into his rucksack, he made his way along the paths back to the entrance to Hyde Park and Marble Arch, where a great multitude of nationalities were speaking in disorderly arranged groups, taking in the warmth and beauty of the weather and the city's hustle and bustle.

Luke spied a well-known sandwich store that he knew sold vegetarian meals. Their ingredients would always enliven his taste buds, and stimulate his gustatory sense. While he lingered inside the store just in front of the sandwich selection, he felt the glowing warmth of the sun beating on his back through the plate glass window, which fronted the edge of Oxford Street. He inwardly delighted at the simple pleasure of the heat and golden mellowness that had spread over his back, with a giant, warm, bear-like embrace. He appreciated the simplicity of it all, amongst the turbulence and complexity of what modern life had become for the majority of people.

As he made his way out of the store, he thought that he would eat his sandwiches just at the front of the store, amongst the snaking throng of shoppers, workers and holiday makers. There were no seats, but Luke felt emboldened to just stand to the side of the pavement, and eat his meal in full view of all who walked past. The genuine confidence that Luke sometimes exhibited, was, even by his standards, surprising. Not only had he planted himself firmly at the edge, amongst a constant moving stream of bodies in muted colours, interrupted by splashes of bold, vibrant colour, with just a handful taking time out to pause near him, but he also set about wolfing down his supper, and thoroughly relishing the discreet exhibition he was making of himself.

He wallowed in the gorgeous nature of this spot, not only because he had a view of the beautiful park but also the golden liquid sun was enlivening his face and body. However, the contrast could not be starker, due to the juxtaposition of Luke, who felt still and composed, while all around him varying shades of anxiety and stress were inscribed on the faces of passers-by. He felt so happy to have ditched his last job, and to have taken the leap into the unknown. He did hope that his previous employer would not be picking up too many loose ends that he might have left, and that his architectural business would still continue to flourish.

After having polished off his meal, and washed it down with some still water, he dutifully waited for the traffic lights to change to allow the cross-flow of pedestrians over the busy street. Quite often, as a teenager, he would try and dodge traffic when it was the vehicles' right of way, but he very rarely attempted such foolhardy behaviour, while in the heart of London.

Luke remembered back to one particular occasion when he was at the Oxford Circus junction with Regent Street in his late teens, and he went out into the road, to suddenly see a double decker bus come to a screeching halt right next to him - within a few inches of his life. After this incident, he became much more aware that he needed to abide by the green man signals at pedestrian crossings, and not take the law into his own hands.

After having parked himself on a stone slab that ran in segments by Marble Arch, near the side of the entrance to the park, he suddenly became aware of his own inner emotional world. Luke felt very alive and present to his experience, but his heart area was charged with a fire and heat. This was not a confused or erratic heat, but one with a genuine, sustained force behind it. Still he could not help but think about what was in stall that night, and felt his pulse quicken fractionally more than before.

Gradually over the last two to three weeks the fire in him had been getting progressively stronger and more powerful in expression. He still wondered whether he was actually getting more muddled in his thinking, or else he was breaking through to new levels of insight and awareness of the world around him. Not being entirely sure, he thought that the primary symptoms of his illness were manifesting themselves, which he had never experienced in the seventeen or so years that he had been on that particular drug.

Turning his mind away from what he would say to the Leamington surgery, he gradually weaned himself off a potentially spiralling negative train of thought towards the future exchanges he might encounter there. Instead he let go of any need to be anywhere other than the present moment, and appreciated the golden orb and the combination of a peaceful yet somewhat frenzied melee occurring around him. His worry for now was plateauing.

Chapter 10

After Luke sat on a deck chair, freely available for anyone to use in the park, dusk was setting in, and the tendrils of light from the sun were steadily diminishing and fading around them. He had decided to resume his original position below that magnificent oak tree, grab something sweet to eat that he had brought as provisions for the evening, and stood attentive, while slowly munching on his almond-coated-sponge slice.

Once the light in the sky had completely turned black, with it being a clear night and the stars visible from where he stood in the park; he laid out his warm blanket before him, and donned a very thick jumper, as well as his trusted duffel coat that had remained on him most of the afternoon and early evening. He then unfolded his meditation stool and quickly found a comfortable and relaxed yet upright posture on the grainy, nobbled ground.

Closing his eyes, he could hear sounds of boisterous laughter at the end of the path, where it split off in direction, but no sooner did he become aware of it than they started to diminish in volume and recede from his hearing. It was then that Luke acknowledged that in this part of the park, at least, he was now on his own. Luke was now experiencing a mixture of emotions: on the one hand he was a little tense about the possible threat from a group of rowdy delinquents, and on the other side of the coin, he was delighting in a joy that would come to him in waves. After thirty or so minutes sitting quietly and firmly on the stool, he began to grow somewhat restless again. He said to himself kindly that he was nowhere near the development of Siddhartha Gautama, and he could definitely excuse himself for feeling agitated and wanting to move from his spot.

He thought he would change his tack, and he made a firm resolve to sit on for another ten minutes, doing the practice of the mindfulness of breathing that he had been engaged in. This practice developed integration of one's many different selves or sub-personalities into a harmonious unified self, plus it cultivated a greater degree of concentration and focus.

The idea that emerged in his mind was to venture into Mayfair, and sample the atmosphere in a few of the pubs in that quarter. Also thinking that it was not late enough for him, and by experiencing city life a little that evening, he would be nearer the silent but possibly deadly action that might await him in the middle of the night.

After having ordered his third soft drink at a well-known bar at the edge of Oxford Street, he occupied himself by making overt glances in the direction of a few pretty women - not being particularly discreet and subtle about it. When he was distracted like this, most women he encountered would not meet his forceful gaze, which was sometimes close to being an outright stare. His sister had confided in him on a few occasions that this bold eye contact could be viewed, by a lot of women, as threatening and intimidating, but Luke had always maintained that he was only being true to himself, and he would only act out how he was naturally. In recent years, he did temper his look by looking away every now and then. Luke somehow sensed that people saw him as different, eccentric and odd.

Luke left the pub after a good while inside, and then let himself be spontaneously guided in his choice of the next pub or bar. He did not have any plan of his subsequent venue, but chose dark quiet roads to test his nerve and fear towards unknown drinking establishments. There were moments on this stroll, when he was starting to sense what it might be like to be a fearless warrior.

It made him feel exhilirated in the courage he was displaying. Slowing down his walk towards a bar, prosaically titled as the name of one of the streets in Mayfair, he fancied the idea of having a swift alcoholic drink amongst those who he thought would predominantly be office and city high flier types. Glancing at his metal strapped watch, it said it was coming up to 10:30pm. He was glad that it was becoming sufficiently late for him that after one more drink, he could head back to the park, and then be able to resume his late night meditation. All this evening's entertainment was a prelude to the real reason he came to London that day but still all vitally necessary.

He crossed the open door threshold into the warm and invitingly lit bar, and saw nearly all the seats around him taken. He did not feel intimidated by the quantity of handsome and possibly materially successful young people around him. As he entered the space he paused for a few moments, and surveyed all around him in a cursory way the whole lively spectacle. He then proceeded to head straight for the bar, where he patiently waited his turn to be served. He ordered himself a bottle of beer. It was going to be his one and only drink that night, so he would slowly savour it, and allow the alcohol to relax his mind a little more than it already was.

Carrying his bottle of beer, Luke found a two person table with wooden seating, set by the entrance to the bar, and casually ensconced himself in one of the chairs, while leaning part of his back against an ornate free-standing timber partition. He felt very self-assured and confident in this setting, even though he was sitting all on his own. His body language definitely displayed this quality, by having partially splayed legs, open shoulders, and one arm languidly hanging behind the back of the chair. His overall orientation was split between some of the other customers in the bar and the entrance doorway.

A good ten years ago, he would not have even contemplated going to a bar or pub on his own, let alone a smart, well-to-do bar like this one. In the last two to three years that he had been teaching at the Buddhist centre, it had given him a much greater measure of inner strength and robustness in character. His work at the University of Warwick was also invaluable in building his confidence, as he quite frequently had to chair meetings.

As he sat in his seat, feeling very integrated and in command of his emotions, he spotted a group of thirty-something women, engrossed in what seemed like a meaningful discussion. He wondered that instead of them talking about current affairs, or something of a more serious nature, they were probably dissecting and sharing tales of their partner's peculiar but annoying habits at home. They looked the types to have other halves, as they were not distracted by other men around them, and were content to be absorbed in each other's company. They seemed a mature, sophisticated and well-heeled group of women.

One of the blond women did steal a look in Luke's direction, but quickly averted her gaze, when Luke turned his head in her direction. He registered her barely noticeable interest, and he tried to pursue a subtle, distant, visual flirtation further. She did not reciprocate with playful wandering eyes towards him, although as Luke was getting close to sipping the last remnants of his bottle - she got up and walked past, flashing a lovely warm and sweet smile at him. This was a moment that Luke relished, with the pleasant joy lingering while making his way back from the bar to his solitary spot in the park.

Looking at his watch - and just about ready to get into his meditation posture underneath the dark, black friendly giant - he observed it was now just after 12am. He had leisurely made his way back from the bar, and on a few instances in the park took the opportunity to gaze upwards at the wondrous cosmic display. It was not the brightest glimpse he had ever had of the star-lit firmament, but it was enough to inspire his imagination and child-like wonder.

Settling down on his meditation stool and getting comfortable, he made a definite resolve to sit for at least fifty minutes without moving. He thought that if he gave himself a realistic target, he would then be more likely to achieve that aim, than to proceed with the wishful and vain hope to meditate indefinitely into the night. The total reality was now thrust upon him and nearly always in times of existential crisis, he would rise to the challenge with a grit and determination within. Although there was a scant hint of worry, the major emotion, in him, was feeling emboldened and together. The open air scenario lent this emotional strength to his situation. As Luke sat there with the very faint hum of vehicles diminishing in intensity in the far distance, a profound silence slowly began to descend on him and this part of the park.

There was a famous Zen story about a Zen abbot, who had been told that newly accomplished samurai warriors would often test their new swords that they were given on homeless vagrants in a certain part of Japan. Their way of testing the swords would be to sever the heads of the vagabonds. The abbot spent some time with the homeless people, and decided one night that they should make themselves scarce, while he would sit in the location, where the samurai warriors usually appeared. He was not deterred by this threat to his life. That night the abbot calmly sat in that particular area, in a meditation posture. While he was positioned in this spot, a samurai warrior nimbly and quietly came towards him, unsheathed his sword, and then exclaimed to the abbot in a loud voice,

"Prepare to die!" to which the abbot did not move a muscle or flinch at all but continued sitting like an immovable but peaceful rock. The samurai warrior was so shocked at the strength and courage of this individual that he panicked and then fled from the scene - not having the tenacity to carry out his threat.

Zen Buddhism was often about conveying to people and monks, stories and paradoxes. This specific story had lodged itself firmly in his psyche, and he too felt that he could be as strong willed as this abbot in the face of impending danger.

He wondered whether there were agents with guns directing

their cross hairs straight at Luke's head from the protection of the adjacent bushes, but patiently waiting for their orders to fire their weapons. These mercenaries would be as silent as was necessary for Luke not to hear their movements. He could not be sure, but with the past week's events he would not put it past the secret service to be involved in such a malicious strategy. He still believed that they considered him to be an insidious threat to the whole of civilisation.

About ten minutes before the end of his fifty minute sit, where a deep silence had descended everywhere; he heard behind him a branch snapping as if someone had accidentally trod on it. Suddenly, his heart started to beat faster, and a fear gripped him tightly. He now knew, this was the moment of truth and he would just act like the abbot had done all those hundreds of years ago. Although, he felt fear, he continued to remain rock solid on his stool. There was no exclamation or spoken word uttered, just a resounding stillness in the depths of the park, and yet what Luke imagined was a looming menace in close proximity. He was open to the possibility that it could have been a fox, but somehow Luke thought that the sound of the branch snapping was more akin to a heavier weight being loaded onto the wood. From Luke's perceptive ear, the timber breaking definitely had a deeper resonance than if a fox had landed on it. Luke waited - still sat like a staunchly defiant yet motionless king - with his fear gradually dispelling into a refined calmness.

Looking at his watch with the help of a light, he observed that he had been sitting very still and poised for almost an hour. He could not however sustain a longer sit, as his body was feeling the discomfort with the knobbly surface beneath him.

Lifting himself in a slow and gradual ascent from his stool, he delicately unfurled his legs from his meditation posture, being careful to allow his ankles to adjust to a normal standing position - and generally being kind to his body. He packed everything away, but decided to finish the two remaining almond-coated sponge slices, and then stuffed the packaging back into his rucksack.

From where the sound came he could only see complete darkness, and presumed that whoever had made the noise had stealthily retreated to a more secure vantage point - in a well-trained and managed operation.

Finding the tarmac path with relative ease, he followed it to where it split off, where a pool of luminosity covered his frame in a ghostly wash. He paused briefly, and deliberated on which path to take. Was he going to follow the tried and tested path or else go towards the more unfamiliar and somewhat alien territory in what was practically complete darkness? He chose the former but as he came nearer to the entrance to the park, he veered off towards the other end of the park, still maintaining his alignment with the established hard surface pathway.

After walking for what seemed like three hundred metres; a lone slim dark, silhouetted figure shot across the path about a hundred metres in front of him, and disappeared into the blackness of the park, without making a single iota of sound. It was almost dreamlike in its apparition. This ghostly appearance really rattled Luke, because up until then, he had not actually seen anyone. He suspected that this singular person was one of many lurking in the park because of Luke's presence that night. How many more were in this park, watching his movements?

This specific observance prompted Luke to flee from the confines of the grounds as soon as he could. His breath had now become more audible and shallower, as again the harsh light of reality had announced itself to him. Changing his orientation, he headed straight for the nearest park fence, which was very ornate and refined in appearance, being of royal commission. They were particularly high but fortunately, there was a low standing wall below the wrought iron posts, which Luke used as a ledge to give him a prop up. Being quite a tall man himself, and having sufficient muscle power in his arms, he managed to lift himself up to its highest level, and slotted his trainers between the arrow heads on a flat continuous piece of wrought iron. He was positioned at the corner of the railings, where another set headed off perpendicular to the set he was precariously balanced on.

Thinking that the best approach would be to now jump off from the great height onto the dimly lit flagstone floor below, he wavered for about a minute before plunging to the ground outside the park. Just as his body lurched forwards, his right foot with his trainer got momentarily stuck in the vice of the arrow heads, which caused him to land almost squarely on his right knee, while the left foot landed directly onto the ground. A sharp and searing pain shot through his knee and right leg. He immediately worried if he had broken his knee, due to the impact. He rolled up his jeans to where the blow had occurred, and saw that blood had been drawn and was slowly oozing out. He unrolled his jeans, and hoped that, over a short period of time the jeans would absorb and stem the flow of blood. Although Luke felt decidedly tense and worried at this juncture, a kind voice in him whispered that his wound would heal with time, and he did not need to fuss over it. Another voice in Luke suggested he could liken himself to the mythic spy, James Bond, and this was all part of the trials of his night-time adventure. It was as if he was the shadowy spy fighting a lone struggle against the system that had created him, but without the use of weapons. Luke then had conceited notions that he really was that mythical superhero spy.

He felt convinced that the agents would have attempted to have a pop at him during his courageous excursion in Hyde Park. The streets were now deserted, and Luke imagined the scene to be like something out of an end-of-the-world apocalyptic nightmare.

While he hobbled with no particular destination in mind, but keeping a steady momentum going, his thoughts would intermittently gravitate towards his injury, and whether it would actually heal. For all the bravado of him thinking he was like the archetypal spy; he still felt vulnerable and slightly stupid at his fanciful imagination.

After spending about a good hour-and-a-half, or what seemed like that length of time, aimlessly ambulating through the built-up streets of inner-city London, he stumbled across a small park area, demarcated by some high hedgerows, and made his way to a bench within the adequately sized public urban garden plot. Reclining on the bench, he wondered whether he could get a few winks of sleep, before he would resume his meandering path through the heart of the city. He felt empathy for all the homeless people, who struggled to find decent places to sleep in built-up areas, and thought he was lucky to be able to go back to a warm flat, at the end of this ordeal.

After about five minutes in an uncomfortable and awkward position, he intuitively believed that he really needed to push on with his journey, and now not delay in finding his way back to Marylebone station. He felt very muddled as to his orientation in the city, and he was not at all sure, he would be able to successfully navigate his way back. Suddenly, after having resumed his path on the streets again, with a huge stroke of luck, a taxi drove by with its light on, and came to a halt at the red traffic lights about 50m ahead of Luke. Immediately, he sensed that this was his moment to flag down the taxi. With all his reserves of energy and hobbling momentum, he moved, as quickly as he could muster, towards the taxi shouting for him to stop and give him a lift.

"Hello there! Thank you so much for stopping. I'm after a lift to Marylebone station please."

"Sure! You're very lucky, as I was just about to finish my shift, and I was just starting to head home. You're out late tonight. Been anywhere nice?" asked the taxi driver.

"Actually, I've been in Hyde Park, and then I decided to wander the streets," Luke thought that there was no point in lying to him, but he was nevertheless being a little economical with the truth.

As the taxi driver continued to speak, Luke felt he was a friendly and kind man and felt very safe being in his company. He was quite talkative, without being excessively so, and he was quite happy to keep the conversation light-hearted, without delving into the reasons for Luke's midnight excursion. The conversation, while being ferried to the station, just seemed to glide by effortlessly, and there was no suspicion on Luke's part that he might be taking a circuitous route to build up a greater charge for the ride. He just seemed a very honest and decent man, and Luke expressed this, just before alighting at his destination, with a generous and handsome tip.

Once Luke had raised his hand in gratitude, and the taxi receded into the distance, he was then left at the entrance to the station with an eerie, otherworldly silence, yet with a profound peace in his heart. He would now bide his time by loitering in the immediate vicinity, and wait to catch the first train back to Leamington Spa, which he assumed would be a very quiet and subdued affair.

The pain in his knee still throbbed and surged through the lower half of his body, but he felt the main part of his adventure was now over, and the rest would now be comparatively plain sailing - in contrast. He could now remain mindful and vigilant during the ensuing hours, feeling very awake and alert to his environment without needing to be particularly worried or fearful.

He rested his body against a metal electrical box, folded his arms, and just observed the surrounding architecture – imagining the problems and issues that the construction teams would have had to overcome to achieve the architect's vision. He admired the black wrought iron filigree pattern of the large entrance canopy, adjacent to the main entrance and thought of how many hours of craftsmanship had gone into achieving these swirling, refined patterns. So many more hours of investment from all parties would have gone into these spectacular edifices, than the time and cost parameters prevalent in today's society. In those earlier times, quality of product was the overriding concern, while cost and time would be pushed more to the background.

After lingering with his body inclined against the electrical box for a good half-hour, he felt impelled to take a little walk around his immediate environment. Walking at a slow and deliberate pace, he came to the corner of the Marylebone station building, and turned into one of the side streets. He was suddenly aware of someone walking almost a couple of metres behind him. Luke had not spotted him before. It did feel like an encroachment into his personal bubble. As Luke had done in the recent past, he fixed his attention on what was ahead of him, to convey a degree of naturalness as if it was a training that had been imparted to him in a school of espionage.

Luke had been shocked by this personal intrusion, and his heart had begun to beat faster, with his palms becoming decidedly moist and sweaty. He looked at the posters lit up in the windows to the side of him. He decided to adopt the ploy of moving in an exaggeratedly slow way to suggest to the other lone individual, 'Give it your best shot mate!' The man then walked past just a little faster than Luke's snail's pace, and Luke spotted in the corner of his eye, what seemed like a can of some description, which Luke presumed was some kind of powerful alcoholic mix. However, Luke could not detect any hint or whiff of alcohol wafting in his direction - so was open to other possibilities, and not that he was a drunkard or homeless person, which was his initial impression on observing the can in the man's hand. Being still a little shaken by this close proximity to a complete stranger, Luke felt no real desire to then continue down this side street, not because he feared for his life, but just because he felt he did not have anything to prove with this unkempt individual, who languidly proceeded away from him and the station. Luke gracefully did an about-turn and headed back to the station entrance.

There were streetlights lighting the entrance area and a solitary Metro paper was gently rustling on the ground in front of him. Bending over to pick it up, he started reading some of the columns. Although he was generally a serious minded individual, and concerned with the world's state of affairs, he was a sucker for the trivial that came in the form of what was going on in the various star's lives. The column about a suave and sophisticated actor getting married after all these years of living a celibate lifestyle, and being adored by a massive women fan base, got him captivated. There was a flattering photo of him and he thought how devilishly handsome he appeared in the photos. Although Luke felt there was a certain vulnerability to him that he was keen to conceal to the public's watchful eyes. Luke felt he had a charm that was not altogether sincere but he sympathised with him, thinking that that was the modus operandi of so many famous people around the globe. The moods and attitudes they displayed in public never quite matched their character in their private moments, and to get a truly all-round authentic person in the public arena was a rarity. Checking his watch, it was coming up to 4:30pm. There were lights on in the station concourse and a staff attendant filed through the large metal gates that were slightly ajar. Luke felt very appreciative of all the many people making his life easier in every respect. This was fundamentally the law of conditionality, commonly spoken of as dependent origination, or even as the Tibetans sometimes termed it - interdependent origination - which determined the reality of every being's existence. This was a vast infinite network of conditions that contributed to each moment to moment experience of every living thing in the cosmos. These conditions would arise, play themselves out and then cease, in a state of continual flux. Each living thing was in some way connected and not isolated from everything else in the universe. The Buddha had enunciated this in a very pithy short phrase, which encapsulated this teaching, and Luke had subsequently memorized the saying. It went as follows:

'This being, that becomes, from the arising of this - that arises. This not-being that does not become, from the ceasing of this - that ceases.'

It could be seen by most to be a very elementary concept, but to directly see, experience and realise its implications was to see it as unfathomably deep and complex. This concept, which is also the concept of impermanence, goes to the very core of Buddhism.

Seeing that the large entrance door was left open, he thought this might be an invitation to be allowed to enter the lit concourse area. Being now calmer than his earlier encounter with the stranger, he nonchalantly entered its domain. Finding one of the few metal circular benches, arranged in the large space, he slumped in its unforgiving steel support and continued to wait patiently.

His mouth was starting to dry with lack of fluids, and he remembered his two litre bottle of water that he had brought with him from home. He had completely forgotten about it, due to the nature of the night's events that had, as it were, swallowed him up in an encircling flurry of muted activity and drama.

Luke had waited for a good hour-and-a-quarter on the bench, shutting his eyes from time to time for what he hoped would be a moment's kip. Unfortunately, no such luck was in store for him that morning, although admittedly he still felt alert and present at this particular hour. He then saw a couple of separate men making their way onto the station concourse, and they immediately darted for the nearest available seats nearer the digital screen display than he was - all in a state of half-slumber.

The coffee stall attendants had arrived, and were slowly setting up shop. Luke was now desperate for a cup of coffee. He got up from the bench and made his way nearer to their stall, and sat on another similar steel bench - and waited. Almost a few seconds after he had sat down, quite a large and tall guy decided to sit directly next to him. Immediately, his heart started to pound with a momentary dread. He saw this as a very odd move, and without a moment's hesitation he lurched forward out of the seat, and found one of the coffee stall's own seating, which would be highly unusual for someone else to sit with him - at the same compact table-seat arrangement.

Earlier he had stuffed the copy of the metro inside his rucksack, and decided now was a good time to retrieve and sift through the paper again, so as to keep his cognitive mind active and be emotionally engaged. During his reading, he looked up, and noticed a bleary eyed office worker had parked himself a couple of tables opposite him, and was flicking through the contents of his own metro paper. Luke could not help thinking that both the large person, who had decided to sit right next to him, and now this supposed office worker, might not be genuine – being at the station at such an early hour. Might they again be undercover agents still monitoring his movements at very close quarters? Although the suspicion was rife in his mind, he inwardly said to himself that he needed to try and let go of these unhelpful thoughts that were trying to crowd his consciousness. Even if these two men were spies, they were just trying to do their job, and they believed that what they were doing was the right course of action. All they wanted, or anyone else for that matter, was to be happy. Ultimately, their happiness was misguided, but the same could be said for so many other people on this planet. Happiness was not dependent on external circumstances, but on an inner contentment and peace that comes about through a transformation and development of self. This view was so self-evident to Luke, but one which was also unsurprising due to his twenty-one years of on-and-off Buddhist practice, which had finally stabilized into a path of consistent, regular steps and a well-established spiritual routine.

After delicately sipping the very hot coffee he had bought, he looked at the digital display for the next train to leave for Leamington Spa, and saw one was already waiting to depart from platform 4. With a huge inward relief, he left the metro paper by the coffee stall, kept hold of his coffee, slung his rucksack over his shoulder, and went to board the train. He now felt his mission had been accomplished, and he could sit back restful and contented for the journey back. However hard the intelligence services tried to kill him off in stealth-operations; the more he would be protected by the benevolent gods.

Chapter 11

The following morning on the Thursday, after returning from his intrepid trip to the heart of London, Luke started turning his thoughts towards the Buddhist movement that he was affiliated with. Could the ordained members of the Buddhist community really be who they say they were? He believed wholeheartedly that the founder of the movement, Leander, was of pure and noble intent, but as for some of his followers and disciples - Luke could not be so sure. Although they taught a principle called 'metta,' namely universal loving kindness, Luke felt that some of the order members did not in the slightest way display this principle, even though they claimed to practise it in meditation. A friend of Luke's, who had gone on one of the Buddhist courses, remarked that she found one of the order members to be not very open-minded in terms of more New Age beliefs and she alleged that he seemed to dismiss her claims, she put forward to him, in a slightly condescending manner. She had espoused those beliefs to Luke, and he had been a lot more receptive and open to them, even agreeing with most of her ideas.

As Luke continually mulled over the various order members he had come to know and trust over the course of his engagement with the movement, he became more and more certain that there was something untoward with certain people and their activities. Had they been set up with their sole aim to find a convenient way to eradicate this elusive figure? He still believed that the teachings of Leander were exemplary and perfectly suited to the Western mind-set, but he felt that some, but definitely not all of the order members, were only paying lip service to the teachings, and half-heartedly living them out in their own lives. His associative train of thought began imagining the group he had joined as some sort of covert religious cult. He had been completely taken in by their web of deceit. They were probably part of the spy world's conspiracy, to do away with Luke - this genuine, warm hearted individual - and one who actually possessed real potential for enlightenment and Buddhahood.

When Luke pondered over the characteristics of some of the order members he had come to know and respect in his time with the movement, he became aware of attributes that could make for very effective and lethal secret agents. Most of them were well educated and quite a few had been to boarding schools, while some had gone on to study at leading universities. They were mostly slim but wiry individuals. Some of them could be very assertive and bold, and they were mostly very competent and able people.

He pondered that the further up the ostensible spiritual hierarchy it went, the more capable and deadly their attributes became. The most senior order member in the movement, just below the founder, was an extremely charismatic and gifted speaker, with an astonishing command of the English language. He was above all erudite and eloquent in equal measure and he had attended a prestigious boarding school. He also had an uncle who had been an admiral in the navy.

He remembered how he had been on retreat over half a year ago with this order member leading it, and the order member had for the whole nine days on retreat worn the same smart, grey waistcoat. Luke convinced himself that this article of clothing was synonymous with that of a secret agent's attire. He also liked to don a black trilby hat, which made him look even more suspect.

Luke wondered whether his life in the movement had been one where some of the order members were secretly trying to plot his end with the most allegedly accidental of causes. Another leading order member on this retreat had suggested that Luke could go and talk to this most senior disciple, while on the retreat. As Luke remembered this incident, he shuddered at the idea that if he had done so, his life could have been in peril. He surmised that this particular man would have had no qualms or reservations in inflicting a killer blow to his life, either with a sharp blade or else a gun with a silencer.

Over the next few hours, he allowed these anxious thoughts to proliferate and cement into a vicious reality in his mind. On that Thursday afternoon it dawned on Luke that he now needed to extricate himself from this insidious Buddhist movement. He would write an e-mail setting out his views, and send it to as many of those he knew in the movement, without hesitation or deliberation. He was becoming more assured that he had seen into the truth of the matter. Getting out his laptop he waited, for what seemed like an age, for his computer to be activated. After logging on to his Hotmail account, he proceeded to write vigorously.

Dear All,

I have had an epiphany moment and certain things have become clearer to me. This comes after 21 years of reflection on the nature of existence and the law of conditionality, as it applies to all beings. This includes trees, plants, animals and what you would normally see as inanimate objects. I see all life imbued with energy and consciousness.

I truly believe not all of you, but quite a lot of you in the movement are not genuine and your motivations are not pure. I believe you have been recruited by government bodies to ultimately, have the intention of dismantling the very structure of what Leander has espoused. This has been done very subtly, adeptly and dare I say skilfully and intelligently. Any person who believes can take this teaching further, and lead us into a new society, is in your eyes truly a threat to the established order. Although you preach a new order, you do not want it transpiring, and you have been recruited to eliminate any real and genuine hopeful to the emergence of a new order. I believe you are all aware that this person is me!

One of the things, which had given your game away, is that you are all too bloody confident!! In my years of reflection this has always stumped me, but now I can truly say it is clear to me. Most of you are just FRAUDS!

I am aspiring to be a true Bodhisattva on the path, and I truly believe that the Buddhas and the gods are protecting me on my continual journey through the realms of the cosmos, with their great compassion for the sufferings of all beings.

With compassion to you all, may you one day realise the unadulterated bliss of release and liberation.

Luke Trevelyan.

He realised that metta, an old Indian Pali word, which meant universal loving kindness, and its development in meditation, was one of the movement's defining standpoints. He believed this principle was just a front for the more wicked aspects of the organisation.

Luke was sad to have to write this e-mail, because over the years he had developed a real fondness for the people he had met. He knew now that he was formally severing links with the movement, and there was no way he was going to reengage with the people. He was now fully aware that he was on his own, and he would perhaps have to explore other traditions or movements - to try and continue some semblance of Buddhist practice.

Luke also wrote a letter to his sister, as he believed she was also duplicitous in this drama. He was extremely reluctant to write it, as she was family, but he could not ignore the fact of her grand deception yesterday on the phone.

Dear Rebecca,

I really did not want to speak to you on the phone, until I had formulated my thoughts in an e-mail to you, and thereby setting them out coherently.

We have all heard of the prophesies; namely that there will be a second coming, or a Jesus like figure that Christians believe would come to save humanity and in Buddhism the belief that there will appear a future Buddha. There is also a notion of the Devil that is often portrayed, waiting for the right moment to come to Earth, once evil has increased sufficiently.

GCHQ, MI5 and MI6, some of the most brilliant minds of this country were trying to locate where this possible Devil character might be born into. I am sure the minds of GCHQ would have assumed that this figure would be deceptive, charming and not to stand out too much, but to still possess a lot of wonderful qualities - not only in terms of abilities but also in terms of looks. For the record, I do believe in the Devil, but not as some charming man, who is pretending to be humble, but instead someone who is actually intent on world domination, with a gigantic ego. By the way, as a Buddhist, I am trying to diminish the pull the ego has on me, and I am seriously trying to pursue the important idea of humility – which is essential in the spiritual life. The actual Devil will be a raging inferno of a being, able to overcome any extreme pain whatsoever. He will look like a true monster, and he will be immense in stature – towering over all beings. I truly believe he will arrive with a scene of lightning bolts and thunder, and that will be the start of hell on this planet, where he will rule supreme for many, many millions of years, with the planet getting progressively hotter and hotter and more evil.

I, on the other hand, would want to be part of a new world order, amongst the realm of the gods, basing my life on the three qualities of love, contentment and wisdom, and fundamentally aiming to lead a truly ethical life.

Returning to the point of GCHQ, when they had found this potential Devil hate figure, they would tune into every part of his life, from the moment he was born, with the government's sophisticated satellite technology, and use the images that were being messaged out, to create a new reality TV show of this character that could

be displayed all around the world. I hasten to add that this would
not have been to everyone. There are people on this earth, who
are longing to lead a spiritual life, and are aspiring to do so. These
particular people, who are many, would not all have access to this
reality TV show. I believe one of the key messages about this reality
TV show, which would have been displayed – is if you meet this
person then *Terminate his Life!*

Those who are in on this reality TV show, (as an aside, is it
not interesting to note that when the *Truman show* came out, the
main character had a passing resemblance to myself, and a couple
of people have commented that I look a little like him! I do not think
this is just a coincidence!) As I mentioned before, those watching the
reality TV show would have had to sign an official secrets act to state
that they would never divulge this piece of information to the person
being watched – namely myself, and not to discuss it with anyone,
who was not in the know.

On Wednesday afternoon, I received a call from you, which was
very odd for you to do. How would you know that I was in my flat,
and would you not realistically have assumed that I would be at
work at that time, and there would be no point in ringing me? You
then opened the dialogue with "What are you doing?" and not "Hi!
Al, I was not expecting you to be at home at this hour," in a friendly,
congenial manner. In my opinion, this slip-up on your part gave the
game away, and proved to me that you are in on the conspiracy –
with terminating my life!! I am convinced though that Mum and
Dad definitely do not know what is going on, and I can fully trust
their genuineness and concern for me.

With this knowledge that I have gained, I can truly say – hand
on heart – I do not want anything to do with you, Robert or Alex
ever again, and I will not be making any visits to your lovely home
in Oxfordshire. It is not your fault, and you are just a pawn, who has
been sucked into this world of duplicity and deception. I am sure
you feel you are doing the right and noble thing for your country.
Ultimately, there is no-one to blame, and it is just the way things

are and always have been. We are all in this wheel of life together, making our journeys through the cosmos – constantly being reborn until one day, we reach the end of our immensely long journey, and find inner contentment and supreme peace.

I hope that you fare well in the endless rounds of existence, and some day you will find your complete liberation and bliss. This also goes for the whole of humanity in this world, and the innumerable beings in other worlds. My notion of space and time is epic and vast, and we are all guided by two things – namely to be happy and to be free from suffering.

With compassion to you all,

Luke

After this explosive letter to his sister, over the coming months he managed to salvage his relationship with his sister, as he was told that she had been called by his previous employer just before his Hyde Park outing, to say that Luke had not appeared in the office since that last Friday, and that Brian was very concerned about his welfare. On discovering this important fact and after a few soothing words of reassurance, Luke was able to resume a very friendly relationship with Rebecca and her whole family again.

Chapter 12

It was Friday 21st March, the following day from sending his explosive two e-mails, and Luke desperately needed to turn to a genuine companion and friend in this time of need. He racked his brains a little. There was a particular woman, who he had got to know from first meeting her at a meditation class, and she was definitely open to alternative points of view, and seemed genuinely spiritually inclined. Her name was Imelda, and she worked as a writer of children's novels. Already she had two books published, and was working on her third novel. She had been quite successful with her first two books, and was starting to make a genuine livelihood out of them.

After looking up her contact details on his mobile, he decided to call her. He would see if she was free that evening, as he could really do with someone lending him a sympathetic ear.

"Hi Imelda! How are you?"

"I'm doing well thanks. It's nice to hear from you. Is everything okay though?" She could tell from his slightly quavering voice that all was not well with him.

"I'm in a little bit of a pickle. I have left the Buddhist movement I was with, as I suspect they aren't genuine, and they are not who they claim to be. I think that they probably have some ulterior agenda that is of a sinister nature." Luke confided in Imelda.

"I'm really sorry to hear that." Imelda said with authentic concern.

"I'm also in need of some friendship, and you were the first person I thought I could genuinely turn to - as a trusted companion and friend. Would it be possible to come and visit you this evening, I wonder; if it isn't too much of an imposition." Luke delicately asked.

"Yeah sure! I haven't got anything on tonight, and you would be more than welcome to come over this evening. If you want - we could go out for a meal?"

"Thanks Imelda that would be lovely! I'll tell you more when I arrive at yours. Can I come over for about 5ish?"

"No problem! I'm working from home today, so come over whenever."

"Thanks Imelda, you're a lifesaver."

Luke was truly grateful for her willingness to meet him at her place, and from what he knew of her she was a loving and caring woman, who would lend a very sympathetic ear to his plight. Although, he was sleeping a little better with the help of his meditation practice, he still had a heat inside him, as if he was some kind of human pressure cooker simmering at a low temperature. He was still convinced his life was being played out on satellite TV in most people's homes around the world, and that his life was still in mortal danger.

Imelda lived in Belbroughton, and Luke's journey there was very mixed. To begin with, along the stretch of the motorway, he drove considerately and responsibly, while towards the last part of the trip, off from the motorway, he drove as if someone had given him a shot of pure adrenaline. It was as if he was the main protagonist in a car chase of a notable action film. His driving was very skilled, but definitely on the dangerous side in these closing miles towards her house.

Finally arriving at her house, after some wrong turnings and routes; he got out of his car, ventured over to her side door, and rung the bell. A few seconds later, the oak door opened, and he was greeted by a gentle smile, with the slightest rumblings of worry detectable in her eyes.

"Hi Imelda. I'm not too early, am I?"

""No not at all. As I said you were welcome to come over at any time, but now is actually perfect for me, as I'm just wrapping up my writing for the day."

"Great! Thanks for being able to see me. I see you as a friend and someone who I can truly turn to – and also someone who would probably be supportive to my problematic situation," said Luke, as he started to relax a little in her homely and comfortable setting. Before he proceeded to tell her about the recent unfolding of events, he started to become a little more agitated again, thinking that what he was going to say would be viewed and judged by millions of people around the world, and this thought remained during the early part of their chat.

""I really believe that my life, and what goes on, is being shown to millions if not billions of people around the world; as if I'm some Big Brother spectacle. Already by saying this to you I feel uncomfortable, with the knowledge that I'm being judged harshly by so many people. I know there will be some members of the public who will really get me, but so many will not. My view is also that some members of society won't be party to this secretive world – like you for instance," said Luke.

""I really have no knowledge of what you're saying, but that doesn't mean it isn't true," said Imelda tactfully.

Luke found it suddenly very difficult to go on, and he took a deep inhalation of breath with a strong internal tension manifesting around his heart area.

""I don't expect you to believe what I'm saying. All I would encourage you to be is open-minded," said Luke hopefully.

""Don't worry. I'm listening to you with an open mind. Do you want to tell me about your thoughts on your Buddhist friends as well?" Imelda enquired in a maternal way.

""I'd placed so much trust in my Buddhist friends, and I'd also become so fond of them that to find out they have hoodwinked me into thinking they were bona fide Buddhists – really hurts. They claimed to preach metta, or universal loving kindness, as being as elevated as mindfulness, but most didn't seem to embody that quality much - if at all."

"I agree with you. The order members I met didn't seem to be as kind as I was expecting them to be. In some ways they seemed to be a little on the gruff and serious side, not really showing much love or open-heartedness," she said in agreement.

"I also believe that some of the order members have sided, or are working, with the government to help eliminate me. I believe they agree with the authorities that I'm a genuine threat to the established world order," added Luke with a modicum of anguish etched on his face.

"I'm sure the order members aren't in collaboration with the government to terminate your life. Do you really think that you pose such a threat to the established world order?" She asked sensitively.

"I just think they've been monitoring me for a very long time, and they see a lot of idealism in my nature. I am sure they spotted and took notice of my youtube video, which I aired last year," said Luke, as his internal tension started to soften and mellow a little. It seemed that to her it all appeared a little far-fetched, to say the least, but he imagined she was listening attentively to Luke's theories - and respond sympathetically where appropriate.

They both went to her office, and Luke talked to her in sporadic bursts, while she busied herself with completing the remaining tasks on her computer – partly concentrating on her work, while lending a slightly distracted ear, to now Luke's slightly more mundane concerns. There was a low setting sun, and the day was ending on a particularly warm note, with Luke enjoying the stillness of her home, and the sun's inviting rays reaching out over the green landscape, which accompanied their exchange.

She suggested they eat out, and he jumped at the chance with her proposal. She gave Luke a couple of options, and a restaurant with a regal sounding name sounded, by far, the most appealing of the selection in Belbroughton.

After about twenty odd minutes of wrapping up her writing, they both agreed that they would go for a drink at one of the pubs in the village, before having a meal at the royally named restaurant.

They both walked a short distance into the heart of the village, and called in at the local pub. As they entered the warmly lit old pub that had been given a contemporary make-over, a woman was sat in one of the leather armchairs. She was in her fifties, and greeted Imelda warmly. She asked Imelda who this young man was she had in tow on this early evening.

"What's your name?" the woman asked Luke.

"Luke. What's yours?"

"Joan. I bet you're an architect. Something tells me that you are," she enquired in a direct and forward manner.

Luke was starting to think that here was his first example of a woman, who knew the intricacies of his life, but had few qualms about revealing in small part her knowledge of him. He went along with the charade. She did not subsequently divulge any more ostensible guesses about Luke and his history, but kept remarkably restrained towards Luke for the duration of his sojourn to the pub.

As Imelda got into dialogue with Joan, a man with short brown hair and a kind and inquisitive face looked at Luke, and smiled warmly. He suddenly felt that this is what the upside of being famous would be, and responded with an equally endearing smile. Luke got into a short conversation with this interesting individual, but Luke thought to himself that this man was finding him equally as fascinating and alive, as Luke was of him. Could these two short exchanges be further evidence to Luke, that his life was definitely being streamed to millions or billions around the world? The counter thought still did emerge, from time to time in his mind, that he might be seriously deluding himself with this seemingly outlandish idea. Could such a claim really be genuine?!?

After one drink at the pub, Imelda and Luke headed for the restaurant, which was delightfully situated by a gently flowing stream and a dark wooded backdrop to the side of the stream. Luke and Imelda both agreed how relaxing and comforting the sound and sight of a gently flowing and meandering stream was to them.

"So this is the restaurant. A very regal name it is too," Luke felt kingly in stature by exclaiming this fact, and noticed he felt very inspired in his speech, with it taking on again tuneful cadences and a commanding resonance.

"Do you know that I have only been here once before for a drink, so I'm not sure what to expect from the food being served here." Imelda stated slightly anxiously, as if she was going to be judged harshly by Luke for her choice of restaurant.

"I'm sure whatever we have will be excellent and very tasty, what with a name as regally sounding as this. I'm sure we can't go wrong – don't you think?" Luke proffered to Imelda.

"I'm sure you're right. Let's go in and hopefully enjoy its culinary delights," Imelda said, as she and Luke motioned towards the large oak door entrance.

Once they had gone in, they were invited to sit at a two person table, against a patterned floral wallpapered wall with an oak timber mantelpiece in the centre of the wall and framed pictures above. Luke sat with his back to the wall, and had a good view of the other guests seated amongst them.

They looked through the menu and decided they would each have a starter, as well as a main course. Interestingly, they both opted for the same fish dish for their main course. They both chose a glass of red wine to accompany their meal, with also a bottle of sparkling water.

A thought of an objectionable nature arose in Luke's mind. What if the chefs now had the perfect opportunity to poison Luke with either his starter or the main course? He did not confide in Imelda this idea of poison, but instead chose to try and dispel the low level worry that was lightly bubbling away underneath his contained exterior. If he mentioned this to her, it would only mar the beauty of their evening together, and he was sure it would cause her to feel utterly disturbed. He just hoped that if the chefs were going to sprinkle some cyanide or other deadly concoction, then the gods would exercise their magical powers in turning it into something neutral and harmless. He started to feel a little more at ease with this new reassuring thought.

As they ate their main course, Luke noticed a couple beside them not saying much, and also being a little discreet in what they did say to each other. It was as if they were trying not to be overheard by the other guests and in particular Luke, and were slightly embarrassed about sitting in such close proximity to him. They very rarely glanced in his direction, but they seemed to have a strong awareness of his indomitable presence.

Imelda then said to Luke,

"How would you like to meet my spiritualist friend, who also lives in Belbroughton. Perhaps you can explain your ideas to her. She's a wonderfully warm and compassionate woman, and she has a definite positive and radiant energy. One of the things she likes to do when you greet her is to give a big hug, and she will undoubtedly give you a very warm embrace, if you do meet her."

"That sounds lovely. I need to meet more open-minded individuals, and also those with depth and more rounded spiritual interests."

"I could take you there tomorrow, if you like. Her name's Linda. I have spoken to her to see if it's okay. She told me it would be fine for you to go over tomorrow morning."

Luke had asked Imelda if he could stay the night at hers, because he did not feel up for driving back home that evening. She was perfectly happy for him to bunk out in the office, which doubled as a second bedroom. She said that anyone staying there normally had a very good night sleep, as it had a particularly good energy and orientation to it. Luke was still suffering from a considerable lack of sleep, and hoped that this night would prove to be different.

After Luke settled the bill, they both walked out into the clear night sky, with stars sprinkled all over in the jet-black cosmic backdrop. Once they arrived back at Imelda's house, she offered him a tea, and he opted for a camomile tea, to help him try and sleep better. After a brief wind down with Imelda, he polished off the tea, said goodnight, and headed off to bed. Imelda followed soon after.

Although Luke could feel a distinct calming and positive energy with the bed and its arrangement, he could not manage to quell his restless body and anxious mind sufficiently to get a good night's rest. The room's powerful and restful energy did however give him some broken sleep, which he was grateful for.

The following morning they both went to see Linda near the heart of the village. She lived in a relatively new estate, which was well-established with a profusion of greenery in the form of bushes, trees, and flowers that beautified the front lawns of the properties.

The meeting with Linda was everything he imagined it to be. She seemed to him to be larger than life. With a certain distinct, positive aura to her, she explained to him that she was in touch with other heavenly spirits. She could communicate with them through messages sent via instruments she had in her possession. Luke was open-minded to these abilities, but he did not accept everything she suggested was in her power. Her claim to be living within higher states of consciousness, and having to make an effort to come down from these exalted states of mind - he saw as dubious and remained internally dismissive.

Imelda had left early, and was only there to introduce Linda to Luke, but after Luke had spent a while in the company of such a loving presence as Linda, he parted with a strong bear-hug embrace. This refreshing physical contact lingered for quite a number of seconds, and one that Luke was keen to maximise the duration of. He confirmed that he would definitely like to visit again soon.

Walking back to Imelda's place, he was suffused with a warm glow. Thanking Imelda for the stay at hers, he got into his car, and drove back to his flat in Leamington.

Chapter 13

The following Wednesday 26th March, Luke was due to see his doctor and the nurse, and confront them both about what he saw as their scurrilous activity. In a perverse way, he was sympathetic to their plight, as he believed they were just following orders from the secret service and the government, and in turn the government were only conditioned by their misguided ideologies. He could really see how everyone was enmeshed in an unfathomably deep and complex web of conditioning, and he should only be compassionate towards them all.

On that Wednesday, he went about his new found daily morning ritual to drink coffee, and read a book in one of the coffee shops. As he turned the corner, where the Town Hall proudly stood, and entered into Regent's court, he spotted in the corner of his eye a man of what seemed like Indian descent, and who was very smartly dressed, leaning expectantly against the wall of the hotel. Luke's first impression of the man was that he was some sort of diplomat. He had that air of calm assurance, and he carried himself in a dignified manner. On seeing Luke, he came away from the wall and hovered by the entrance to Regent's court. As Luke proceeded to walk at a less brisk and more measured pace than his walk leading up to the Town Hall; he saw that this distinguished looking gentleman was now starting to follow him. On this occasion, he decided against entering his favourite well-known store, and carried on to the next coffee shop in the court. The interior of this other coffee shop felt a little like a time warp. It was rustic yet sophisticated, and it had a lot of dark timber panelling and pictures of screen idols dotted on the walls. Only two or three of the staff would communicate with him on a friendly, but slightly disconnected basis. He was never quite sure if the staff regarded him with suspicion, and consequently with a little detachment.

As Luke comfortably planted himself in a two person table by the entrance door, the sartorially elegant man entered the domain, and purposefully head straight for the staff in the kitchen. He whispered some words discreetly and conspiratorially into their ears, and then left the premises. At no time did he make eye contact with Luke. Luke noticed how he tried pushing the door away from him to leave the coffee shop – floundered - before pulling the door inwards to exit the building. Immediately, a powerful vice-like grip of fear seized Luke's body, and he thought that this brief event could only mean one thing. The government wanted to try and poison him again. He thought it could be so easy for the staff to slip some belladonna or deadly nightshade into his coffee. It would take about a few hours to kick in, and then back at home he would quietly pass away. The emergency services would then be told to put his death down to unexplained causes. They might even claim he had a heart malfunction that can strike people in their 30's and 40's, to assuage the grief his devastated parents would have. Luke had completely forgotten the comparative reassurance he felt with his meal at the restaurant in Belbroughton, and this time Luke believed that the possibility of success for the authorities seemed greater.

At once Luke decided he would take pre-emptive action, and politely said to the waitress that he would like to change his mind about ordering the latte, and could she cancel the order for him. As the obtrusiveness of the man had been overwhelming, and his little slip-ups with not being aware of the fine detail of the door and which way it opened - helped Luke obviate the possibility of his death in this instance. He was a little shaken up by the incidence, and was struck by the reality bearing down on him.

Later on that afternoon, he walked to the surgery from his flat, and, over the last two weeks, he had been experiencing an expanding heat and fire inside his body. He felt in control, yet a little out of control at the same time – a dichotomy of moods. It was not that he felt anxious, just an undeniable heat.

The receptionist at the surgery had slightly reddened cheeks, which Luke put down to the stress of the job. Ultimately, she looked a little frazzled, and wore a stern expression with Luke.

The nurse called him into a different treatment room from her usual one, and she sat down behind the desk, while Luke sat in a chair, adjacent. She then enquired in what seemed to Luke like a mock-concerned way (Luke could not be sure if it was his bias towards her that was clouding his judgement).

"What can I help you with Luke?"

"I need to say something quite frank to you, and it relates of course to my medication." He paused to muster his inner resolve and strength, before launching into his accusation.

"I believe you haven't been giving me the correct medication at all. For the last three to four weeks, I've been labouring under sleep deprived nights, which has caused my performance at work to deteriorate, and for me to subsequently give up my job. I've been on the medication for about seventeen to eighteen years, and nothing like this has ever happened to me before. I can only put it down to one thing, and that is you've been negligent in your duties." Before the nurse could retort, Luke continued in a demonstrable fashion with his line of reasoning.

"Ultimately, I don't think you're at fault because you're only following orders from the authorities," Luke expressed vehemently yet sympathetically.

"I can assure you hand on heart that I have in no way given you the wrong medication, and I'm sure you are just imagining it," she retorted. Luke was convinced that she was lying, yet found this conversation futile, as she would just stand her ground, and so would he.

"The proof of the pudding is in the eating, and the symptoms of my condition have been manifesting themselves over the last four weeks. How do you explain this?"said Luke with a raised and amplified voice.

"I really don't know. All I can say is - hand on heart - I didn't tamper with your medication." She responded in a dead-pan way, with no visible sign of feeling or emotion."There's never been a time, when I have come to see you, where you've let me come into the treatment room, and then shown me the ampoule you were extracting the medication from - before subsequently injecting me," said Luke with an escalating confidence and boldness.

"This is the procedure I follow with all the patients I see," she replied.

"Well, that procedure is ultimately flawed!" Luke retorted with a riposte that sounded very satisfying to him. He thought if that was the case then he had no other option, than to withdraw his involvement with that surgery, and return to the Crick surgery at his parent's home. He did not divulge this to the nurse, but he said that in the future, and especially tomorrow when his injection was due, he would want to witness the nurse drawing out the depixol drug from its ampoule, as a definite priority. She confirmed that she could definitely oblige with this request.

After talking to the nurse, he waited in the upstairs waiting area, to meet with his doctor, who he had not seen until today. He was told that she was a female doctor of the name Watson. Once he was ushered in, he started to spill his thoughts of spies out to get him, yet maintaining that he felt totally at ease with himself, due to his steady Buddhist practice.He highlighted that he was an intelligent person, and saw the world with sense and reason, even though his views might sound extreme. Luke got the impression from her body language that she thought he might be seriously loopy in the views he was espousing, or else he wondered whether it could be that she could not reveal something to Luke, because she had been instructed by the government to keep silent about him. These conflicting ideas seemed to ricochet around in his spinning head. He was a little unsure, as to what the actual reality was. Was he a crackpot or was there some truth in what he was confiding to the doctor? Ultimately, he felt a little unsteady in his opinion, while talking to her so intimately and also because he was speaking to her for the first time, and barely knew her.

The following day Luke had his injection with a different nurse, and this time the woman, who was a petite, anxious looking woman, showed him the ampoule before administering it. With her hands trembling and her general demeanour jittery, he thought whether his seemingly outlandish views had been bandied about by the staff, and this was causing her to be intimidated by his presence.

After a couple of days of receiving the medication, he started to sleep better, which was long overdue having been a good four to five weeks that this had been denied from him. His worried parents called to see how he was, and there was overwhelming relief that his sleep patterns were slowly returning back to normal. Luke told them about the nurse showing him the depixol ampoule, on this occasion. Both Luke and his parents were more than ever convinced that the surgery had either been negligent, or else they had been underhand in their dealings with him. They both thought it would be futile to press charges. What evidence would they have against the surgery? All Luke knew now was that he would immediately revoke being a patient there, and return to the Crick surgery, where they were much more understanding and sympathetic to his needs. Luke had also developed a personal and friendly relationship with the nurses, the doctors and all the staff at his former surgery.

Chapter 14

It was Wednesday 2nd April. Luke went to see Linda, the spiritualist woman again, without this time meeting up with Imelda, to discuss his views and beliefs of a supra-mundane nature. The last time they had met, he was reluctant to mention his intrepid trip to Hyde Park, either to her or Imelda, as it was then so fresh in his mind, and he needed time to process the experience. This time he had managed to absorb it into his life. The pain in his knee would still throb sporadically, and it looked as if the knee plate had been set slightly different to how it was before – due to the impact from the fall. A feeling of worry enveloped him again about the healing process of the knee. Would he be able to run as before and play tennis easily, or had he disfigured it, to the extent that practical concerns might even become an issue? A more positive but quieter thought countered the negative train, and mollified his anxiety. He sincerely trusted the thought that believed his knee would make a full recovery with time. For now he would live with this constant ebb and flow of painful sensations, which he had begun to inure himself to.

When Luke had last visited Linda, he felt the house possessed a strong, even powerful positive force, which was her aura and energy leeching into its fabric. He thought he might make quite a habit of this, by dropping in to see her for a chat, and to explore ideas about themselves, life and the universe, which he knew she was as fascinated by, as he was.Once he had pressed the doorbell, the door opened evenly, and there was Linda with a big beaming smile. She appeared other-worldly, and with what seemed like the faintest impression of a halo around her head.

"Hello Luke. Lovely to see you again!" she said.

"Hi Linda! It's lovely to be here again." Luke entered the living room, and gave her a very warm and long, emotionally nourishing hug. Linda offered him biscuits and tea, and then they engaged in small talk for a few minutes. She then asked in a curious and interested way,

"Luke. What would you like to talk about this time?"

"I thought I would tell you about my intrepid excursion to Hyde Park. I went there two weeks ago, just before I first met up with you here, to test my nerves and try to overcome some of my fears. I sat in the middle of the park in the middle of the night and meditated, while also making a point of sampling some of London nightlife. I really believe that I wasn't alone, when I was sat in the park, and there were probably secret agents trying to shoot me dead, although I can't be sure. I did, however, see a lone silhouetted figure race across my path about a hundred metres in front of me, just as I was making my way out of the park. In the ensuing drama, I damaged my knee quite badly from climbing over the park's railings, and jumping down from them." Luke began to roll up his jeans to show Linda the darkened, reddish, mauve scab encrusted on his knee.

"I know what the knee injury signifies. It means you were being too wilful, and not listening to your kind inner voice. Sustaining an injury like that, with the brief story you've just described, usually implies stubbornness and being too head-strong," Linda replied matter-of-factly.

Luke nodded and murmured in agreement, realising that she could well be correct in her assumption, and also not knowing better.

"What mental condition did you say you have?"

"I'm diagnosed with schizophrenia, but I'd been well and functioning in a healthy manner for about seventeen or eighteen years, until this psychological upheaval happened in these last few weeks. All I can put it down to is that the nurse at the surgery, where I live, did not administer the correct treatment, for one reason or another."

"I will fetch a little device, which divines your actual symptoms. You could of course suffer from a bi-polar condition, and not schizophrenia." On their last meeting together Linda had shared with Luke that she had been a nurse, before later in her life she turned her time and attention to spiritualism. She came back from her bedroom with a pretty, ornate and bejewelled object, and said,

"This object requires to be balanced. You at first determine which rotation stands for yes, and which rotation stands for no – either clockwise or anti-clockwise. You then pose it a question, with the answer to be yes or no. If it rotates clockwise, with the question being asked, then that implies a 'yes', and if it revolves in an anti-clockwise direction – then that means 'no'. Obviously, I'm posing the question to the angels, or as you had termed them the gods above us," Luke had always been extremely open-minded in areas of the unexplained and mysterious, and he felt that he could only go along with Linda's mysterious diagnosis, thinking that with this divining there would be a definite but unmistakable and irrefutable truth presenting itself.

"As I thought to myself, she murmured. "The pendulum rotates clockwise, when asking it if you have schizophrenia, and anti-clockwise, when asking it if you have a bi-polar disorder. This means that you have schizophrenia and not bi-polar." To Luke this was disconcerting to hear, as he would have far rather been termed a bi-polar sufferer than a schizophrenic, with all the latter's accompanying negative and unhelpful associations. He talked more with Linda, but he was feeling a little deflated with the outcome. Now he would feel forever wary of mentioning his condition, unless it was to those friends of his that he deeply trusted and could confide in. He realised that the stigma attached to mental conditions was becoming ever more eroded in today's society, but the mention of schizophrenia still seemed to play on a lot of people's doubts and fears, as there was still a lot of uncertainty surrounding this particular mental condition.

Luke shared with her his belief about being filmed 24/7, as like a Big Brother contestant, and also the idea that the authorities saw him as a devil incarnate figure, masquerading as a spiritually minded figure. He tried to explain to Linda his theory that reality in its wholeness embraced both dark and light aspects of life, albeit rejecting evil acts of body, speech and mind. He maintained to her that he did believe that demonic energy was within us all, and this energy should ultimately be harnessed within the greater overall goodness and purity that was essential to leading a spiritual life. This demonic energy had the power to drive us forward, and had immense energy and momentum. Luke cited the listening to dark, gritty songs on the radio or in his CD collection, as a way of evoking the passionate and wild flavour of that energy. Also its energy could be expressed in eccentric, flowing and staccato dance movements, while at home or in clubs. It could also manifest in the honesty of his personal exchanges with people. His teacher, Leander, had stated in a pithy maxim, 'Rather honest collision, than dishonest collusion'.

"I'm happy to meet with whoever comes through my door, whatever their beliefs or underlying motivations are. I feel very safe and protected, and I've no cause to worry that any harm will come to me," Linda said in a calm and unruffled way.

Luke took this to mean that she was a little disturbed with his open, provocative and revealing dialogue. Luke sensed that she was indirectly admitting that she found Luke a mild threat. Her tone of voice remained constant, and it did not suggest her underlying concerns, she might be having. Luke tried to dispel any fear she might be labouring under, confirming that he only had honest and honourable intentions to her, and anyone else for that matter. After she suggested he pay some money for her time, which she had not asked for at the start of their encounter, but was implicit that this was the form these meetings would take; he realised that it would forever be a spiritual consultancy service, and not a friendly meet-up. He parted from her with a little feeling of resentment simmering away below the surface, as he could not now meet up with her as just a friend. A financial transaction would always come between them. Feeling that somehow this was probably the last time he would come to visit this remarkable woman, he had thoroughly appreciated the wise counsel she had imparted to him in the small time he had known her.

Chapter 15

After knowing that Luke had been given the correct medication this time at the Leamington surgery, he had made swift and pressing moves to change back to his old surgery in Crick. He knew he could rely on the Crick surgery to do the right thing, as he had witnessed in the past. They were truly responsible and caring in their actions. The main female doctor at the Crick surgery suggested Luke should look up a psychiatrist of the name, Doctor Goodyear, who worked at Daventry Hospital. He had come highly recommended to her, and she felt this would be the best doctor for Luke to get good psychiatric advice from.

Luke had polished off an Americano, which was now his more preferred coffee of choice, as he had to be more careful with money, and he had begun to grow used to a stronger, sharper and more bitter taste, compared with the Flat whites, which were slightly too sweet for his now maturing taste buds. As he was not working, and was living off savings and some inheritance, he had to manage his finances more carefully. Luke left the coffee shop, and hung around nearby to make a discreet but much needed call to Daventry Hospital. Once he got through, he asked the secretary to book him an appointment to see Doctor Goodyear for a consultation. Even though he was ringing on Tuesday 8th April, a space in the doctor's diary had presented itself on that Wednesday, and he jumped at the chance to have himself booked in on that close and convenient date. An evening slot was arranged at 7pm. Luke got back home, and then contacted his father to tell him of the appointment, as his father had requested.

"Hi Dad - just to let you know I've booked an appointment with the psychiatrist, who'd been recommended to me. I managed to get an appointment for this Wednesday at 7pm. Would that time and day suit you?" Luke said with a hint of resentment that his father had to tag along with him.

"I can definitely make that date and time," said Jeremy with an audible relief."You know Dad, it isn't necessary for you to come with me. I can go on my own you know," said Luke, feeling as though his independence was being usurped.

"I think I really need to be there, at least for the first part of the meeting, so I can set the scene, and explain things about you and your potted mental history. I don't intend to be there for the duration of the meeting, but I will allow you, once I've finished, to tell your side of the story to the psychiatrist. What's his name by the way?" Jeremy enquired.

"It's Doctor Goodyear." As Luke said this name, he inwardly thought how he enjoyed the positive associations it conjured.

As Luke ended the call to his father, he contemplated how he was sleeping so much better, and also how his thought patterns were unravelling. He was starting not to see the sinister nature of his predicament as much, and he was becoming more and more positive to the people around him and his surroundings. Not everyone seemed like a threat to his life anymore.

*****

Once Luke and his father Jeremy had parked in the fairly empty car park at Daventry Hospital, they wandered up a flight of stairs to the first floor in a fairly modern brick building. The reception counter was diagonally opposite the top of the stairs. A very warm and friendly secretary asked Luke if he could fill out his name and the details of his car and registration for her. Although Luke found her pretty; he noticed how he felt uncomfortable, because of his particular mental condition, and that he might be perceived by her as fragile and of a nervous disposition. Luke knew this could not be further from the truth, but laboured under this perceived interpretation, with all its prejudices and judgements.

As they waited at the top of the stairs in a small waiting area, Luke noticed that one of the walls had been painted a purple colour. He wondered to himself whether this colour was deliberate for putting the minds of the patients at ease, or was it that the staff chose it for its more upbeat qualities. Luke appreciated the colour, and it was one of his favourites.

After about five minutes of waiting, the door to the corridor leading to the consultancy rooms opened and a young, friendly-faced man greeted them.

"Hello! You must be Luke Trevelyan," looking at Luke in a gentle but direct way.

"Yes, I am. My father wanted to come along as well," before Luke could continue, Jeremy had interrupted Luke's explanation.

"Hello. Doctor Goodyear, I believe. I would like to tell you my side of the story about my son, and his mental history, and also explain to you about my brother's condition, which was very similar to my son's. Then I thought I would leave you two together, while I work on some papers I've brought with me."

"That's quite alright with me. Are you okay with that Luke?" Doctor Goodyear asked Luke in a professionally considerate manner.

"That's perfectly fine with me – thanks," Luke said reassuringly.

Once Luke and his father had both positioned themselves in the chairs provided, opposite Doctor Goodyear's chair, which stood behind an oak veneered table - the psychiatrist offered them both water. Luke accepted the offer willingly, and saw it as an opportunity to stop his mouth becoming parched from speaking about his past mental history. Jeremy took the lead, and talked to the doctor about his brother and his history. Jeremy explained to him how his brother had suffered from bi-polar and not schizophrenia, and that he had taken the same medication as Luke was taking. Jeremy said how he was convinced the medication Luke was getting, did the trick in keeping him consistently healthy and mentally together. He mentioned the concern, both Jeremy and his wife had, about the surgery in Leamington, and that things for Luke were getting markedly better - now Luke knew he had been given - in the last instalment - the correct medication. Jeremy also explained how they all felt more comfortable with Luke going to the surgery, by his parent's home, and they were a very supportive GP surgery, with excellent staff across the board.

The doctor listened and transcribed feverishly what was being said, as Jeremy was speaking. After Jeremy felt he had explained enough about what was pertinent, with regards to Luke's and his brother's mental health, Jeremy suggested he leave them to talk to each other, while he retreated to the waiting area.

Once Jeremy left the room, Doctor Goodyear asked Luke,

"It would now be good to hear your side of the story. Firstly, what did you make of what your father said to us just now?"

"I would say most of what he said is spot-on. I would like to think that I'm like my uncle with a bi-polar condition, but I had a spiritualist woman tell me, through a divining instrument, that I am actually a schizophrenic and I don't suffer from bi-polar."

"I will endeavour to look into that. As I said to your father these conditions can overlap with one another. It does sound however that you definitely experience manic and even psychotic episodes, but as your father stated, you do not seem to experience the lows or depressions that most of the time come with bi-polar. However, it is possible to be bi-polar, and only experience the manic phases without the low points. This would effectively be termed bi-polar affective disorder. It does also seem that the manic episodes are not without a degree of psychosis attached to them, which is one of the overlaps between schizophrenia and bi-polar," the doctor reliably informed him.

"I thought I would also add that I'm never violent, hostile or aggressive to people, when I'm labouring under an episode. In the distant past, I would feel a strong wave of self-loathing. However, with this last episode it was different. I felt more empowered, even though I believed I was locked in a struggle with the secret service. I found myself ruminating over a spiralling cathedral of thought, related to the government's secretive and malicious endeavours against me."

The doctor started to ask Luke to give him a potted history, right from his upbringing, through to the present day, in particular highlighting the key episodes in his life. The doctor was quick at writing down the salient points, of what Luke was uttering.

After quite a long while of opening up to the doctor, Luke was relieved to have the glass of water by his side, so as to give his drying mouth some much-needed lubrication. Luke wondered if the doctor was analysing his little mannerisms as well as taking notes, or was this Luke's own misguided interpretation of the consultation process. Luke very much warmed to the doctor – who was a young man in his thirties – and was of a similar background and age, albeit a few years younger than Luke. The doctor mentioned how he had been to a concert with a certain band that was big in the nineties - playing a set. Luke responded enthusiastically to the mention of that band, and asked if they had played the song, 'Sit down' at the venue. The doctor, who loved the band, was a little disheartened at the concert, as they had not sung any of their hit melodies, especially that song.

Once the doctor enquired if Luke had anything further to add – Luke believed he had said everything that was noteworthy, and they both stood up and warmly shook hands. The doctor decided he would come to the waiting area, and say his goodbyes to Jeremy as well,

"Mister Trevelyan – I'll be seeing your son in a few months' time, when I should have a better assessment of his condition. I suggested he go back into architectural employment to keep his mind busy and occupied. Hopefully, by the time I see him again, he will be gainfully employed."

"I'm in total agreement. There's nothing like work to give a boost to one's cognitive faculties, and stop the brain from slowly wasting away," said Jeremy, with a sense of comfort and relief that the doctor was seeing his son's situation similarly to him.

"I'll see what I can do," Luke pitched in, with a sense of resignation. He had come to appreciate the time and space he had to himself, and he was reluctant to return to work so soon, although he knew that it was probably a necessary activity.

Chapter 16

On Saturday 12th April Luke made another trip to London. The weather was glorious, and it was surprisingly warm for that time of year. He decided to dress in a more visceral and raw ensemble. He chose a black, long sleeve T-shirt, some dark blue jeans, a brown plain but stylish leather jacket, some comfortable but trendy looking dark brown leather shoes, and an ochre brown beanie to complete the look. Compared to his previous attire, it seemed more brooding, and hinted at a dash of menace.

After arriving at Marylebone station, he decided to walk the route to the Tate Modern, rather than taking the tube to either Oxford Circus or even Charing Cross, and then walking the remainder of the stretch. He felt impelled to see as much of London, and the people who would pass him on his way, as feasibly possible. He still experienced a residual heat and fire inside himself, but this time, compared to a little over a week ago, it was now a much more contained and subtle force.

While walking along the Southbank, past the National Festival Theatre, he was aware how quiet it was still at this relatively early hour. He had left Leamington particularly early, and he had arrived at the Southbank, before it had become busy with hordes of people, sampling its wares and food delights. Remembering that he had read an article about how a certain actor thoroughly enjoyed lying down on park benches, or on the grass in parks and looking up through the spindly branches and leaves of the trees to the sky above. He did this totally unselfconsciously, and he had no concern for what other people thought about his antics. The joie-de-vivre of this actor Luke very much admired.

Seeing as it was not busy with the hustle and bustle of people; he chose a suitably clean park bench, overlooking the Thames. Lying down in a supine position, he gazed mindfully through the myriad fingers and blossoms of the couple of tree canopies above him, to the cloudless blue sky above, just as the actor would do and had done. After indulging in this restful yet alert posture for about five minutes, a helicopter from the distance began to get ever closer and louder, until it seemed to be hovering directly overhead. As far as he could make out, it seemed like a police surveillance helicopter or even that belonging to a special branch unit.

This rather put him off the tranquillity he was previously basking in, and he felt the need to reluctantly move himself from this space. He thought whether MI5 were continuing with their many attempts to erase him, through a sniper discreetly located inside the helicopter. Luke was not paying much attention to the details of the hovering machine and the occupants inside, but instead calmly rose from his seat, and walked nonchalantly from the bench, heading towards the direction of the Tate Modern. Their weapons could not hurt him as they would be disabled by the magical power of the gods.

Luke now, in this instance, felt utterly safe and secure with this heartfelt belief. After a couple of minutes with it lingering in that aerial location, the helicopter banked back towards the heart of the city.

While inside the Tate Modern, he arbitrarily ventured into one of the free exhibition spaces. Not being very focused on the artwork, he was instead a little distracted by the motley arrangement of people passing him by, or going partially in his direction. After about an hour of scanning the exhibits, it seemed to Luke that he was becoming emotionally saturated with the artwork on display, and feeling a little overwhelmed by the many individuals coalescing in small groups, or meandering through the spaces, and tracing their own unique paths.

He went out of the exhibition space, and opted for a comfortable leather armchair among a series of sofas and armchairs to relax on. These were situated on the middle level, with a large bank of windows opposite them, in which to survey the large turbine hall.

Ensconcing himself in a rather indulgent pose, with his legs dangling over the side of the leather armchair on the middle level; he directed his gaze towards all those, who would wander by behind the armchair - with a level of keen interest. It was slightly quieter on this level, and the quantity of people walking past was inwardly more manageable for Luke's soft temperament. He loved being inquisitive about people, and thoroughly appreciated trying to delve into the psychology of strangers and those friends and acquaintances he knew. It was as if he was drinking in their faces and physiognomy, and gleaning some partially hidden truths about their histories – their hopes, fears, struggles and joys – the bittersweet symphony that was their lives. His attention was not restricted to those who were attractive, popular or successful but he surveyed the whole gamut of people that fell under his radar with a feeling of metta. Luke really appreciated the word metta or the equivalent in English being an unconditional love, or a boundless love that had no self-referential quality to it.

After enjoying the relative quietude, interspersed with sporadic bursts of big groups passing him by, he left the Tate Modern, and noticed from his watch that it was time for an early lunch. He crossed the Millenium Bridge, which was humorously termed the wobbly bridge after its opening because when the public walked over it, when it first opened, it would sway precariously. The ensuing battle between the architect, the engineer, and the client was ironed out, after considerable time and expense in lengthy court battles - with the resultant action taken to fit dampers to the underside of the structure. As he reached the other side, he ambled in the direction of St. Paul's cathedral.

By St. Paul's tube station, he spied a French restaurant chain, and thought that would be the most appropriate place to get some sustenance. He entered the premises and was greeted by a very polite and friendly looking woman, who to Luke's ear seemed to be of Eastern European descent. The restaurant was practically empty, seeing as he had arrived just after midday. She enquired with him, where he might like to sit for his meal. Very much favouring the corner seat by the plate glass window, he could then have his back to the window, in order to face towards the interior of the space.

Almost about a minute after he had sat down, and had grabbed a menu in front of him, he was perusing the dishes, when two very muscular and dominant males entered the restaurant. They looked towards where Luke was situated, and they chose to sit directly adjacent to him in the corner by the window.

Immediately, a wave of fear gripped Luke tightly, as he tried to come to terms with what he perceived were these two menacing presences, sat next to him. The person who sat with his back to the window seemed like the more dominant individual of the two, and he was also the taller of them. The other individual had light blond hair, and although he was looking in the direction of Luke's table, he could not seem to meet Luke's piercing gaze.

Luke wondered about this, thinking that the blond brute probably had a guilty secret he could not bring himself to acknowledge the reality of. What Luke also noticed is that they both were talking in, what appeared to be, Russian. This fact heightened the drama in Luke's mind, as he connoted their Russian speech with potential physical violence and maliciousness, due to the stereotypes he had come across in so many films. From their overall physique, they looked as if they worked out regularly in the gym, pumping iron, and probably engaging in cardio-vascular work-outs to keep their bodies as fit as a fiddle. The overall impression Luke got was they were in to do someone real damage, and the person on the receiving end was unmistakably Luke.

Once Luke had ordered one of the vegetarian dishes, namely a cheese toastie filled with mushrooms, plus a side order of chips;

he did not need to wait long before the order arrived at his table. He then proceeded to battle with his fears and demons, by feeling very threatened and intimidated by these two handsome brutes. He did not let the fears consume him, but rather chose, in his own inimitable way, to surmount the mental obstacles in his path. As he was eating, he did just that, and continued engaging with the activity of mastication of his food. Though he felt his nerves and his pulse racing; he just mindfully pursued the task at hand. He did not need to engage in any mantra to give him solace - just by the act of eating with awareness, was enough to keep him focused. He knew this moment would pass, and there would be no violent ramifications that would result from this close shave to his life.

After having consumed his satisfying lunch, and having just paid; Luke got up from his seat and headed for the toilets. As he entered the toilets, he did not let the panic overtake him, and just went about his business, taking a pee - steadily and efficiently. He was half expecting the door to open and one of the brutish men to confront him, if not both of the physically powerful men. They would then clobber and maim him, possibly to his death, and then run away from the scene of the event, with no genuine wish from the authorities to pursue these nameless thugs.

Luke exited the toilet to see no-one coming his way, but while he was ascending the second flight of stairs - the larger of the two Russians, emerged at the top of the staircase. Luke opted for not engaging with him in eye contact and kept himself strictly to the left hand side of the flight, but kept his posture tall and erect. They passed each other with no event to speak of.

Luke acknowledged the waitress, and said goodbye to her courteously, with which she appeared to be reduced to a sweet, giggling yet slightly embarrassed girl of her youth again. As Luke exited the restaurant, he took a brief moment to pause - to take a deep inhalation of air - collect himself - and then advance westwards between the large, opulent historic blocks of buildings. He decided not to look over his shoulder, to see if the two men were following him, but for a brief time he heard no sound of footsteps trailing him.

Suddenly, after about five minutes of leaving the restaurant, he could feel someone was directly on his tail. He smoothly turned his head around, and observed a man in his early thirties, and of fairly stocky build, looking a little sheepishly into his mobile phone, as well as making shifty glances at him. At this juncture, there was a turning into a very quiet side street. Luke could choose to continue on the busier road with more pedestrian footfall, or else opt for the quiet side street with no discernible movement of human life. With a sense of boldness and courage, Luke chose the quiet side street, and internally said to himself about the rogue individual, "Let's see what you are made of. If you think you are so tough, let's see how willing you are to embrace the unknown."

He purposefully strode down the quiet street, deliberately not shifting his head to look round, and waited with bated breath to see if the particular man would follow. Luke just continued with his regular pace, and seemed to slowly let go of his fears and worries, within a matter of minutes. The man who had been by his side at the earlier specific junction had now scarpered from the route Luke was taking. He walked past a site with building work happening, and a fairly large group of operatives from a firm of contractors were huddled together, discussing their build strategies. As Luke approached, and sauntered by, their voices lowered, and they all wore expressions of deep curiosity.

Reaching the embankment, he decided to stroll along the bank of the Thames. He had no particular destination in mind, and was content to just absorb and appreciate the atmosphere and people, while maintaining a steady momentum forwards. It was as if he was some sort of lion, who had made the separation from the group, and was on a quest to search for a pride of lionesses, he would become head of. There was even a leonine step to his gait, and what felt to Luke like an indomitable courage.

After having passed lots of people, mostly sitting on the

benches, periodically situated along the bank of the Thames, and basking in the glorious weather - he had reached the Houses of Parliament. There was an emotional response of awe and respect for such grandeur in this conglomeration of gothic architecture. The mass of people in this specific area was a little overwhelming, but Luke managed to find a spot that was not so busy with pedestrian footfall at the edge of the grassy square overlooking the side of the vast historic edifice.

Feeling a desire to lie down on the low stone plinth surround, he calmly and deliberately took off his shoes, and made them as a rest for his head, and planted his tall frame on the very low wall. He then proceeded to close his eyes, and started letting the sounds of bodies walking by and the cacophony of the vehicles, wash over him. He imagined what the general public would be making of this comparatively strange occurrence.

The sun's warmth and light was wonderful, and an overwhelming stillness seemed to descend into Luke's heart. He was totally at peace with himself, yet all around there was the sound of the chaos of traffic, and people frantically living out their lives.

After lying there in a supine position for about half-an-hour, feeling utterly rested and still, Luke mindfully put his shoes back on, and favoured a different orientation he would go in. After skilfully negotiating his way across the wide traffic congested road, he headed towards Buckingham Palace, along Pall Mall.

Arriving at St. James Park, he found a quieter spot in the open area, lay down and closed his eyes again. This time he drifted into a short doze. He woke up with a startle, and lurched forward onto his feet again, thinking he was in a very exposed situation. This would be a perfect opportunity for a satellite laser gun, to pinpoint its terminal aim at him, and kill Luke cleanly and surely. He was now becoming a little weary of his endeavours that day, and plumped for making his way back home. He walked back along Pall Mall, and once he spotted the first underground station available, he found his way back to Marylebone station.While sitting on the tube back, he observed a clean cut, slim, handsome individual with an earpiece in one ear, sitting directly opposite Luke. He was not making any eye contact with Luke or anyone else for that matter, and had turned his focus inwards, but he looked decidedly tense and nervous. Luke surmised that he might be a novice spy, and had been given orders by central intelligence to do away with him, with a clean shot from a silencer to Luke's heart. By his facial and bodily expressions, it was as if he was having a serious and anxious internal tussle, and therefore unable to act out the direct orders from central command. All Luke could feel was compassion for his plight. He wondered if, from the back of this crucial event, the individual's job would become more precarious, due to his slip-up in espionage.

A thought then crossed Luke's mind. As much as his life was in danger, not one person could bring themselves to end his life. It was not that he was invulnerable, just his life was too precious in the grand scheme of the cosmos. Even if spies did have the gumption to try and end Luke's life by whatever means available to them; then the gods would always magically intervene, and prevent him from coming to any harm.

Chapter 17

Luke often went with his mood, when it came to his choice of coffee shops, and the coffee shop in the Royal Priors arcade in Leamington Spa became his haunt in the mornings. The manager was a friendly man, and always engaged Luke in polite and interesting conversation, normally sparked off by Luke's choice of reading material. There was also a very friendly Welsh woman, who was particularly keen on discussing Luke's books and the one's she had been reading herself. They both lifted his spirits, with their interest and enlivening communication. Somehow these were the only two members of staff in the coffee shop he warmly connected to, while most of the others were frostier towards Luke.

It was the middle of April, and Luke had begun to go wandering a bit after his coffee. There was quite a wild expanse of ground adjacent to the river, on the east side of Leamington. He had been to the grounds on a couple of occasions before, but on this day something felt a little different to Luke.

It was a sunny day with no clouds present, and he had with him a copy of the Dhammapada, which was a translation of the words of the Buddha. It was a profound discourse expressed in beautifully poetic form. As he approached the entrance to the open parkland, he heard loud calls and noises from youngsters in canoes on the river. They were shouting and yelping with delight and excitement.

As he walked near the edge of the river, the path then took him to the middle section of the large expanse of field, and after a pleasant five minute stroll through the open parkland, he thought he would sit down on this gorgeous day and soak up the atmosphere – with a lovely view of the backdrop of the mature and majestic trees, marking the boundary of the open field. Within a couple of minutes of settling down into a comfortable posture where he crossed his legs, and felt firmly supported, he heard a whistle go off. Luke could have sworn that it came from someone in the trees near where he sat, and not the river further upstream. It went off again on a couple of subsequent occasions within half-a-minute of each other. Luke could still hear the party of children in canoes, but their voices were very faint, so he jettisoned the notion that the whistle came from their instructor. He heard behind him the sound of a few clicks, and he was sure he heard too the faint noise of rustling in the long grass, as if someone was trying to very stealthily make their way towards him.

He did not at any time turn his head round to see who was making the noise. Taking his book, he started reading the translation of ancient and pure text. Hearing the clicking behind him again, he thought it might be coming from a weapon. Again, there was the repeated rustling in the long grass.

While he was reading he noticed quite a strange feeling envelop him. He imagined it to be like an invisible serpent was climbing up his spine and offering complete protection to ward off attacks from outside. In Buddhism, there are such things as nagas, which are mythical serpents, which reside in the depths of the ocean of one's unconscious mind. They are seen as possessing spiritual qualities, and are not of Christian mythology - as embodiments of evil. It was as if the king serpent Mucalinda was affording him complete insulation from harm.

After about fifteen minutes of remaining extremely peaceful in that spot, he decided to make his slow but measured way out of the park – not being perturbed by what he had just experienced. On one of his previous occasions to the park, he had sat down in a similar spot as today, and a bespectacled middle aged woman had come by with her small furry Yorkshire terrier. When they both approached very near to Luke, she carried on until she turned round to see that the dog had frozen about a few metres away from where Luke was sitting.

Somehow there was a force in Luke that the dog was picking up on. The woman was baffled. She went to grab his collar slightly confused and frustrated, and then dragged the dog past Luke. He wondered if all this was being picked up on some satellite TV, and transmitted to a billion homes around the planet. What would everyone make of this particular event? Luke thought it would stir up debate, as to what his true intentions were. Personally, he would put it down to overcoming recent fears through a multiplicity of scenarios and events that made him much more in touch with his body and mind, and the by-product was it gave him a subtle but deep internal fire. He was sure that some would probably misread this event, as a sign of something much more sinister and evil.

Once Luke had left the park on this day with the particular whistle noise, it would be the last time that he would venture into the park that year. The idea of strolling through the park, and sitting in the middle of the expanse of land just did not appeal to him anymore. His activities on subsequent mornings became more orientated around the centre of town and the coffee shops. Luke still felt whether he was just deluding himself with all these theories about spies in the Buddhist movement, and over the course of the next month, he would slowly start to dismiss these views completely. His sleep patterns had pretty much returned to normal, and the residual fire in him, over the weeks, would gradually ebb away with a much cooler and more stable temperature residing in his body. However, he still felt isolated by separating himself from his former Buddhist friends, and he decided near the end of April to look up a different tradition that allegedly practised a modern Buddhism. Perhaps he needed to join another tradition, as he had imbibed the teachings of Leander for over twenty-one years, which was a good measure of time with one school.

After looking up the Dappa tradition in Birmingham, he

made plans to go and attend a short urban retreat, located in a large Victorian house in the outskirts of the city.

Chapter 18

It was Wednesday 23rd April. On arriving at the well maintained Victorian house Luke rang the bell, and was duly greeted by a friendly and welcoming individual.

"Hello! Have you come for the three day urban retreat?" the man enquired with a warm complexion and kindly eyes.

"Yes I have. I hope I'm not too early arriving?" Luke said, being about three quarters of an hour early. He had deliberately planned this, so he could potentially speak to the senior monk or nun of this tradition, and hopefully quiz the individual about their practice and doctrinal viewpoint. Luke got into conversation with the man who had greeted him at the door. His name was Jay. Being of Indian origin, he had been brought up in this country. After some much needed pleasantries, Luke started pointedly asking Jay about pertinent aspects of the Dappa tradition. He interweaved the more serious discussion with dollops of light heartedness and occasional bursts of frivolity, which seemed in keeping with the one-to-one and unfamiliar context.

Luke discovered that the monks and nuns wore robes and that they had all made vows to observe the various rules, pertaining to the established code from the Buddha's time - a total of over two hundred rules. Already Luke inwardly pondered this fact, and thought that although they described themselves as modern Buddhists, they were quite heavily steeped in history and tradition. Their tradition placed high demands on monks and nuns compared to the laity, and in our times of multiple distractions, here there and everywhere, Luke felt it would be almost impossible to uphold all those rules, especially the vow about maintaining chastity throughout one's life without subsequently denying one's fundamental life force.

Above all, Luke pondered that we had to acknowledge where we were at, and try and walk a fine line between hedonism and an ascetic path, but taking into account the darker as well as the lighter sides of our lives. Luke understood these darker aspects to be primarily that of fear, anger and desire. These shadow sides should not be repressed but instead one should try and turn towards, acknowledge, observe and experience them, with the ultimate aim to eventually let go and transform these strong forces. It is important though, as much as is feasibly possible, to try not to mindlessly indulge in them. With gentle but steady effort, one should try to overcome and transform these darker aspects of our psyche.

There were however dark elements in life, like anger, which could have a drive and power behind them. These could express themselves as uncomfortable truths in some music, films and sections of the Arts. He also recognised these dark forces in understanding where we were at with regards to sex. He thought very few could deny sex from their life, and ultimately this denial could lead to repression of one's baser forces. He was not in favour of a complete free sexual expression though, but instead saw that it should be practised in a healthy moderation - set within an overall context of invaluable friendship with people who shared one's spiritual values of growth and development in consciousness.Luke did believe that the more one was able to access and maintain higher states of consciousness through meditation, and experience feelings of more and more spiritual bliss, then one could let go to a greater degree the attachments of the cruder and baser sexual urges.

In the movement Luke had left behind, he believed they had got a much healthier understanding of the idea of the monks and the laity. They did not have a definite distinction between them. They had people who were ordained into an order, and they observed ten fundamental and overriding negatively and positively formulated precepts, which were considered training principles and moral guidelines. These precepts were not generally taken as vows, but instead were areas of one-self - in body, speech and mind - which were there to be worked on and improved – they were ultimately guidelines and not rules. The positive formulations were what the Buddhist practitioner could ultimately aspire to, and forever better in themselves, until they became perfected when enlightenment was reached.

After about half an hour of conversation with Jay; the senior nun of the tradition came through the small but cosy seating area where Luke and Jay were sat down in. She turned her head towards Jay, and said to him that they would begin the retreat in a quarter of an hour. Jay said to her,

"We've got one person here for the retreat. His name's Luke. I'm correct aren't I?" Jay said in a friendly tone.

"Yes, you're right" said Luke amenably.

"Hello Luke. Welcome to our place. Is this your first time here?" she enquired.

"Yes it is, but I've been with another movement before this. It was called Vandana. I've fallen out with them, as I believe that some of them might not be who they say they are, and I'm quite keen to now try your tradition, and see what it's like."

"Sorry to hear that. Perhaps we might be able to entice you in to our collective throng?" she said with a mixture of innocence and cheekiness in a half wince and half smile expression. It did not dawn on Luke that morning, but the more he reflected on this particular senior nun in their tradition, the more he felt that she was repressing a very strong life principle, through the many monastic rules she had vowed to observe and uphold.

Another nun and also a girl named Leanne, who was in her thirties, had joined the group of them. Jay made it clear to Luke that both, Leanne, Luke and him would venture up to the large hut at the back of the garden, where the retreat would be held. They would then get prepared in their respective seating positions, either on cushions or chairs, and they would wait for the two senior nuns to arrive and take up their sitting positions. The senior nun would then begin the retreat.

Inside the shrine room Jay got the sound system ready, and the specific music track waiting to play. Once Luke, Jay and Leanne had got ready, and waited silently for the two nuns to enter, Luke spotted the array of different unopened biscuits and sweets, dotted around the shelving on the back wall, which had been draped with beige cloths, behind the raised platform of the retreat leader. Amongst the biscuits were framed pictures of their particular teacher, and lights that he later found out were permanently left on as a mark of continual offering to their main living teacher and an ancient Buddhist, Je Tsongkapa, whose teachings their tradition stemmed from. He thought the assemblage of sugary foods and lights that were continually left on were two odd practices to Luke's more refined sensibilities. He understood the sentiment of using objects to reverence their esteemed teachers, but not with the use of biscuits, and other sweet foods that were on display. Also they did not seem to respect the environment with a continually powered electrical light source. Luke much preferred the simple gesture of Vandana, whereby they offered candles, symbolizing the enlightenment of the Buddha Shakyamuni – flowers to represent impermanence, through being beautiful and scented one moment, and then becoming faded and fallen in the next instant – and incense to symbolize the perfect community pervading in all directions. These he believed were more appropriate forms of offering, and especially that the candles were always extinguished once the celebrations had been made.

To Luke the sweet comestibles only seemed to highlight the fact that the denial of sensual pleasures in so many other areas of their lives was in some way compensated by the indulgence in these sweet foods. As Buddhists, Luke felt that there needed to be more a healthy balance with all forms of desire; not trying to stamp out some unwholesome desires, while letting others run wild and rampant, as a way of keeping a semblance of internal harmony. A path that Vandana subscribed to - steered itself more towards refined sense pleasures, but without denying our strong, base urges. Luke wondered if due to their many vows as nuns or monks, tasty sweet foods were a source of comfort and solace, and therefore precariously kept them from breaching those many vows - passed down from ancient Buddhist tradition.

Luke believed that these historical principles and rules did not work well in their current age of mass information, communication, and consumption, and other modes of operating, such as Vandana's approaches were necessary as a Buddhist to meet with the modern Western mind-set.

The two nuns entered the shrine room, and Sarah and Jay clasped their hands and bowed their heads. Luke felt a touch uncomfortable with this mark of respect, being given to the women, but reluctantly yet obediently followed suit – so as not to appear unruly. The senior nun assumed the position on an elevated platform, while the other nun sat in the audience. Jay fumbled with the electronic music device, and experienced a little complication before succeeding in playing the right track. A few moments after the music started playing, all four of them broke out in song form to a tuneful but slightly syrupy melody. Luke wondered whether it was his past conditioning that was baulking at the sound of their voices and the tune, or else the general atmosphere did not sit comfortably with him, and would never do.

Luke thought it would help his slightly begrudging mood, if he joined in with the singing. He used the book that had been given to him earlier, to help with knowing what the words to the songs were. He tentatively joined in with the unified vocal expression. It helped him to get a vague understanding of their particular interpretation of the Buddhist teaching. This combined rendition of tuneful verses lasted what seemed like a good hour. Once the music ended Luke waited with slightly bated breath for the senior nun's first quasi-public utterance.

Luke believed that this elevation of teacher over disciples that had been handed down from Tibetan teachers was something else that did not fit in with the spirit of exploration and openness - here in the West. He felt this act of formal separation between monks or nuns, and the laity was more a guard against their fragile egos – and not what was conducive to a healthy human exchange. He believed this was one more thing that was not congruous with our modern times.

The head nun spoke about karma, rebirth and all actions have consequences quite convincingly; interweaving stories from life and her own life to substantiate her valid points. Luke had no reason to call into question any of her views, and in some ways responded favourably to these points. He was encouraged by this exposition, and he believed that there might be some merit in pursuing this tradition further.

After ending the talk, some more music was played with verses being collectively sung, and then, once the music had stopped, the two nuns left the building, while Luke, Jay and Sarah helped with putting away the cushions and mats, while conducting a general clear-up. While they were clearing the room, Jay said to Luke,

"Did you feel the strength of energy with the Vajrayana ritual we undertook? I definitely noticed it, and in fact I felt it to be quite strong."

"I perhaps found a little of the energy you are talking about, but I can't say it was anyway near discernible," Luke replied in a conciliatory tone, as he had in fact not felt even a glimmer of raw energy. Vajrayana literally means: the way of the thunderbolt, and was meant to be the third and last way to gain enlightenment. It was meant to be the speedy path to awakening, but depended heavily on the guru-disciple relationship. If the guru was very skilled, and the disciple was willing and able, great progress could be made by the disciple through the guru's initiation and instruction. Great forces and energies could be invoked from the subconscious, yet if the disciple was not calm, tranquil and together in mind and heart, it could result in a mental collapse of the individual. The Vajrayana was not a path Luke was willing to explore in any depth yet, and preferred to stick to the Mahayana with its emphasis on generosity, altruism and the will to enlightenment for the sake of all other sentient beings, while adopting a steady but consistent development in all aspects of one's life - in one broad sweep.

Luke therefore preferred to adhere to meditation techniques that would cultivate concentration, integration and positive emotion, in the form of mindfulness of breathing and universal loving kindness or friendliness - respectively. These were the basis of samatha, the Sanskrit word for calm and tranquillity, from which vipassana, the Sanskrit for insight, could be established.

Luke stayed for lunch with all of them still present, but before the meal he engaged in conversation with the head nun on an outdoor seating area in the well-maintained garden. The weather was, yet again, bright, blue skies and glorious sunshine.

"I would love to become a monk, but I feel the demands, placed on all of you, are extreme with the many strict vows you have to abide by," Luke said with mild concern.

"If you find the vows too difficult, there would always be a possibility to become part of the laity. They've a more restricted set of precepts that they follow, and try and adhere to," the Head nun said trying to appease him.

"The only downside for me would be that as a lay person, I wouldn't have the opportunity to teach Buddhism or meditation, unlike the monks or nuns who are able to do so," Luke responded.

"That's not strictly true. We've a number of laypersons, who teach just like the monks or nuns do. You'd have to go on a three year course though, and you would have to teach in the style of the Dappa tradition, but if you felt we suited your understanding of Buddhism, and you were prepared to undertake the three year long course, which would involve some teacher training - then this tradition might well suit you," she willingly offered.

"When you mention that laypeople do have the opportunity to teach; that fact really interests me. I had been teaching meditation myself at my former Buddhist place, and I truly believe that in my situation, teaching is so fundamental to my spiritual growth," Luke said passionately.

"If you wanted to know a bit more of our tradition, I could point you in the direction of some good books to read, by our highly esteemed teacher. Or else, there is a spring festival and retreat near the Lake District at the end of May, you could go on - to find out more about us."

"I think a retreat near the Lake District does sound a very appealing prospect. I'm pretty sure I don't have anything pressing around that time. How many people normally go there?" Luke asked.

"You probably would find that it's attended by thousands of people, and most would pitch tents, all dotted around in their grounds. It's all very well managed, and the retreat talks and meditations take place in quite a newly designed, decorative and harmoniously arranged large building, whilst other activities are centred in the old Priory building, which is a vast historic edifice," the head nun said, enthusing to Luke about its merits.

"The more you mention it, the more I think it would be ideal for me in my current situation. I also miss not being on retreat or at Buddhist festivals, so it would come in quite handy in my present circumstances."

After more discussion about his situation with his previous Buddhist movement they both went inside and joined the rest of them, who were beginning to tuck into a light vegetarian meal. He was encouraged by their vegetarian habits, which was not so prevalent in the more historic Buddhist traditions - in South East Asia and the Far East. As Luke sat down amongst them, and helped himself to the food on offer – he listened attentively to the ensuing discussion.

The subject was skirting around the issue of the mind and ethics. Luke felt suddenly impelled to mention the first verses of the Dhammapada that he had on a previous occasion memorized.

"In my previous Buddhist group, we quite often stress the first couple of verses of the Dhammapada, which was a sutra meant to be one of the most poetic and timeless words, the Buddha had ever uttered. It goes like this:

Experiences are preceeded by mind, led by mind, and produced by mind. He who speaks or acts with an impure mind – suffering follows, even as the cartwheel follows the hoof of the ox drawing the cart.

Experiences are preceeded by mind, led by mind, and produced by mind. He who speaks or acts with a pure mind – happiness follows, like a shadow that never departs."

The other nun remarked to Luke,

"That's a lovely and very beautiful quote."

"Thank you," Luke responded. He was happy that he had imparted this nugget of wisdom. Thinking that the ramifications of what he had just said might filter and percolate through their minds, but might not necessarily plant themselves there and take root. The overriding view he had though, was that their tradition spoke a similar language to his previous movement, but with different emphases, especially around the area of karma, rebirth and emptiness.

After lunch Luke decided to leave as he felt he had sampled enough of their particular approach to Buddhist practice, and one that he was not familiar with. That evening, back in his flat, he went online to book himself on their Spring festival and retreat. He thought why not try them out, as he was now no longer affiliated to Vandana. He needed to get a sense of their retreat and festival format. If all else failed, he could see it as a holiday in lovely countryside.

Chapter 19

Over subsequent days Luke spent quite a lot of time on his own reflecting, in a somewhat restless and isolated situation in his basement flat. Were the people in Vandana actually frauds, or had his earlier unstable mind been subtly distorting reality – so thereby deluding himself? The more he contemplated the facts, the greater became the realisation that he had made a serious mistake with his interpretation of past events with a lot of the individuals in his former movement. From his experience of the Dappa tradition, he strongly believed that the way Vandana explicated the Buddha's teaching was more in line with what his heart and reason were telling him. Vandana's approach was more progressive and modern, than the Dappa tradition or any other alternative, for that matter.

It was Wednesday 30th April, and after days of deliberation, he took the bold step to write a very conciliatory e-mail to all those, who he had sent the previous vicious e-mail to. He had to, in some ways, try and heal the rift he had caused between him and Vandana. Luke proceeded to write,

Dear All,
About the start of this New Year, I changed medical surgeries, as I receive a fortnightly dose of medication that is administered to me by a nurse. I used to attend a surgery local to my parent's home, but I now registered with a medical practice, local to where I live in Leamington Spa – thus trying to further erode the ties that bind me to my parents. A distinction could be made between the two

surgeries – my previous place cared for patients –the Leamington surgery processed patients.

By about the early part to the middle of March, I was starting to sleep less; I was starting to develop ideas of being closely monitored by spies from Intelligence Services, and I was starting to become a little paranoid and delusional. One of the main ideas I developed was the notion that I was some kind of Truman show style figure being watched by millions, if not billions of people around the world. However, no-one could reveal anything to me for fear of being prosecuted by the authorities. I was convincing myself that all the signs, in my life, pointed to this assertion.

It is interesting to note that the nurse, at the new medical practice, did not open the medication in front of me, like what was done in previous places, but as soon as I walked into her treatment room, she had the syringe fully loaded, and with no ampoule in sight, I can only conclude from this that probably on more than one occasion, she either diluted the medication, or else she gave me a different drug or just water. What the underlying reason and motive was, I will never know. As the saying goes, "The proof of the pudding is in the eating", and this past episode I experienced, serves to substantiate the fact that I was not being given the correct treatment. I had been on the drug for over 17 years, and up until this time I had been well and healthy.

This brings me round to apologising profusely for the last e-mail I sent all of you, and the worry and concern it must have caused. I also truly and deeply regret the sending of it, which when I read it back to myself, sounded hostile and venomous, in the nature of its content. This is the antithesis of my loving nature. In my defence, I was still in the throes of my episode with a confused and delusional head on me. I can assure you all that I am now 100% fully recovered, and I do not intend to ever go through that experience again. This time I will have checks in place i.e. making sure I witness the nurse opening the ampoule in front of me, before administering it.

I lost my job, through this turbulent period, but a few good things have come from this ordeal. I have upped my game with meditation, and now meditate daily 2 to 3 times a day, each for 40 to 50 minutes. Now I am out of work, I can devote more time to the study and practice of Buddhism. I very recently inherited money from my uncle passing away last year, which could keep me comfortably going for the next couple of years, while I look for the most appropriate architectural practice to work in.

I have left the surgery in Leamington and, for the time being, I have gone back to the one local to my parent's place, which I know well and trust. With my involvement at the Birmingham centre, I will start to attend events and courses very soon. All this re-engagement will be taken steadily and tentatively at first, but I want to fully immerse myself again with Vandana, and almost start where I left off – which seemed to be on a very firm footing.

With much metta,

Luke

Over the coming days Luke received a number of messages of well-wishing from a few of those he had written to. In particular, they commented on how brave he had been in his last e-mail, and how the writings in his first e-mail did not reflect the person they knew, who came to the Buddhist centre. They only knew someone, who was a warm, friendly and engaging individual, who had a lot of empathy for those he met and encountered. Luke was touched by the overwhelming support from a lot of his former Buddhist friends, and this seemed to confirm to him their authenticity. He knew Buddha Day was going to be held on Sunday 11th May, and he decided that that day would be his first chance to meet and explain himself to some of his fellow companions on the Buddhist path.

The Ordination Team in Norfolk sent an unequivocal e-mail to Luke, a few days after his conciliatory e-mail, stating he would not be welcome on the first retreat, he had assigned himself to that year. They had to seriously consider the wellbeing of the other retreatants, and they needed to be thoroughly convinced that Luke had fully recovered - which at the moment they were not. They suggested to Luke that he re-establish contact with members of the Birmingham Buddhist community, and only when the community felt comfortable that his health was fully restored, would the ordination team feel reassured of his return to retreats in Norfolk.

Luke had asked for ordination into the Vandana order about five and a half years back, and inwardly felt that this dramatic episode was another setback to his ordination into the movement. Some of the order members highlighted to Luke and others on the path that one needed to view it as a process, and therefore one should try and enjoy the journey, rather than grasp after the goal of becoming ordained. One did not have to be an order member to make spiritual progress. Luke was especially appreciative of his opportunity, over the last two and a half years, to teach meditation to beginners at the Buddhist centre. It established a strong sense of purpose and confidence in him, and bolstered his Buddhist practice.

On Buddha day, on Sunday 11th May, he arrived about five minutes before the meditation in the morning, with a mild degree of trepidation, but also an accompanying exhilaration in his heart. Here was a chance to re-engage his practice with a movement he wholly endorsed. Not only did they look far and wide, exercising critical evaluation of most Buddhist traditions and schools, but they also directed their gaze and focus on pertinent aspects of Western civilisation: appreciating a lot of Western literature, philosophy and the arts, throughout the ages of civilisation. The movement cast their eyes on whatever artistic works surrendered their egos to higher, more visionary forces, in particular works which were the realm of an illumined imagination, and not the product of a selfish or fanciful imagination. They also strove to become a more socially engaged Buddhism, than most other Buddhist traditions or movements he knew of.

As Luke entered the café area with a bright sunlight streaming through the long skylight overhead and washing over the congregating melee of people; he was greeted by Mahina, a female order member of a very pleasant and robust nature.

"Hello Luke. Welcome back," she said with a wonderfully warm and inviting timbre to her voice.

"Hello Mahina. It is good to be back. Sorry about what you had to be party to, and I hope to never have to go through that again," Luke said trying to reassure her of his new-found mental health, while manifesting a broad smile that reached from ear to ear.

"Gawain heard that you were coming today, and sent his warmest wishes to you, from the Malvern Hills. He was really pleased that you've got it together again," she replied.

"That's lovely of him. I'll have to get in touch with him soon," Luke said.

"We were all really concerned for you. There has been a lot of metta from all sorts of people who know you, towards you and your situation. It was lovely to witness their concern for you," Mahina said with genuine warmth, and heartfelt sympathy, which noticeably lifted his spirits.

The day at the centre ended with a puja, the ancient Indian pali word for a devotional worship. This consisted of reciting beautifully poetic verses, and chanting mantras, which reflected the attributes of certain archetypal Buddhas and also the historical Buddha. The verses that are recited are there to invoke seven different spiritual moods and emotions in the participant, ranging from worship to rejoicing in merits, and culminating in a verse to do with the transference of merit and self-surrender. This is embellished with an exquisitely decorated shrine, and offerings that people can make during the chanting of a particular mantra, near the beginning of the ceremony.

Once the clear-up had happened, and Luke was driving home, he pondered that although it was a very positive initial meeting with some of his Buddhist friends, it would take quite a long time for their wounds to properly heal. The trust he had earlier forged had been severely weakened, but thankfully not irreparably so.

Chapter 20

The days to the Dappa festival and retreat were fast approaching, and Luke decided that he needed to purchase a decent tent for himself, and some waterproof outdoor clothing. After buying a suitably robust tent that would not cave in or disintegrate with bad weather, he set about the night before his departure, to pack a large travelling bag with all the necessary items he might need. He planned for there being either hot or wet weather, and stuffed as many different items of clothing, as the large bag could handle. Better to take precautions than be caught short of essentials, he pondered to himself.

Luke never paid much attention to weather forecasts, but he was made aware by one of the members of his coffee shop in Leamington that it was predicted to be a wet weekend for much of the country. Knowing that with a positive mental attitude, he would not feel despondent at this weather report and it was the company of people that made a festival and retreat, or for that matter a holiday, pleasurable.

It was the Thursday, on the bank holiday weekend at the end of May, and Luke had now let go of the view that he was a Big Brother spectacle, for all to tune into. After a relatively long journey on the motorway, and a few wrong turnings, nearer the destination - Luke spotted, as he slowly drove down the tarmacked drive, a large, highly ornate building, which he knew, from flicking through the Dappa retreat brochure, was their crowning architectural achievement. It was partially hidden behind a large reclaimed brick wall, and amongst some beautiful oak trees, situated just outside the retreat compound. The visiting cars were parked in open fields outside the grounds, and two individuals, one young Scottish man and an elderly woman greeted him at the entrance to the verdant makeshift car park.

"Have you come for the festival and retreat here?" the handsome Scottish guy dutifully asked, with a very warm and welcoming manner.

"Yes I have. Would you like to see my pass number that I got from the internet," Luke said pre-empting what the Scottish guy was going to ask next, and offering a warm smile in return.

"Thanks. That would be great," he said. Luke proffered his printed slip with the retreat details to him, and he then courteously waved Luke through.

The Priory building was a gigantic and historic edifice, and Luke was asked by assembled staff, dotted at various points along his route to the Priory, to make his way to the reception area in order to register. The majestic nature of the old building was hinted at by a very tall spire in the middle of the complex, but the majority of the vast historic pile was screened from Luke's initial view by some two storey dwellings that sat alongside the impressive hub.

As Luke sat obediently in the waiting area of reception, along with quite a few other retreatants, he observed how most of the staff, registering the procession of people, were wearing matt red robes, either as monks or nuns. He also became aware, over the course of his stay, by noticing and speaking to various people that the nuns definitely outnumbered the monks in this tradition - by a considerable margin.

Luke had slight difficulty pitching his tent, although he had the instructions laid out before him. It had been many years previously, whilst in his teens, when he had last pitched a tent. A young black South African man was also starting to pitch his tent nearby. He could see that Luke was struggling a little, and he asked Luke,

"Do you need a hand with that?"

"That would be brilliant if you could help. I haven't put these up in donkey's years," Luke openly admitted.

"I do a lot of camping, so I'm very familiar with how to put them up. Back in South Africa, there've been many opportunities to go camping," he said.

"Whereabouts in South Africa, do you live?" Luke asked interestedly.

"Johannesburg. Where do you live?"

"Leamington Spa, in Warwickshire. Nowhere near as far or as exotic as where you've come from," Luke said being suitably impressed with this individual's commitment and dedication.

Luke found out his name was Tony, and he was also dazzled by his expert hand at constructing Luke's tent, with a small part played by Luke. He offered to help Tony erect his much larger tent, and this was gratefully received. The weather that late afternoon was of a soft, warm sunlight, unlike what had been forecast. Luke thought a little pessimistically that it would probably be only a matter of time before it worsened.

After supper had been and gone with two time slots, one at 6pm and one at 7pm - at 8:30pm it was time for the evening singing, and a brief talk by one of the leading nuns in the tradition. From the programme it was mandatory for informal retreatants to sit outside of the main hall, under protective tent canopies, as they had not been formally inducted into the tradition. Luke entered the confines of the retreat building and temporary structure - and for a few moments stopped and paused to take in all the many different individuals - mingling or seated. He noticed three large flat screen TV monitors fronting the immediate collection of people, who would be seated under the closed tent canopies. He pondered that this particular tradition were definitely not short of money, and they probably had some very wealthy donors, who had contributed large sums of cash.

Luke sat by where there were a row of empty chairs, and parked himself on the seat at the edge of the row just in case he needed to make a quick getaway. Most people came without their children, as couples, and there were others like Luke, who had arrived on their own. Luke sat in his metal-framed cushioned chair feeling slightly apprehensive, of what was to await him. He was wondering if they would play that sickly sweet tune, and then everyone would sing along to it. What grated a little with Luke was that, in his opinion, the music was far removed from the shades of dark that reality could also manifest as. The music displayed a definite one-sidedness to the light aspect of reality. To Luke's more refined ear, it seemed to filter out the deeper, darker underbelly that lurks in reality's union of opposites. He could now see why there were so many nuns in the tradition, as this sentimental music might well appeal to their more sweet natured temperaments than the men's.

During the start of the service, there was a video of the founding monk of the tradition. He was walking around a newly opened temple, and commenting to the camera about the edifice. What struck Luke most about this particular individual was that although he came across as a very kind and sweet man, with a definite aura, he just appeared to lack a depth and the quality of being rooted to the earth. It might have been his age that was tainting Luke's view of him, but he had read somewhere about a very well-known Vietnamese monk, who had settled in the States, and was probably quite similar in age. His qualities were described as being like the combination of a snail, a cloud, and a heavy piece of machinery. He really got this description, when he had subsequently seen a video clip of him giving a talk. The clip somehow seemed to confirm these attributes of the Vietnamese monk. Luke just did not feel totally inspired by this founding monk of the Dappa tradition. However, Luke was impressed by his dedication and tireless effort to disseminate the teachings of the Buddha to a much wider audience, and he also thought that his writings, especially on the nature of emptiness, were exemplary, after he had read one of his books before embarking on this festival.

After about three quarters of an hour with singing, interspersed with videos of the founder; the most senior nun of the order, who was already sat on the central podium at the far end of the hall, began to deliver an address. Luke was impressed by her confident demeanour, and she definitely held the stage, but a third of the way through he started to get restless on his chair, as she was talking about empowerments, which was a concept Luke was unfamiliar with, and which, at that time, he was a little wary of. After a little internal tussle and dialogue, he rose from his chair, and made a measured but determined route for the exit. He smiled graciously at the young woman, who was marking the exit of the tents, and she warmly reciprocated.

With an unexpectedly goodnight sleep on his first night, he unzipped the tent, and spied, with slightly bleary eyes, sunlight streaming and hitting the Priory building. He also observed the trees on one side were basking in the warm, rich early morning glow. They were defining the edge of the main lawn to the building. His tent was deliberately set under tree canopies, so he would not experience the full force of the sun's morning rays, and he could therefore extend his sleep that little longer. He glanced at his watch. It read 6:25am. Thinking that it was the appropriate time to go and do his morning ablutions before the morning service, he would hopefully beat the marauding retreatants, who would descend on the single sex communal bathrooms. No such luck was had, and he patiently had to wait for his turn in the queue.

Once he had attended to his shower, and had gone back to properly, but with a little difficulty, dress in the slightly awkward shape of the two man tent, he decided to venture into the Priory building while the service in the huge shrine hall was being conducted. There was a particularly friendly security guard sat at the entrance area. Immediately Luke engaged him in convivial conversation, and said to him,

"Are you okay?"

"Yes, fine thanks. How are you?" the conversation continued

briefly with light-hearted small talk, until Luke felt compelled to ask him whereabouts in Liverpool he came from – noticing the Liverpudlian accent. His name was Mick, and he said he came from an area that Luke was not familiar with. In fact, he was not acquainted with most areas of Liverpool, except for where his grandparents and uncle had lived, by Sefton Park. Luke knew Lark Lane quite well, as when he had visited his uncle Terry in the past they would gravitate in the morning and evening to that road with its lively bars, pubs, and coffee houses.

"So your grandparents and uncle lived off Sefton Park, hey. That must have been a pleasant experience for them. Sefton Park is a lovely park – very green and lush – also there are the big, impressive houses at the edge of the park. Did they happen to live in one of those properties?" he asked with benign curiosity and with no hint of mischievousness on his part. "No, they actually lived on one of the streets that came off the big road, which was Egberth Drive," said Luke.

"That's right Egberth Drive. I was trying to recall what that road was called," said Mick. Luke found from his exchange that he came across as a kind man, and he did not want to labour any of the humour aspect in their chat. Thinking that in a previous incarnation Mick might have suggested from Luke's accent that his grandparents would have been the perfect candidates for one of those houses, along Egberth Drive – with a retinue of servants. If Mick had posed that humorous response to Luke, he would have taken it with the jest with which it was intended. However, Luke believed that through Mick's practice as a Buddhist, he did not want to conform to any of the usual stereotypes that so often were planted onto people, in order to label and categorise them.

As Luke left Mick to continue with his duties; just behind where Mick was sitting, there was a very large Buddha in a seated position with a purple halo around his head. Luke had noticed this statue on his arrival, the previous evening. After spending a few moments appreciating the aesthetic aspects of this seated Buddha, he went back to Mick and asked him,

"Which Buddha is that statue meant to represent, Mick?"

"It is depicting Maitreya, the future Buddha," said Mick in a matter-of-fact way.

"Thanks Mick, I'll see you soon," replied Luke, who was instantly taking in the magnitude of what Mick had just said.

Luke took one more look at the seated figure, and thought that it was ironic with the purple halo that it was one of Luke's favourite colours. Something in him felt it was portentous. Also the statue was a seated Buddha, and not one in a full lotus posture on the ground, as was so often depicted of the historical Buddha. Could it be that this future Buddha would emerge from the West, as opposed to the East, as he was more accustomed to sitting on chairs, than being at ease sat on the floor - due to a particularly Western upbringing and conditioning. Over the following days, he mulled this over, from time to time, in more quiet and reflective moods.

He spotted amongst the throng of people on the retreat, a particularly grounded yet effervescent and attractive blond woman. Having consumed his lunch, being with the first lunch slot, he made his way to the light and airy tea shop, set in a conservatory adjacent to the main lawn. As Luke strolled there, his eyes met with the blond woman's. She was waiting in the queue for the second time slot, and they both gave each other warm beaming smiles. Luke felt a frisson of delight in this pure and innocent, but brief, non-verbal exchange. Ordering an Earl Grey tea from the shop, he sat on some outdoor furniture, which was conveniently provided. The sun was wonderfully strong and warm, and furnished Luke with an optimum temperature.

After quietly sipping his tea, and watching the various motley characters walk past and a few sitting amongst him, he decided he was going to have a brief lie-down in his tent – for an afternoon nap.

Once Luke had rested for about three quarters of an hour, he went out of the tent, zipped it up, and strolled slowly from his tent to the main building. On his way, the blond woman happened to be just coming out of her tent. Luke then felt impelled to speak to her,

"Aren't we really lucky with the weather. It's so gorgeous today,"

"I know! It's wonderful, and to think they had forecast bad weather for much of the country, it therefore seems amazing that this is what we're getting," she responded with verve and enthusiasm.

"What are you planning to do now?" Luke enquired innocently, but with a sneaking hope that she would join him in conversation.

"I was just going to have some tea, and go indoors and read this book. Would you like to join me?" she said expectantly, inadvertently flashing one of the Dappa tradition books at him.

"That would be lovely. I suggest we could go upstairs into the main Priory building, where it is quieter and cooler. I'd earlier noticed that there is some comfortable soft seating up on the landing. Does that sound okay to you?" Luke suggested invitingly, and appealing to her senses.

"Sounds perfect to me," she said with visible delight in her expression.

They both ordered tea in disposable cups, and made their way to the upstairs landing, slumping themselves in opposing sofas with a thin, old oak table in between.

"By the way, what's your name?" he asked.

"Sarah, what's yours?"

"Luke. How long have you been engaged with this tradition?"

"Not long, probably only about a year and a half. I'm not always able to manage the weekly group study meetings, as I live in Essex and work in London, and I normally don't get back home until quite late," she said with a forced smile that betrayed a hint of weariness with her predicament. Luke sensed that she was probably contemplating, in a sudden flash of memory, all those early morning rises and thousands of hours of commuting she had to endure, which was the downside of her job in London. After talking about what they thought the festival was like - Luke asked, "What's your job in London?"

"My current job is as a marketing manager for an environmental waste management company. I tend to work as a contractor rather than being PAYE. I like the freedom of working for a couple of years with a company for a decent salary, and then taking three to six months off by going travelling," she said with obvious joy welling up inside her. Luke was reluctant to continue with the discussion on her job, for the moment, and focussed on her travels, which would hopefully brighten her mood.

"Where was the last place you had visited on your travels?"

"It was Malawi. I spent six months out there. For three months, I taught in a primary school, and then for the two months, I travelled the country with a friend I had made at the school, and then in the last month I went around parts of the country on my own," Her face seemed to be glowing. He could not be sure if it was due to the sunlight streaming through the high and broad ornate Priory windows, and catching the side of her face, or else it was the joy she was experiencing - emanating as a natural healthy glow.

"That sounds so thrilling and adventurous. By what you're telling me, it does make being a contractor, and with those benefits, an exciting and seductive prospect. I guess it helps to be also working in London, where jobs now seem to be plentiful. I think employers jump at the chance to recruit people like you. I'm sure it would impress any future employer, by having a six month break, where you also show that you've been doing something worthwhile with your time," said Luke with a great deal of interest in her situation. "You're right, employers do love that, and because I've been told I'm good at my job, it makes me even more marketable. I've started thinking recently though that I don't just want to take any job that presents itself to me. With my limited Buddhist practice, I'm looking for jobs that have an ethical standpoint, and so I'm a little more discerning than before. That's why I am so chuffed with myself in finding this job, as I sifted through quite a few adverts, and held out until this post came along. The company's got very good credentials towards their staff and the environment," she said with a degree of satisfaction and healthy pride.

"Impressive! That sounds really commendable. I hope I would do the same thing, if I was in your position. Do you have many friends in Essex that you keep in touch with?" Luke changed the subject to bring it more in line with human-interest topics.

"It's funny you ask. I've quite a lot of male friends, either with exes that have stayed in touch, and remained friends, or else male friends, who I've shared accommodations with, and also kept in touch with. Where do you live?" Sarah asked.

"I live in Leamington Spa, in a basement flat near the river. When entering the flat on a wet day, I normally have to wear a mask and snorkel to get around my pad," Luke quipped.

"Don't forget your flippers that you would need in addition to help you move around your submerged premises," she said with a faint smile crossing her face.

"No don't worry, the flat is perfectly fine, and issues to do with surface water run-off have been dealt with by an extra drainage system being installed after a flood that occurred a few years back," Luke added sensibly, and then continued,

"I've been really enjoying my time off work over the last three months, as I've managed to inherit some money. Since my time off I've ploughed myself into my Buddhist practice, and developed my friendships by having meaningful and soulful chats."

"You mean like the one we're having now?"

"Except I'm still getting to know you, so we are still only skirting around fairly superficial topics, except for my basement flat, which is deadly serious!" Luke said trying to keep a mock stern expression on his face.

"You mean your quasi water pressure chamber. Do you keep exotic fish in your giant tank?"she playfully teased.

"Only the best kind from warmer climes with beautiful iridescent colours."

"I expect you've given them all names?" the edges of her mouth started to creep further outwards.

"Yes, I have. There's Harry, Jane and Peter amongst others."

"You mean to say you can tell which sex they are?" By this point she was positively beside herself with laughter.

"I'm on familiar terms with all my shoal of fishes being couped up in such a confined wet space," Luke was also now grinning like a Cheshire cat.

During their conversation Luke noticed her cheeky sense of humour would surface every now and again. Luke was turned on by women, who were in touch with a darker side of their personality, as well as being complemented with a lighter and more buoyant side.

Luke launched himself into explaining his version of the Vandana movement to her, and what their fundamental philosophical standpoints were. He talked to her about the act of Going for Refuge to the three jewels, namely the Buddha, the Dharma, and the Sangha, being in fact the central and definitive act of being a Buddhist - to things like the importance placed on spiritual friendship in their movement. He explained how his teacher, Leander, an Englishman, looked to the pali scriptures for guidance, and from the wealth of knowledge he had gained from many teachers, whilst living in India for twenty years. These ranged from Thervadin monks to Tibetan lamas. There was another interesting angle to this incredible man. He had read very widely indeed, especially the classics in literature, philosophy and religious texts while he was growing up, and he had an extremely retentive memory. Luke had witnessed a hint of this when he went to meet him briefly about four or five years ago, while Leander was in his mid-to-late-eighties. Luke happened to mention William Blake, and in particular his poem about a world in a grain of sand. Even Luke struggled to remember it word perfectly, but he dazzled Luke with a recital of that poem - verbatim - without any pause uttered. It might be that it was a poem that was close to his heart, and which he remembered especially well, but Luke was sceptical of this notion.

They both went downstairs, and immediately, once he had set foot on the ground floor, and he had said goodbye to Sarah; he was verbally accosted, but in a kindly and good-humoured way, by a seated blond Russian woman and a sweet natured man accompanying her. They were assigned to try and recruit as many volunteers in helping with the multitude of tasks that were required around the building.

"Hello there! I'm sure you'd love to get involved with the many tasks needed. Just think how much merit you will accrue by giving your time to some worthwhile activities. You'll also help to expend your energy in healthy channels," she said with vigour and bubbliness, which Luke found hard to resist.

"Sure! I'll sign myself up for some duties, if that's what's needed," Luke replied. Luke found that he was not attracted to her, like he was to Sarah, but she definitely had a palpable charm and appeal, through the sheer force of her personality. Her name was Nastasia, which he found out during their brief chat.

Sarah had left for the late afternoon singing in the main shrine hall, while Luke, once he had resolved what his cleaning or helping duties were, decided to go to the North wing in the Priory building. There he sat on a cushioned chair, and meditated in the silent medium-sized shrine room. This would become the place, where he would meditate on this festival, due to its consistently quiet and peaceful setting. He had earlier been made aware of this room in his conversation with Mick.

Luke had decided that he was going to see this festival more as a holiday, and therefore he had planned to mostly do his own thing, while still undertaking his cleaning and preparation duties. He spent quite a lot of time, over the span of the festival, savouring his teas in the Tea shop conservatory, or sat outside in the sunshine. Here he would read, or merely observe people or the nature around him. The weather was unexpectedly good, and when he returned home he found out that much of the country had rain than sun, which Luke saw as a little mysterious and magical.

While Luke sat outside in the late afternoon with the mellow light enlivening him, a young guy, with a slightly rounded face and a boyish enthusiasm, approached him. He was wearing khaki coloured combat trousers, and wore a dark T-shirt, with a logo emblazoned on it. Luke paid no attention to what the logo said. He had a charming way to his manner, and Luke realised from his accent that he was also from Liverpool. Asking Luke if he could sit down with him, Luke was more than favourable with this friendly request.

His name was Dave, and he told Luke that he was living in a community, but he was seriously considering coming to the Priory building to work and live - all year round. Luke asked him directly,

"Would you like to become a monk?"

"I'm not sure it would work with all their vows they need to adhere to, although I've managed to give up watching porn, so that is, I feel, some achievement," he replied with a hearty satisfied look.

"Definitely! I agree with you," Luke was amazed at this achievement, as he still found it so very difficult to renounce the watching of porn. Admittedly, Luke would be very selective in what he viewed, but nonetheless in the realm of spiritual life it was not a wholesome medium. However, it still had an extremely powerful hold on Luke, and probably the same for so many men in the world, who had access to the internet.

"I think what you've achieved is truly amazing, and I definitely aspire to totally renouncing its viewing. Although unlike monks, I'd be unable to let go of masturbation, which for me is necessary in my current mental state. It's a way of keeping me emotionally and psychologically healthy, and in touch with my life force. I'm sure that when the time comes, when I hopefully access and maintain higher states of consciousness that'll be when I can relinquish my hold on having sex, but until then I'll continue with the way I am," Luke said emphatically.

"It took some time with me, but with a bit of gentle perseverance I managed to, at least, overcome my porn habits. I know how it is though - sex is such a powerful drive, deriving from millions of years of biological evolution," responded Dave sympathetically.

"The Buddha is alleged to have said that if there was another vice as strong as the vice of sexual craving or lust - then it would be impossible for anyone to achieve enlightenment ever," said Luke, passionately believing in the validity of this claim.

"I can really see that might be the case. Do you know where you got that from?" Dave asked inquisitively.

"I'm not sure where you can find the reference to it, as I was told it by a Buddhist friend, and I've never subsequently looked up its origins in the scriptures," answered Luke honestly.

The singing had nearly stopped in the main shrine hall, and Luke checked his watch. He knew he was down to help with the serving of supper, and suggested to Dave that he would get ready for the supper preparations. Dave acknowledged this, and responded by saying that he was down for the same activity.

The following day in the early afternoon with some more superb weather, Luke came past Mick sat at his desk by the entrance, and asked him how things were with him. Mick replied with a seriousness tempered with a degree of positivity,

"Things are quite good, but we had a little incident arise last night. There were some intruders in the grounds. Obviously we weren't sure what they were up to, but we've been instructed not to allow anyone into the grounds, and the safety of the people taking part in this festival is paramount to us. My security men, that were on patrol, rallied round, and they got a few more of us from our beds, to help out with the commotion. It was a little disturbing, to say the least, but I guess all part of the job."

"That does sound a little scary to me. It's good that you have such a disciplined and willing workforce. I suppose that's all your collective Buddhist practice coming into play," Luke said commiseratively.

"I think you're right there!" said Mick. Just then he got a radio call on his walkie talkie, which buzzed with a crackling reception. Fortunately, Mick could make out what was being said, even though to Luke it was barely intelligible. He then answered the call with,

"We're not supposed to let anyone, who hasn't paid, into the grounds, and you are saying that even though we started the festival on Thursday he'd like to pay the full sum for the rest of the festival and retreat."

From what Luke could make out from the poor reception on the walkie-talkie, this person was insistent and he was in a fancy car, which seemed to suggest he had money, and probably felt that with cash and worldly influence he could be much more persuasive.

"I really don't care if he's a famous dignitary - he hasn't paid and registered in time, and my orders are not to allow anyone, who hasn't met those conditions to come to the festival."

"He says he would like to speak to you. He does have a very fancy car," were the garbled words that came back from the receiver.

"Go on. Send him up to me, and I'll tell him categorically that he cannot attend," replied Mick forcefully yet with a modicum of composure.

Mick signed off with the member of his team, and he swivelled his head towards Luke, who was standing patiently by the side of his small plain desk.

"Some people really don't understand. They somehow feel they can pay their way onto events with their bulging wallets, and with what they feel is their degree of power and position," Mick was starting to get a little angry, and was speaking with a little more vehemence. Although, he spoke to the other security guard in a relatively composed fashion, his raw and visceral emotions were now bubbling their way to the surface, and he was finding it a little difficult to contain his anger and frustration.

About five minutes had elapsed, when a middle-aged man came through the main entrance door. He was well-built and tall, dressed in conservative summer clothes, and he had some designer sunglasses perched on the front of his quite fulsome shock of light brown hair. Luke guessed he was in his mid-forties. Luke did not know what car he drove, but immediately as he clapped eyes on him, imagined he drove a very fast and aggressive looking sports car. It was as if Luke subconsciously linked the person with that type of car, as though they were synonymous. Luke noticed an immediate twinge of dislike towards this individual. Much of the man's overt values and attributes, which Luke was registering, were mostly what Luke was trying to move away from in his life, or, at the very least, lessen his attachment to. He spoke with a cut-glass English accent, and said to Mick,

"Hello, you must be Mick, the chief security guard. I've been trying to persuade your personnel that I should be allowed to attend this event, as I am willing to pay the full price."

"Well I've been given strict instructions from the organisers that once the retreat has started, I should not let anyone else attend," Mick replied assertively but courteously.

"But I've driven all this way from Surrey, and I thought you would show compassion for my plight. Isn't that what you, as Buddhists, promote?"

"We might preach compassion to all beings, but we are not pushovers by any means. We're also not doormats to be walked all over. I'm sorry you had to drive all this way to be told that you can't attend, but I'm under strict orders, and so my answer to you is still no," Mick was still managing not to lose his temper, and remained admirably calm.

"How can I try and convince you? Perhaps if I pay you more than the going rate?"

"I'm sorry, but my answer is still categorically no, and I will also not be bribed as well," Luke detected the faintest hint of anger in Mick's voice.

"Where do I stay for the night then?" said the gentleman with rising indignation.

"You'll have to work that one out for yourself. There are plenty of B&Bs around this area or even hotels. You could also drive back home now, and perhaps make it back before the end of the evening," responded Mick, knowing that his resistance was rock solid.

"I thought you Buddhists were better than that!" he retorted and then stormed out of the building. The last trace of him was the sound of his loud, gravelly turbo engine receding into the distance.

Luke thought that Mick handled it beautifully. He was direct and assertive, yet kind in his delivery and manner. For a brief instance, Luke felt a sense of *Schadenfreude* towards this well-heeled individual, but it quickly fizzled away when Luke thought he might have found himself in a pickle - for the night at least. He did however think that as the man seemed to have money, he would not be in too much of a scrape that evening, and if all else failed he could drive back home that evening in his fast sports car. Luke did think it rather odd though that he should have come all this way, and try it on with the staff to end up being turned away, which seemed to Luke to be the inevitable outcome. At the time, he did not ruminate on this incident, but later in the year, Luke felt that the previous night's commotion with the security team, and the rich man's boldness and cheek were in some way connected to Luke being there in the grounds.

The following day in the afternoon, Luke happened to meet up with Sarah again, and they both went for a long walk in the direction of the small town.

"Have you had many boyfriends in the past?"

"Yeah, I've had quite a few, but I nearly always stay in touch with them after we break up. I'd say that one of my exes, who I had a fairly long relationship with is probably one of my best friends now," she said.

"I wonder why that is?" asked Luke inquisitively.

177

"I guess it's possibly because I'm so relaxed around men, and that I'm accepting of their foibles. We all have dark spots and things that irritate us about someone else, but I remain open to those blemishes as well as their more favourable aspects. It's probably also due to having a brother, who is schizophrenic, and he's been holed up in a psychiatric ward for years. It makes me more understanding and empathetic towards people. I'm sure that's partly why I was drawn to Buddhism, because of its emphasis on compassion to all beings, and seeing that all our actions are determined by the myriad conditions from this and previous lives," she responded.

"You're so right! I couldn't agree more! I'm sorry to hear that about your brother. Do you get to see him much?" asked Luke tactfully.

"I usually try and see him every other weekend, normally for an afternoon visit."

"How is he these days?"

"Jack can get very angry at times, and can sometimes say some nasty, or at least, hurtful stuff to me, but I know he's suffering and that this is his way of coping with his condition," she replied.

"I thought I would let you know, but I suffer from schizophrenia myself. I've had it since I was nineteen, but I've been predominantly well and healthy for about the last seventeen or so years, since I've been receiving a regular course of medication that works for me," he stated.

"I don't think anyone of us are actually 'normal', and we all have the potential to manifest mental disorders given the right conditions. Who wants to be normal anyway," she said.

"You're right! I think so many people are living their lives trying to conform to one another's expectations of what we consider to be normal, and we're all actually a mixture of the sublime and the ridiculous. When the Buddha cast his spiritual eye over the limitless beings throughout the infinite universe, he said that the overwhelming majority of beings were actually mad

– chasing after pleasures that were transient, and repelling or pushing away things that caused them emotional pain, and not resting in an open way to their mixed, bittersweet experience. Beings need to turn towards their pain, and bring kindness to themselves and others. Acknowledging their suffering, they then need to let go of the anger or hurt inside. Peace and bliss come from within and not outside of oneself," Luke remarked.

"I'm sure most people are so worried about what other people would think if they appeared anyway different to the so-called established behavioural norm. I love getting to know more interesting and eccentric people. They make the world so much more radiant and colourful. Life seems to burst from their seams," she declared convincingly.

"I try and aim to be different, and walk a fine line between madness and genius," he said.

"Is that how you see yourself then, as a possible genius?" she asked cocking her head to one side.

"Well, I do feel that I might be a genius of the spiritual kind, without trying to sound self-righteous. I am continually trying to transform my negative emotions into one of calmness and stillness. I'm sure it will take a very long time though to reach my goal of supreme enlightenment."

"Well good luck to you, if you think that's possible, but to my mind it feels like an impossible task," she uttered.

"As a wise man once said, and I think it might have been the Buddha who said it, although I'm not sure, but a walk of a thousand miles starts with a single step," said Luke satisfactorily.

"I like that, pithy and profound!"

He found himself getting sexually charged, through their honest and intimate exchange, which was analysing the differences between the sexes, and how it did not have to be that way. They stopped to have tea at the first main pub they came to, on the fringes of the town. The weather still was uncharacteristically warm and sunny for that part of England, and this just amplified

Luke's strong, passionate emotions towards her. She was not slender, but she had an endearing chubbiness with an attractive full and revealing cleavage. Her face, eyes, bosom and personality were unequivocally the most enticing qualities that enraptured Luke, like a bee drawn to a sequestered beehive.

Being down to stay at the festival and retreat until the Wednesday, he decided on the Monday that he would make his way home - rather than wait another couple of days. The weather had become overcast, on this last day of his. He had exchanged numbers with Sarah, yet she was scheduled to stay on until the end of the retreat, and so she said her goodbyes to Luke before breakfast. She was happy to see him wearing his purple trousers on this last day, as he had mentioned his fondness of them, in passing. Having breakfasted with Nastasia and a few others; the Russian woman generously and very kindly bought him a book, written by her founder and teacher, to take home with him. She was a woman with a lot of energy and drive, complemented with a sense of fun. She urged Luke to stay in contact with her, and if ever he was near Chester that he should pop in to see her.

After he had said his farewells to nearly all those he had encountered on the retreat, he set off back for home, leaving a little before lunch, but getting a bite to eat in a supermarket café in the town of Ulverston.

The following morning Luke sent a text message to Sarah, which said,

Hi Sarah, It was really good to meet you at the festival. You are so easy and interesting to talk to. I can see why you have so many guy friends. You have an inner and outer beauty. Speak soon and enjoy the rest of the now retreat. Luke x

She responded later that evening with,

Ah such a lovely thing to say wow! Ditto, lovely chatting to you and getting to know you. Hope you got back safely. Much love x

Her text message was the last time he heard anything from Sarah, even though he tried phoning her on a number of occasions, where she did not respond. Luke initially thought this was peculiar, as she did not have a boyfriend, and he thought that she had been interested in him. Later in the year, her silence would feed into his burgeoning imagination, and act as evidence that things were not what it seemed in his world.

Chapter 21

By the end of June Luke had found a new architectural post in a company that predominantly designed high quality hotels, amongst other notable building types. The location of the office was in an easy commutable distance - nestled in the countryside. The offices were in a converted barn, and it was of a high architectural specification. The interior of the office was clean and simple with whitewashed walls and white office tables with sophisticated and comfortable office chairs.As soon as he started on his first day, he was given the assignment of bringing together a working drawings package, or in layman's terms - a detailed construction set of drawings, for the refurbishment to a high quality hotel company. Luke was tasked to single-handedly bring it together, and to have the bulk of the drawings and a building specification completed by the end of July, to show at a design team progress meeting.

There were about thirteen members of staff, who worked at the company. There was quite a relaxed atmosphere, although lately the work pressure had mounted greater than at any other time in the firm's history. Occasionally, tempers would fray, as the pressure escalated for most of the staff.

Not all pulled their weight, and behind where Luke sat there was an athletic brown haired, Caucasian man of the name Joe, who always left at 5:30pm, on the dot, while in the morning he would often turn up at about 9:15am – so a good quarter of an hour after work was officially meant to start. His attitude was very relaxed and *laissez-faire* even though he had recently joined, and was still working out a probationary period. What Luke found bizarre was that he had a family to feed, and a mortgage to pay, yet his attitude, not only to timeliness, but also his application to the work, was questionable. Did he not worry that everyone could see he was not putting in the hours for specific deadlines?

The managing director, named George, was getting very twitchy with the possibility that Luke would not complete the body of work by the prescribed date. One sunny morning he came upstairs to where Luke and some of the others were sat at their desks, and beckoned Luke with a jerk of the head, to follow him downstairs and outside the building.

"Luke, I'm getting really concerned that you aren't going to have the majority of the work finished for that design team meeting."

"George, I'm working as fast as I possibly can on this project. Firstly, I'm working late into the evenings, and I've also come into the office on the past two weekends. I know you are getting restless, but I do believe that it will come together by the end of July, when the meeting's scheduled for."

"As I have explained to you before, there is so much riding on this! The drawings have to be correct and in perfect shape, as the work will be tendered to a very problematic contracting firm. If the drawings are not flawless, then the contractor will have ammunition against us. I don't want that happening at all," said George sternly.

"I will try my hardest to get it right, but I can only do my best at the end of the day," said Luke trying to keep a fabricated upbeat persona, but feeling genuinely a little weary inside from this brief and unappreciative attack.

"As long as there are no mistakes, I'll be happy," said George emphatically. Luke thought to himself that a drawing without any mistakes at all was impossible, and that is why a contract will always have a contingency sum, to soak up any oversights and discrepancies, which later get spotted by the eagle-eye contractor.

Fortunately, in the last week of the looming deadline, Luke pushed himself that little bit further, to prove to the boss that he could manage the work in the tight timeframe. For the first three nights in the last week, before the submission, he worked until about 9:30 to 10pm. On the Thursday he stayed in the office until midnight before going home. The following day was crunch time, and after having had little sleep, and starting to live off the power of adrenaline, he was back at his desk by 7am, and working methodically but manically.

That day, by lunchtime, he had successfully finished the remainder of the drawings and the building specification. He had begun to develop a headache from all his mental exertion over the past few days. Seeing that he had finished, and he had put in a considerable amount of overtime; he went to George, and asked if he could take the afternoon off. George was reluctant to give him time off in lieu, but acquiesced on this particular occasion. He insisted that he would not allow time-off again in this manner, unless it was part of Luke's holiday entitlement. As Luke was driving home that early afternoon, he pondered on what a hard task master George was. Luke felt, in work, there needed to be a little give and take, and giving him the afternoon off was the least George could do in return for his many hours of hard mental labour and exertion.

The following Tuesday at the end of July, George took Luke in his modest car up to Yorkshire, where the hotel company were based. Although George was speeding on the motorway to their destination, Luke was not fazed by his frantic driving. On the odd occasion he would worry about the pressure George was putting other drivers under by his intermittent tailgating, but more often than not, Luke just acquiesced to this particular driving experience.

At the meeting in the main boardroom of the hotel's offices situated on the first floor; Luke felt emboldened in his discussion with the client, project manager and his boss. Although he was not in charge, the ability to create the majority of the drawings in such a restricted timescale made him feel an indispensable and vital member of the team. Brian, who was the project manager, had an especially commanding and domineering presence, to the point of steering the meeting to his own personal agenda, even though Luke had prepared one that they as a group should probably have followed. Inwardly, Luke thought that these business and boardroom meetings could sometimes be a clash of egos with little opportunity of resounding harmony. However, he tried his best to be a catalyst for concord rather than discord. After a long, extended meeting, he felt elated that a good outcome had been achieved, and the client and project manager held him in higher regard for the quantity and precision of the drawings, which Luke had so arduously produced. Luke also listened attentively, and took on board their feedback.

✱✱✱✱✱✱

He was coming up to the end of his probationary period in the office, after almost three months of being an employee at Winton architects. It was Thursday 18ᵗʰ September, and Luke had given his medication himself that day, as the nurse was on holiday that week. The Crick surgery had established a long standing agreement that Luke was responsible enough to administer the drug himself, in times when it was not possible for the surgery to carry out the procedure. He had kept it safely stored in his kitchen cupboard, and on that day he self-medicated.

That evening his parents were coming round to see him for a meal out. They had decided upon a restaurant on the Parade in Leamington. Luke's mother relayed to him over the phone that on the Wednesday, when she had booked the table, the woman on the other end of the line apparently knew exactly who Luke was.

"Yes, I know Trevelyan", as if to say the name was familiar to her, almost to the point of being a famous icon. This made Luke think back to his earlier views on him being a Big Brother reality figure. How could the woman possibly know who he was, if he very rarely frequented the restaurant? The woman answering calls would surely be inundated with calls for bookings from so many different people. What was it about his name that was so recognisable? He initially held the view lightly of a Big Brother conspiracy, but the implications would steadily mount in his mind - especially during his work that Thursday. It had been quite some time since he had been out to a restaurant. As the thoughts grew during the day, he pondered on his hypotheses earlier in the year that the secret services were still attempting to eliminate him. This particular evening would be another opportunity for the chefs to slip some poison into his food - at the behest of MI5. This pernicious thought started to disturb Luke. He was not sure he could completely believe that he would be protected by unseen forces, which would exercise their magical powers, and transform the poison into a harmless and benign substance.

At work there was a certain individual, named Robert, who displayed a high percentage of frivolity and tomfoolery, during work. He was an ardent Christian, and he took his religion very seriously, yet would act inanely in the office - yet today even more so. Luke was suspicious of him. Like most Christians, he was convinced that Robert believed in a distorted and unhelpful idea of what Satan or the devil would manifest as, and not one that accorded with reality or reason.

That evening his parents arrived around 7pm, and he provided them with nuts, crisps and drinks. They sat outside in Luke's small garden patio area, talked about work, and how he was getting on. Luke expressed his frustration with one of the projects, and how he was set with an impossible task to get the drawings perfect without any loopholes or errors. He mentioned how the company would be working with a very contractual building firm. The building contractors were also unreliable in finishing projects to time, which provided Luke with more anxieties. His father, Jeremy, enquired,

"Did you take your medication today?"

"Yes Dad, I did." Luke preferred not to be too honest with his father on this occasion, and omitted to mention that his heartbeat was slightly accelerating, and this seemed to be a little unusual. How could his heartbeat be starting to gradually increase, when he had administered the correct drug himself - only that morning? He tried to push this slightly worrying idea from his mind. As the minutes ticked by, and they were soon to go to eat out - Luke was experiencing heaviness in his mood, as he briefly and morbidly turned over the thought that he might not see the light of the following day.

The restaurant and wine bar was in a basement, and was well known in that area, for producing quality food and also serving top quality wines. The main section of the basement was internally lined with exposed coloured brickwork, and because of the lighting it had a soft, mellow ambience.

Luke and his parents arrived at the back entrance. They were greeted by a young blond English woman, with quite a stern expression that along with her physique and slightly defensive body language, belied a much softer and more caring type of woman. Immediately, she opened with the words,

"Table for Trevelyan?

"Yes that's correct," said Luke's mother with a polite smile.

Once they had all sat down, the waitress told them of the specials that evening. The main special she brought their attention to was a ricotta and spinach tart, accompanied with mixed vegetables. Normally, Luke's parents would suggest that he have fish, when they dined out. Luke was a vegetarian, and his parents were of the opinion that Luke did not get the necessary health benefits, from being a vegetarian. He tried to reason with them, but often it was futile as they were so entrenched in their views, and they always seemed to have an answer for everything. Over the years, they became less persuasive in trying to change his positive habit, but they also saw that Luke accepted his mother's cooking, even though it contained meat or fish. He behaved in a flexible way to people whose cooking he shared with, trying not to impose his vegetarian habits too rigidly. This less obstinate approach by Luke - his mother warmed to - and she generally felt that although she could not win in trying to change his vegetarianism, he would always partake in the eating of meat or fish that she served at their home.

On this occasion, his mother said to Luke,

"That tart sounds good. You could have that for your main course, Luke."Often, Luke would quip about words of innuendo, and suggest to his parents, if they actually meant the girl or the meal. This evening, however, he felt a weight bearing down on him, and he seemed to be devoid of humour. He replied to his mother with a serious expression,

"That does sound like a good choice."

While his parents were still deciding what food they would have, Luke mulled over the reasons why the restaurant should highlight a vegetarian dish as a special. Vegetarian meals were still not the norm, and unless the staff knew of his eating habits, they would not ordinarily draw a vegetarian dish to people's attention - especially as a special. It made Luke think that the staff could have produced a tart, laced with poison, specifically for his consumption, and therefore they made a point of drawing the Trevelyan's attention to it.

His father had ordered a bottle of red wine and a large bottle of sparkling water to go with their meals. The waiter, who had a line of tattoos along both arms and a black, bushy beard, brought the two bottles over. He had already unscrewed the top of the sparkling water before arriving at the table, and had skilfully placed them on the middle of their round table that they were sat at. His expression was serious, and Luke sensed the faintest degree of anxiety in him, while being in their presence. This triggered internal alarm bells in Luke. He thought whether his parents might be targets as well for the use of poison, in not only the food, but the water as well. The last thing, Luke felt, he should be doing is to express his anxious thoughts to his parents. Firstly, they would think that he had lost it again, and secondly they would not believe it to be credible, thinking instead that it was a preposterous accusation.

Why on earth would Luke be a target for being poisoned – they would think? He also thought that he would have to properly explain himself to them, and in no way did he feel inclined to do so, at this present moment.

Once the main course arrived, they all proceeded to eat. His father like always seemed to be lost in a food trance, while Luke's mother was more attentive to people and things around her, periodically looking up between delicately cutting through her lamb and vegetables. Luke felt like he had a lump of coal in his heart. Feeling like he was being a martyr, and if he were to die he could say to himself that he had had a good life. He totally had belief in the concept of rebirth, and so silently consoled himself with the notion that he would be reborn again, if he were to die that night. A quieter, internal voice whispered to him saying everything would be alright.

He harked back to a couple of memories of magical experiences in the past that he had witnessed: the first being in Yosemite National Park in the States back in 1998, where black bears would roam the area of the park, and the second being a driving incident in his car, which happened a year ago.

The first incidence happened, when he was on a trekking tour with a large group of people - about 26 in total, and they were camping in Yosemite National Park. Luke had not paid attention to the warning from the group leader that they should put all sweet smelling products into the van they were travelling in. This was to stop any possibility of the black bears getting at the scented products, by ripping open the tents with their claws, and either seriously injuring the people inside, or even killing them. That night, after Luke had brushed his teeth, and placed his toothbrush and toothpaste back into the sponge bag with a bar of soap inside as well; he absent-mindedly placed the bag and its contents directly next to his head in the tent. He was sharing the tent with a very tall man from Holland.

That night Luke was out for the count, and he literally slept like a log. In the morning he awoke to find out that there had been utter mayhem in the camp that night. The Dutch man had told him that the bear had come by their tent, prowling by on frequent occasions. The female group leader, who was sleeping on top of the van, was awoken by the noise of violent and sudden movements to the van, by the turbulent rage of the bear. Luke was a little mystified at the time, why it was the one and only time in the tent, where he slept right through, from when he touched the pillow to when he awoke in the morning – even though the night was filled with loud and violent commotion. Years later he had realised and believed that the gods had been acting as guardians for Luke, and this now hinted to him, once again, that his continued survival on this planet and the universe was paramount.

The other story that transpired more recently, and which he brought to mind for comfort and strength, was when he visited his sister in Oxfordshire on a Sunday. On his return he was driving recklessly, testing the mettle of his small fast car, while listening to guttural rock music. He seemed to be evincing a feeling of invincibility. As he came to the Leamington junction, off the motorway, he approached the T – junction, and gave a cursory glance to his left then glanced to his right – and discerned no visible oncoming traffic in sight. He then propelled the car forward. The vehicle suddenly juddered to a complete stop – straddling the road, he was trying to cross over and the middle of the chevron marked central section. Almost that same instance he had violently come to a halt, a very fast car sped by in the lane he was trying to turn into. At the time it was a sobering and humbling experience - and jolted his subsequent behaviour behind the wheel into a much safer and slower driving speed. Later it dawned on him, how his engine had seemed to collapse exactly at the right time, when it was desperately needed. This was one further example to suggest his life was being monitored by cosmic forces, and they were looking after his overall welfare wherever he went.

Once the Trevelyans finished their main course, and they decided against a pudding, as they had commenced with a starter – Luke could feel himself noticeably relaxing, with these two personal stories softening his demeanour.

His parents came back to his flat, and they all had coffee together, outside on the garden patio area. After a pleasant chat about the royal family, Luke felt a little more at ease in his current state. He said goodbye to his parents at just after 10pm, and both of them commented on leaving his flat, as they normally would, how lovely and inviting his place was. That evening Luke wondered if the poison would take hold at any point during his sleep. He found it very difficult to get any beneficial shut-eye, thinking about the incidents that evening and the overall ramifications.

He also ruminated on the belief that had re-emerged only on the Thursday, after about a five month hiatus, that he was on display to millions if not billions of TV screens around the world, and everything that was spoken about was digitally captured and transmitted. During their discussion on that uncharacteristically balmy Thursday evening, he felt really aware of the public's scrutiny, and at times it made him feel silly and awkward.

The following morning on the Friday after arriving into work, and having settled down at his desk, he began to vigorously attend to his work responsibilities. Robert was hidden from view by the two monitors at his desk, while Luke tapped away at his keyboard, and using the mouse to operate the CAD functions. Once everyone had appeared in the office, Luke was aware of Robert passing by his side. Luke's attention was suddenly seized by the sheer moodiness of his expression, and he was looking straight at Luke. This brooding look stood out even more, since he was so used to seeing him play the office clown. Why was he so serious? Why was he now glowering in Luke's direction? What had occurred to him that previous evening for this complete turnaround in mood? Luke wondered whether this could be another sign that Luke was on show. Could it be that Robert was noticeably disappointed that the poison had no effect on Luke, from his meal at the restaurant the previous evening? Luke was sure that Robert considered him to be the devil incarnate. Luke mused that most people were not aware of the real truth around them. The fact that humans, the animal kingdom, birds, insects, fish, the whole natural environment and all other beings in the universe, possessed a consciousness that was mysteriously linked to each other, and each one had a potential for Buddhahood - lying dormant within.

There was an architect, named Greg, in the office, who had been exhibiting poor performance. He had been given a disciplinary on a number of occasions. Once the end of the working day on the Friday had come about; Luke slung his dark navy blue jacket over his shoulder, and made his way to the back exit of the offices, to drive away in his car. Just as he was opening the back glass door, he spotted three of the most senior staff huddled together and whispering to themselves. Luke immediately thought they were talking about Greg, but on registering Luke with heads swivelling towards him, they immediately, but as naturally as possible, disbanded and said their farewells to each other. He was positive that they were talking about him and not Greg. Luke internally commented on this being another suspicious incident, and whether this was further proof, for his now not so seemingly outlandish idea, of constant surveillance into every aspect of his life. The idea began to take on ever more credulity in his mind, and over time through visual evidence, it seemed to ossify and harden into a distinct and palpable reality.

Luke got very little sleep over the weekend, and seriously wondered whether the medication he gave himself was faulty. One notion that crossed his mind, and over the coming days was fast becoming a more and more distinct possibility - was the thought that the gods had miraculously transformed the liquid medication to water, so as to wake him up from his mental dream-like slumber. This would then give him the insight in realising that he needed to make a stand in leading a more creative and fulfilling life - centred primarily on his spiritual development.

On the following Monday he mulled over that the work he was undertaking was not reaping the emotional and imaginative rewards that he had hoped for. He observed how when he was tackling the tasks at hand, he could not help but fixate on the minutiae and specific details of the work without seeing the bigger picture. This was unusual for him. This was normally a sign that there was something not right with the medication. He had however injected himself, and he had witnessed that it was the drug 'Depixol'. This then fed back into his belief of the gods' intervention.

Just before lunch on the Monday, George came to him, and asked deceptively calmly, "How's it going with the drawings?"

"Well I'm nearly there with them, but I still need to make a few alterations and tweaks," said Luke feeling the inability to keep it emotionally together. He responded to Luke saying,

"I'm getting very twitchy with your attitude! We need to finish the drawings straight away, and not dither at all!" He said this with a contained vehemence with the worry writ large on his face. His legs were in a slightly open stance and his arms were crossed defiantly. He said he was going out and he would be back soon, hinting that by the time he returned, Luke would be able to say to him that he will have finished the drawings.

This action and speech of the boss really rattled Luke, like he was some unruly teenager having just been taken off by the scruff of the neck. He realised now he needed to get out of this office, but he would do it as surreptitiously as possible. Luke also felt that like a dutiful employee he would finish the drawings, and hand them into the secretary before departing. He made a plan to leave at lunchtime at about 1pm.

What had worried Luke earlier in the day was he had been told that the firm would be interviewing an experienced senior Architect, who had been working in China, and wanted to settle back in Warwickshire. Luke thought this peculiar, and he believed he smelt a rat. Could this prospective employee be a MI6 agent being reassigned to George's office, in the security services' ongoing quest?

Just after one o'clock in the afternoon Luke calmly shut down his machine, slipped on his jacket, and made his way downstairs to the secretary. He passed her the drawings, and told her to send them to the client with a compliment slip enclosed. He had done his duty as best as he could muster. On walking to his car, Robert was in his car with the associate director, named Patrick, in the passenger seat, and they waited for Luke to pass. Instead of Luke letting them through, he extended a hand towards Robert in a gesture of gratitude, and crossed his car's path. He thought that Robert would love to run him over, and see personally to Luke's death, but unbeknown to Robert, this would be the one and only chance he would get, as this would be Luke's last day at George's office. Luke imagined that Robert would be kicking himself afterwards for this error of judgement, but ultimately Luke believed that Robert would never have the bottle to carry out such a heinous and evil act.

As Luke got into his car, and pressed the ignition button, he was greeted on the radio with the start of The Montagues and Capulets, of Romeo & Juliet by Serge Prokofiev. This was truly uplifting and resounding music, befitting of his current situation – one of drama and intrigue. Something was going on, which revolved around his life being extra significant to both this world and other-worldly beings.

He got home, and after eating some sandwiches; he wrote a short but precise resignation e-mail to the firm. Within about a quarter of an hour of it being sent, he received two calls: one from Patrick, and one from George. His phone was on silent, so they both had left messages for him to call back. On seeing the missed calls on his mobile, he decided to ring Patrick, and try and explain himself. He also decided to be honest about having a mental condition. He did think after the conversation that Patrick was the wrong person to speak to about his condition, and he probably should have divulged this piece of information to George instead, although he was sure in reality that it would spread like wildfire around the office anyway.

Once Luke had spoken to Patrick, he decided to see if he could get any sleep, which at this point was utterly necessary. He got into his bed, and closed his eyes. Suddenly during his attempted snooze, he received a knock on the door. Who could this possibly be he wondered? Opening his bedroom curtains, he saw it was George - standing patiently outside his flat. Luke hurriedly put on his clothes, not quite buttoning up his jeans, in order to make sure he answered the door in time. Luke opened his front door, and observed George already making his way back to his car.

"George!" said Luke with a loud audible tone. George did an about-turn and walked purposefully back to his flat.

"Hi Luke. Thank you for being able to see me. How are you doing?" said George warmly and what seemed to be with genuine sympathy. His mood was such a turnaround from the morning's encounter that Luke regarded it with a degree of wariness and caution.

"Hi George, I'm alright thanks," said Luke amenably.

"Can I come in, and have a small chat about life and work?" asked George. Luke allowed him to go first into the flat. He offered George the red leather armchair to sit on, and George wryly observed,

"You're making me sit in the hot seat then?" Luke uttered a slightly unnatural and hollow laugh in response.

"Patrick tells me you have a bi-polar condition," said George. Luke was more inclined to tell them that he had bi-polar, rather than schizophrenia, as his condition was still being evaluated, and it was a more palatable mental condition.

"That's right. I thought it didn't need to be mentioned, as I've been well and healthy on a continuous course of medication for over seventeen years." He decided to omit telling him about the incident with his last office that happened earlier that year. Luke continued,

"I get an injection every fortnight, and as long as I've received the medication, I'm well. Last Thursday, I administered it myself, and for some reason the drug had no effect on me whatsoever. I can't explain why - I suppose it was a dodgy ampoule." Luke was very reluctant to explain his idea that the gods were involved. This would just cause unnecessary confusion in George's mind, and Luke would probably have to try and justify himself, which in no way did he want to do. Luke carried on,

"The symptoms I show when I haven't had the medication is primarily a heart that speeds up in rhythm and pace." Luke knew that he was again being a little sparing with the truth. He did not want to mention that his internal body temperature also escalates slightly - this probably being a natural side effect of his increased heart rate, but a fact that might raise additional concern with George and his company.

Fundamentally, he did not want to share his most secret and innermost beliefs and views with George.

"Generally, I think you get on well with people in the office. You're a happy and smiley face, and you do a lot of extra work, plus you always come in on time, and leave later than the allotted hours. Why don't you take the rest of the week off, and then give me a ring on Monday to let me know how you are, and whether you'd want to return?" responded George agreeably.

"Thank you. That sounds like a good plan," said Luke. George saw himself out with Luke trailing, and Luke confirmed that he would ring on the following Monday with whatever news he had decided upon.

Chapter 22

That Tuesday he was scheduled to meet his psychiatrist. He went by himself to the hospital, and once he had parked the car, and registered at reception; he waited patiently for the appointment with Doctor Goodyear. There was a middle-aged woman struggling to operate the new-fangled coffee and tea machine. Luke offered to help, as he had seen it done once before. Wondering what this patient was in for, he felt a little embarrassed that he might still be being judged by the secretaries as unwell and insane, like this woman who he was trying to help. The woman by the machine struck Luke as being remarkably normal, and he asked her a little tactlessly, or what he presumed was thoughtless just after he enunciated the words, what she was in here for,

"I'm trying to join the army, and they want me to have a test with a psychiatrist, seeing as I had a mental breakdown about thirteen years ago. This certification of being healthy is the last thing the army are after - for my acceptance. I've passed everything else that they've given me," she confided. Luke thought why would she want to go into the army with a mental condition, albeit one that occurred in the distant past? He hoped that she would be well and happy, if she was given a clean bill of mental health by the hospital's doctor. He hoped she would not suffer prejudice or bias against her, especially in an environment as unforgiving as that of the army.

After a brief chat Doctor Goodyear came striding through into the waiting area,

"Hi Mister Trevelyan. Would you like to come through, please," said the doctor, who was smiling warmly.

"Hi Doctor Goodyear," replied Luke, as he proceeded to his office. The doctor had a full head of black hair, unlike Luke whose fringe was steadily receding with the slow march of time. This little physical fact did not disturb Luke, as he was more concerned with his imagination and sharpening and educating his mind, than the more superficial ageing bodily characteristics that we all have to endure at some point in our lives. As Franz Kafka once said, *"Anyone who keeps the ability to see beauty never grows old."* Luke resonated with this statement, and kept it locked away in his memory bank. He liked trying to memorize pithy and wise sayings or quotes, either from the Buddha, or from distinguished Western philosophers, writers or scholars.

Luke asked the doctor if he could help himself to the water from the jug that was parked on the side of his desk. His mouth was starting to get parched. He was not nervous, but the glass of water gave him not only liquid refreshment but also a sense of pleasant succour.

"Hi Luke, what's been happening over the last five months, since I last saw you?"

"Well, I'd managed to get a job, with an architectural company, which was at the end of June. In the two or three months that I had been working there, I'd completed a detailed drawing package for an important meeting, within a very tight timescale. There was real pressure from the boss on getting me to complete on time, so I managed to put in extra hours and worked occasional weekends as well. In the last week before the submission, I was in the office most nights until about 9:30pm. The night before the submission, I was working to midnight. Then on the final morning, I was back at my desk by 7am, and achieved a completion and resolution by lunchtime. Unfortunately, last week my medication did not do the trick it was supposed to, and in the last four or five days I've been labouring under very little sleep. I've also quit my job yesterday," said Luke matter-of-factly.

"That sounds a little drastic. How do you feel about having

given up your job? The doctor enquired with sensitivity.

"A relief actually! I'm starting to think that I might write a book about the events over this last year, as a way of keeping me occupied, and giving me something to do, but also because I feel inspired to do so," Luke said lightening up emotionally to the conversation.

"What you're telling me about your major deadline, and how you successfully completed it; suggests to me that you definitely don't have schizophrenia. It is almost unheard of for a schizophrenic to hold down a job, let alone be able to finish a difficult project, after they have had a few episodes. Their mental faculties deteriorate with every episode that they experience. In your case you seemed to have thrived under the pressure, and you were able to perform your work duties unencumbered by your condition. Just as you're talking to me now, I would say your cognitive faculties are still very good. I would therefore categorically state that you have bi-polar affective disorder, which is the mental condition I mentioned last time to you. From what you are telling me it fits in with the evidence. With bi-polar affective disorder, you can experience the manic episodes without any accompanying bouts of depression. That is totally possible," illuminated the doctor.

"Why do you think I was diagnosed a schizophrenic, when I had my first episode all those years ago? Luke said eager for a cogent reasoning and explanation.

"A lot of schizophrenics have breakdowns in their late teen years or early twenties, as opposed to those who have bi-polar, who suffer later in their lives. I am sure that will be the reason why you were labelled as schizophrenic, because your first breakdown happened when you were nineteen. As I said before there are overlaps between the two conditions, especially to do with the element of psychosis," The doctor said authoritatively. He proceeded to ask Luke,

"Why do you think some of your symptoms have been resurrecting themselves in the last few days?" Luke paused for a moment, before he began to answer. He was deliberating in his mind, whether he should be candid with the doctor, and divulge his views on the gods having a direct influence with their use of magical powers, and the view of his own personal situation. He then chose to speak truthfully to him and responded,

"I'll be very honest with you now. I believe I'm destined for great things, and I believe I will become Maitreya, or the future Buddha. What I think that means is that I'll become a Buddha in many lifetimes to come, but in this lifetime that will be my Buddhist name. Just to put you in the picture: Buddhism speaks of beings re-becoming or being reborn, and so journeying from body to body over innumerable aeons. My personal belief is that evil is increasing in the world, and the time is now right for a visionary figure to emerge in the world. Although I see myself as growing into the figure Maitreya - it is not the classical portrayal of Buddhist mythology - but a new vision of what that figure represents. I definitely do not hold the view that Maitreya will be a Buddha in this lifetime. The title 'Buddha', which means 'one who is awake or one who knows', suggests an individual, who brings love, awareness and wisdom into a world where it has been completely lost. There are too many people in this world searching for spiritual truth and genuine meaning in their lives for Buddhism to disappear, and if anything that urge for spirituality seems to be gaining ground, rather than diminishing in scope.

Maitreya means friendly, loving and compassionate one. I think that suits my qualities and aspirations perfectly. In the Buddhist movement I'm affiliated to, when we join the order we get given a Sanskrit name, which reflects our main overriding quality. I strongly feel that my strongest quality is my friendly, loving and above all compassionate nature, which still can be taken to ever greater heights, but which surpasses any other quality of mine. I also hold the view that this is the reason why the gods have been seeing to my ongoing protection and safety, whatever I've done, and will do throughout my life.

In Buddhism, we believe in gods, who are more spiritually developed beings than us, and who have cultivated positive qualities in very favourable conditions on other planets - like probably how our earth was a million or so years ago. Their higher power comes in the form of magic or miracles, which can be performed over vast immeasurable distances - as opposed to ours, which would be that of technology, which is of limited value, and is positively primitive in contrast.

I thought I should explain a bit of the background, before telling you my view on why the drug had no effect. As I might have mentioned to you before, I'd been keeping the ampoule safely stored in my kitchen cupboard before administering it myself. I think that the gods had magically transformed the medication into water. I strongly believe that they deliberately did this, so as to wake me up to the reality around me, and help me see that it was in my best interests to extricate myself from that office environment. Yet again they were looking after my continued welfare and security." Doctor Goodyear was taking copious notes, and Luke was helping him, by pausing between sentences when he felt he had rushed too far ahead with his line of reasoning.

"So you think you're going to become this Maitreya figure?" said the doctor in a dead-pan way.

"Yes, I do. Partly, what has shaped this view is that I share quite a few similarities with the historical Buddha. Like him, I'm a very determined individual, and face life overcoming obstacles with immense courage. Also in common with him, I'm gifted with quite an abundance of talents. I'm not only good at Architecture and the Arts, namely painting, music, and writing but I'm also interested and capable in the sciences, especially Maths. Both appeal to me. I'm not only creative but also practical at the same time. From another angle, I'm also an able sportsman, with a good eye for the ball. Another fact about me is that I came to Buddhism when I was eighteen, which here in the West is extremely rare to get involved with something as radical as that - so early on in one's life. I could list other notable areas of my life, which would be revealing," Luke openly shared with him.

Luke was keen to put up as much of a justification and defence of his idea of potential greatness, without trying to sound big-headed or egotistical. He thought that so many people in the Vandana movement and other people would be astounded by these grandiose claims. However, the more he churned ideas about his life and the universe in his mind, the more the notion of him becoming Maitreya seemed to crystallise in a scintillating jewel-like reality. He felt he was somehow the epitome of cultural advancement. Although, as yet, he had nothing much to show for it, but he was sure that with time his name would become familiar around the globe through being a particularly creative individual, which would manifest above all in spontaneous creative actions.

"I think in the first instance we need to prescribe you some sleeping tablets, to help you get some proper sleep. You should also get your injection this Thursday, rather than wait until the following Thursday. I also suggest we raise the quantity you receive to 60 mgs," said the doctor.

"I really wouldn't be happy for my medication to go up to 60 mgs. As I said to you before, I don't think this incident will happen again, and apart from this one event, I've always been very stable and well, being on 40mgs," Luke said this with passionate defiance. He had gone to see his parents before the meeting with the doctor, and his mother had tried to persuade Luke that he should agree to an increase in dosage of 60mgs. Luke had notionally agreed with his mother, but after speaking to her, he felt very strongly, while driving to the hospital, that he was starting to be drugged up to his eyeballs. He did not wish to be cajoled or bullied by his mother, or anyone else for that matter, and made a resolve to keep to the 40mgs, as he honestly felt it was the optimum measure of medication for him. He would stick steadfastly to this resolution.

"Okay. Shall we see how the next few months fare, and take a decision then?" the doctor said with heart and compassion.

"That would be great Doctor Goodyear! I really believe passionately that I can be well with my dosage. If, of course, I haven't improved or remained stable, then I would wholeheartedly agree with you that it should be upped, but let us see first how I fare in the next few months," Luke said in a conciliatory manner.

"You will say something, if you don't feel right?" the doctor asked.

"Definitely, and if I don't then I'm sure my father will get in contact with you - on my behalf." This made the doctor chuckle to himself, and he averted his gaze from Luke, and nodded in agreement. The doctor saw Luke to the waiting area, and bid him farewell. As Luke exited the building, he met the army woman, who was smoking a cigarette, and asked her hopefully,

"How did it go with your interview?"

"The doctor said I was perfectly well, and my mental faculties and resilience are totally intact and good," she said with barely suppressed elation in her voice.

"I'm glad for you," replied Luke.

"Thanks. Good to meet you and good luck,"

"Good to meet you as well, and also good luck in your onward journey," Luke said, as they parted company. He hoped she would enjoy her time in the army, but he thought the idea of him going into the army could not be a job further from his interests and leanings. There would never be a place for him in such an institution, as it went against his fundamental belief in the principle of non-violence.

Chapter 23

The following week on Monday 29th September Luke duly called his former office. Before he lifted the phone from its charger, he could feel his heart pounding, and his pulse quickening to a rapid, quick-fire beat. This seemed like a big event that he was undertaking. There was another aspect that felt significant that day. Luke had decided he would explore another area of London, and he had kept it very much to himself where that would be, due to keeping the secret service in suspense. Ringing the office number, he waited for a few rings before the main secretary answered.

"Hello, Winton architects, Sarah speaking."

"Hi Sarah. It's Luke here. Could I speak to George please, if he's available," Luke uttered with a mixture of precarious poise and jangled nerves.

"Sure. He's been waiting for your call. I'll put you through," she seemed decidedly chirpy, almost in a spurious way – to Luke's sensitive ear. Before Luke had left the office, there were times in his last remaining days, when she would not be so guarded with her emotions, and he witnessed her body language and facial expression displaying a degree of hostility and anger towards him. He had become finely attuned to gauging people's moods and temperaments through his regular meditation practice.

"Hi Luke, how are you?" George enquired calmly.

"Hi George, I'm now a lot better, and I've caught up on my lack of sleep. I've been thinking very carefully about my decision on whether I will continue with working at your firm. I've therefore decided that I would like to pursue the writing of a book, and so I would need space around which to write. With this fact in mind, I would like to act on my resignation e-mail last Monday, and I would now want to discontinue my working relationship with you and your firm," said Luke with his heart stomping in time with every word he was uttering.

"Are you sure about this?"

"Yes – positive. I want to make a fresh start, and make this a new chapter in my life," replied Luke, seeing the irony of using the word 'chapter', in the context of the previous sentences.

"Very well, I'm not sure I can realistically change your mind, but I wish you all the best in your subsequent endeavours, and it would be good if you could stay in touch with us," said George.

"Sure, I will do," Luke had no real intention to ever get back to them in the future, but decided to agree with him, in order to keep a harmony of pretence. Over the past week or so, he had become suspicious of the office's underlying motives. He was not sure if they were helping the authorities in his removal. On a couple of occasions, he wondered whether some of the employees had tried to slip poison into his tea.

On one occasion, Patrick, who normally never made the teas, had decided to make them near the end of Luke's time at the office. Luke had asked for green tea, and was brought a hot drink, which looked decidedly murky brown in colour, not normally what Luke would associate with the colour of green tea. When he had taken a sip, he found that it was unmistakably green tea. He thought it peculiar. Even Patrick had remarked on the colour – perhaps to indicate his presumed innocence in the affair, and to hopefully not arouse suspicion in Luke. Although, there was suspicion - he went ahead and drank it all with the heartfelt belief that the poison would not harm him. It was strange, but Luke would oscillate in different situations between feeling confident and assured to being sceptical and doubtful about the gods' magical influence. These two contrasting qualities of emotion would continue to bounce back and forth in his somewhat fragile yet nonetheless courageous heart.

Another incident which made Luke think there was something going on was when he overheard Patrick talking to Robert, with hushed tones. Patrick remarked that what was happening around them was very strange and mysterious. Luke had managed to eavesdrop on Patrick saying these words, even though Patrick thought that no-one else was party to their discreet and low-volume words.

After he had finished his phone exchange, Luke got ready that morning to depart for London. He was particularly keen to hit one area of London, which in his past had significance to him. Again he was dressed with his purple trousers, the light blue waistcoat, light brown shoes with light under-sole. This time, he decided to wear his black long-sleeved T-shirt, and not the customary white shirt. The reason he did this was he wanted to present a dark base, and not always the light base to his flamboyant attire, and because it was a warm day, being in the low twenties in Celsius. If people were watching him on their TV screens, then another slightly modified image was important, and which subtly conveyed a darker aspect to his personality.

Luke had decided not to tell anyone where he was going that day, so as to keep it a surprise, and make the secret service try and guess where he would go. Luke imagined they had a pretty good idea of where he might be headed, but he was reluctant to present it to them like some kind of *fait-accompli*. He imagined they would bring snipers to that area of London immediately when they knew where he had landed. Stationed very discreetly on the tops of buildings they would patiently wait, being in radio contact with each other and their direct-in-command, until they sighted his whereabouts, and then they would lock on for the kill.

After a pleasant journey on the train, where he viewed the huge expanse of land that was only a tiny fraction of the vastness of Mother Earth, as well as the trees and buildings, which covered that overall area - he realised the enormous and unfathomably deep nature of supreme enlightenment, or Buddhahood - and what he was trying to aspire to. The goal was still so far out of reach, and required perhaps an aeon of time to be traversed before coming to its ultimate resolution and accomplishment – in that of supreme enlightenment.

After arriving at Marylebone station, he made his way to the tube, and connected with a series of different underground lines, before disembarking at the required station. He had now arrived at the place in London, which he had quite a long term connection with. Angel was that place. There was the overt meaning in the name, which would not be lost on people. As he ascended the long flight of escalators, he mulled over where he would venture to. The thought came to him that he would first check out if there was a good movie on that afternoon at the main cinema complex, just off the high street. Scouring the movie display board there was nothing that stood out for him. There were a lot of action movies, but nothing that spoke to him emotionally.

Luke slowly sauntered along the high street seeing a colourful assemblage of different shops, until he passed by a well-known coffee house. He decided to continue walking, until he momentarily reassessed his decision, and retraced his steps, to then step into the coffee store. Luke was aware that while he was waiting to get served; there were a couple of girls seated at a table behind him. While he stood in the queue, they were furtively whispering to each other and giggling frequently. He also noticed that the staff seemed to be slightly amused by something. Could it be his appearance in the store that was igniting their collective mirth? They were being as diligent as possible, but he thought they were a little put off by someone famous, or even infamous, having just walked through their doors. Since it had again dawned on him the realisation of there probably being a constant Big Brother surveillance into his life – a large proportion of those he came into contact with, either smirked, giggled, acted very inquisitively, occasionally ignored him, openly criticised and commented on him, or at odd times, gave him genuine and appreciative smiles.

Now on this specific morning, more than ever, it felt that the public really did know his life intimately – like some open book. He wondered for how long they had known about his actions, and how much time his friends and family friends had been keeping it secret from him. He was not dismayed by this seemingly unpalatable truth. He had in fact wished and prayed for public exposure into his private life, for so long now. The chance to suffer embarrassment and humiliation, and grow in confidence from the experience, was an overpowering volition in Luke. He had come across 'the secret', or the 'law of attraction', on film. The film's premise was that if you truly wish for something to possess and own, or for something to happen to you, then the likelihood of it transpiring is almost guaranteed - if your heart is wholeheartedly intent on it. Luke did think that a little luck was also necessary, and being in the right place at the right time were also key ingredients, but he was drawn to the film's basic assumption and premise.

As Luke perched on a bar stool with a small round high table to plant his Americano drink on, he sat facing the entrance door. He had total visibility of who entered and left the coffee shop. He was generally not conscious of the power behind his inquisitive gaze, which a friend of his had once remarked that it bordered on a passive-aggressive look. He must have come across as quite intimidating, sitting directly opposite the entrance door, and eyeballing anyone who came into the shop. The honest truth was that he was interested and curious with strangers - all of them complex inner worlds and universes. He would drink in their mannerisms, appearances and demeanours.

Suddenly, a person appeared who he had seen before. With not too much racking of his brain, he realised he had seen him at Marylebone station on his first momentous excursion after leaving Brian Levison's office. He was a relatively young man, probably in his mid-thirties, if he was to hazard a guess. Like last time when Luke noticed his presence, he was sporting a bushy dark brown beard, and he had a full head of hair. He reminded Luke a little of a Russian revolutionary figure. It was too much of a coincidence that he should see him on both occasions, in two separate parts of London. Luke was sure he was unequivocally part of the secret service underworld. He directed a look at Luke, but Luke sensed a slightly worried expression on his face, as if to suggest he knew secrets about Luke that were mysterious and inexplicable, and therefore did not fall under the banner of rational logic.

Luke felt emboldened by this brief non-verbal exchange, and he thought that however hard the authorities try; their attempts to rid him of his existence would always be foiled. He was not expecting this singular fellow to do anything other than keep tabs on him. He did not believe this person would try and poison him, or aim a silencer gun his way.

Once the bearded man had left the premises, Luke secretly imagined him making radio contact with snipers, nestled among the rooftops of buildings - to tell them they needed to be on their guard, and await Luke's arrival along the streets of Angel.

After feeling thoroughly relaxed and calm with his time spent viewing the wonderful assortment of individuals in the store, he made his way outside. The weather was uncharacteristically warm for that time of year, but a little overcast with brief spells of sunshine peeking through the clouds. It had been consistently good weather for the majority of the year, which they had not experienced for quite a long time - and definitely long over-due for Britain.

Luke glided along the high street, and decided to cross the road and make a route for the main establishment bookstore in the country. On crossing the entrance threshold of the store, he gave a cursory glance at all the multifarious books on display. One book that caught his eye was about a charming, hapless mother and all her heart-warming tales of success and failure in her love-life. He decided that on this occasion, he would not purchase it, but when he was back at home he would buy a copy. There was a lovely quality about the female character, being genuinely heartfelt and someone prone to mishaps, but always coming through scrapes -

stronger on the other side – not without a lovely self-deprecating humour. She was someone who was quintessentially English, in the most positive sense of that word – a loveable and endearing underdog. In some respects Luke could see a lot of similarities with her and his own life.

As he placed a copy of the book back down amongst others; he raised his head to see a young pretty, petite blond smiling affectionately at him. She appeared to be more interested in him than the books on show. He felt, if anything, a sense that she was a supporter of his life and actions. Even though he would seem to get hostile reactions to how he conducted his life from a lot of people he passed on the streets; there would always be a sizeable proportion of the population who agreed with him, and were perhaps even enthralled by the principles he lived his life by.

Luke ambled out of the store, and thought he would have a drink in a well-known bar and restaurant chain, located close at hand to the bookstore. The place was relatively empty, except for a few couples and a couple of small groups of be-suited businessmen and women. He ordered a sparkling mineral water from the blond Eastern European waitress. She too smiled warmly, and at a distance, every now and then, would look expectantly in his direction, interspersed with quietly talking to her other male and female colleagues. When Luke was settling up, he noticed on the back of the bill a note from her, which said, "Hope you have a great day," with a smiley face rounding off the message. When she came over to collect the money, Luke said to her,

"Thank you for the message. That was a lovely, sweet touch of yours. I really appreciated it."

"It's my pleasure, and I really mean what I said," she said, sealing the brief conversation with a flirtatious wink, and looking gratified that her expression of fondness had been acknowledged. Luke left the establishment with a warm glow and a jaunty spring in his step. Along with the girl in the book store, they had both really buoyed his mood that morning.

Luke was a little tired of going to restaurants, and thinking that the owners might slip some poison or some radioactive Polonium 210, which the Russians use as their weapon of choice, into his food. He therefore opted for a sandwich shop on the high street, where it would be nigh impossible for them to know what he would order, and therefore to have a deadly substance contained within. Instead of being predictable by ordering a vegetarian sandwich, he plucked for a tuna and mayonnaise baguette, to disarm the staff at the sandwich shop. The people working in the store were predominantly male, and there was an atmosphere laden with testosterone - clinging to the warm, stuffy air. They all wore stern looking faces from behind the counter, and a couple of them appeared shiftily. Luke wondered whether it was his presence in the store that caused them to be uptight and defensive. Although, they were very serious, he tried to be as courteous and amenable as possible, to try and defuse the thick tension, which seemed to be hanging ominously in the shop.

It had started spitting drops of rain, and Luke took shelter just outside the sandwich store under the cover of an awning, and sat himself down on a chair provided. He busily munched his way through the baguette, while taking the opportunity to survey the busy street life before him. Once he had finished, and the rain had died down a bit, he went for a meandering stroll – he knew not where. He let his instincts guide him around the area. He first had a drink of sparkling water in a pub with 'Angel' in its name.

It was relatively quiet, as it was a Monday. No-one around him was alerting his suspicions, and the few people in the bar seemed comparatively tame to him. The couple of female bar staff shot him surreptitious glances, and from time to time tittered amongst themselves. Luke was a little tickled by this presumed interest. Wherever he went he would be recognised, and he knew it.

Polishing off the last remaining mouthful of water he left the pub, and ventured along a busy shop-lined side street. Luke let the forces of fate or destiny, lead him onwards. As he was a little over half way down the street, he spied a lovely little shop, selling all sorts of homewares and trinkets. Luke went into the shop, and was immediately hit with a strong, positive, warm and embracing energy. He made his way into the heart of the building, when the shopkeeper emerged from a door next to the counter, and very warmly asked him,

"Can I help you sir?"

"No, I'm just browsing, thanks." After a momentary pause, Luke continued to speak, and said,

"I'm particularly noticing the positive energy emanating from this shop though," Luke was reluctant to express that he thought the same positive vibe was coming from the shopkeeper – being a little embarrassed that Luke might appear to be coming on too strong. The shopkeeper chuckled to himself, and with a really healthy glow in his face replied,

"Thank you. I try my best to make this as inviting a place as possible."

"All I can say is you're doing a good job. Keep it up!" Luke responded affectionately, raised his hand, and then left the shop.

He carried on walking up the side street, with the pavements overwhelmed with a bewildering selection of people. At the end of the street on his right there was another pub, with a name corresponding to the arch-villain in Batman. Luke thought it ironic that he was about to enter a pub, where his attire would suit that of the Joker, from the Batman films. Although he had come across the Joker, as the arch-enemy of Batman, he thought that the true origins of the Joker had been besmirched and tainted by the comic books, where he appeared in an evil and sinister guise. In his mind the notion of the Joker in medieval times was someone who was much closer to reality, and probably more upstanding than most people. He would wear a costume, and act as if he was the fool, but he was far from being the fool. He would often be the one to speak pithy words of wisdom and truth. He would have the close ear of the king, while also being very brave, by being the first one to test the king's food - for any sign of poison.

Ordering a coke he sat down by the window, and pondered the significance and meaning of the name of the pub, and how he had perchance stumbled upon it. He had never been here before, and he had no way of knowing what was on that street. Names and numbers would normally speak to him as symbols, archetypes and myths - pregnant with meaning. As he sipped his coke, he wondered what the large group of foreign thirty somethings were making of his presence, as they sat at a table in the centre of the pub. He meant no harm to anyone, but he presumed that a large percentage of the population viewed him as a dangerous and malign threat to their established beliefs and security. Luke felt a chill run down his spine with this disconcerting notion, which was entering the back door of his mind.

It was nearing 3pm, and Luke had had enough of his sojourn in Angel. He exited the pub, and followed the route he had come down. He popped into a local supermarket, for a bar of chocolate, and then parked himself in a sheltered spot by the side of the store, while slowly consuming his chocolate bar. After a good fifteen minutes of watching people walk by, he saw in front of him a woman older than her years with dark straggly hair struggling to push her trolley, filled with plastic shopping bags - laden with produce. Seeing as she was getting no help from passers-by, Luke stepped in and pushed the trolley for her. He realised why she was faltering, as the trolley seemed to be very stubborn in its motion, and the wheels had become stiff and rigid. As Luke mustered his strength to push the dogged wheeled cage to the main entrance, he looked up and saw a fifty-something gentleman with a tight beard, smiling appreciatively at him. Luke reciprocated, and wondered how many other people were observing his spontaneously generous response. The woman was very appreciative of his efforts, and repeated a couple of times that he was very kind to have helped her. Luke knew that he was in the right place at the right time, and it just seemed the natural thing to do.

After that he made tracks back to Leamington, and mused over the day's events during the return train journey.

Over the subsequent week with the aid of sleeping pills, prescribed by the doctor, and a depixol injection brought forward by a week - Luke settled down again into a stable state of mind, but one which, this time, he started to believe in a few aspects of the views he had formed after his first episode in the early part of that year.

Chapter 24

On Friday 10th October Luke went on a men's weekend retreat, with the members of his Birmingham movement, at a converted barn in the middle of the Herefordshire countryside. He was asked to turn up early to help with the food preparations that needed to be carried out. It was incumbent on him to help with the cooking that afternoon, as they were short of willing helpers, and he had earlier in the week volunteered to assist with the running of the weekend.

At the back of his mind, he worried about his life being in danger out in the country. There were no locks on the doors of the barn, and anyone could freely come and go, as they pleased. He inwardly wondered how the secret service would play it. Would they send someone in as a midnight stealth operation, to shoot him while he slept, or might they have an infiltrator in their midst, who would use brute strength to strangle Luke, while he slept? As he helped chop vegetables for his friend Ian, who was the cook; he waited expectantly, and with trepidation for the other retreatants to arrive. Supper was to be for 8pm, and most of them arrived around 7:30pm. Being by the entrance door, he and a couple of others greeted those who entered.

Two young individuals, who had arrived together, shook Luke's hand. They were both reluctant to give Luke eye-contact, and they both seemed to act shiftily. He could feel the rhythm of his heart increase, with a sudden pang of realisation that they were both the most likely candidates to be involved in his potential death that weekend. Luke could see that they were young, muscly and undoubtedly idealistic. As soon as a few words were exchanged between Luke and them, they both made a beeline for the room that Luke was sleeping in. He was made aware of this because as he peered up from the bottom of the stairs, he momentarily glanced both of them pushing his dormitory room door open, while their respective holdalls were slung over their shoulders.

It was a room with two bunk beds in, and Luke had strategically chosen the top bunk for where he was going to sleep, seeing its height as an advantage – in the event of any nocturnal attack.

That evening, after eating a tasty vegan supper, Aslan, who was leading the retreat, undertook a dedication ceremony, which was a way of marking and purifying the space and building they were in. He then suggested if everyone could be as quiet as possible for those who wanted to continue to meditate on in the shrine room. One of the individuals, who had earlier chosen to sleep in the room Luke was in, was named Ben. He was a young man in his mid to late twenties, and Luke could tell from his physique that he worked out in the gym a lot. That evening he was wearing a tight-fitting T-shirt that hugged his pectoral muscles and his wash-board abdomen. His uncovered arms flaunted a display of rippling muscles, with bulging veins tracing a series of meandering paths. The arms had a profusion of different swirling tattoos on their inner sides. He seemed particularly ingratiating, and was continually being apologetic and humble in what Luke sensed was false and fabricated. Luke knew that something was up.

Staying on in the shrine room, Luke decided to meditate further. He did the metta bhavana or loving kindness meditation. Bringing the two individuals to mind, he wished them well. He truly understood why they were acting in this way, because they had been conditioned in this life and all the previous lives in their past. They did not know what they were doing or the implications of their actions - ultimately they were deluded and spiritually unaware.

Even as Luke was trying to settle his mind with these more mellowing positive thoughts, his heart still continued to pump vigorously. He was one of the last to leave the makeshift shrine room, and he thought he might stay up and read. He immediately found that his mind and body were too restless for engaging in that particular activity. Once he had brushed his teeth, he climbed up the ladder to the top bunk, and tried to settle himself down to sleep.

At about 11:30pm, the two young men came into the room. Luke lay motionless and listened very attentively, as if he was straining to hear the sound of a pin dropping. Once the two had both undressed, one of them got in the bunk below him, and the other one was on the top bunk by the other wall of the room. There was a fourth individual sleeping in the room, who Luke believed was a benign presence.

It was a very tight space that they were in, which, with the tension, added to Luke's oppression and dread. The person, who was on the top bunk, would from time to time put his torch light on. Luke was aware of this gesture, and wondered whether he was communicating to the individual below him. Although the person on the opposite top bunk was tossing and turning and moving incessantly, the person below him remained extra quiet and still. Wondering whether the one below him had fallen asleep, he did however hear occasional languid movements and barely audible groans, so suspected that he might be awake as well – intermittently at least.

Would he come through this night, he pondered. Fortunately, he had little to drink that previous evening, so he did not require the toilet, and so was comfortably settled under his duvet for the duration of the night.

After a thoroughly sleepless night, he got up out of the bunk early at 6:25am, relieved that he still was in possession of his life.

Once some of them had meditated that morning, and they all had consumed their breakfast, Luke and a couple of others helped to wash and dry the cutlery and dishes. Once complete, Luke observed Ben sitting agitatedly at the trestle dining room table. Luke pulled up a chair by the side of him, and with legs splayed, in a very masculine and dominant body posture, asked how he had slept that evening. Luke was very aware of Ben's defensive body language. He flexed his tattooed arms out straight, which conveyed to Luke that he found the situation almost unbearable, by being in such close proximity to Luke. He answered gruffly,

"I had a really bad night's sleep."

"Sorry to hear that. I hardly slept at all myself," Luke had become aware when he had got up that morning that Ben had been sleeping in the bottom bunk underneath him, and for most of the night had lain very still. Luke pondered on the implications of this fact. Usually when you cannot get to sleep, you become restless, and ultimately toss and turn throughout the night, generally making a lot of noise. Ben on the other hand had made very few bed movements, even though he could not sleep. Luke did think that this was not normal, and inwardly questioned what his underlying motives were.

He was uneasy about continuing the conversation with Ben, due to the fact that he seemed to be overtly squirming in his seat – so Luke got up from his chair – said a curt, "See you soon" - and left the dining room space.

Taking in a few deep breaths of the wonderful clear air, and surveying the wonderful rolling hills and tree-filled backdrop; Luke was nestled on an old wrought-iron framed bench with slowly decaying timber seating slats, which had a commanding view of the Herefordshire countryside. He ruminated over how the retreat would progress with these two individuals present. If he had a chance he would try and speak to the other person, named Matthew, and just try and be a friendly figure. This tactic could be potentially disarming, and might work in his favour.

As he strolled back through the wooded area to the converted barn, he just paused for a few moments, and inhaled the clean pure air around him. He dwelt on a few of the positive aspects of the retreat, and remarked to himself, if nothing else, what a healthy natural environment he was in.

On entering the dining area, he saw the other individual, Matthew, was seated almost in the same spot that Ben had been sitting in before. Instead of lunging for the seat next to him, like he had done with Ben, he decided to play it cool, and hung around the kitchen area, which was open plan with the dining area. Luke spoke briefly to Ian the cook, who was starting to prepare the lunch for the retreat.

When the timing was right, he chose the seat next to Matthew, and instead of adopting an aggressive and masculine pose, he sat parallel to Matthew and arced his head towards him. Asking Matthew how he had slept, he mentioned how he also had had a restless night sleep. The difference between the conversation between Ben and Matthew was diametrically opposed. Ben had been totally unwilling to speak to Luke, while Matthew engaged Luke in a cordial exchange, and seemed quite comfortable in their chat together – often smiling with occasional outbursts of laughter. It was almost like chalk and cheese in their respective differences. As Luke listened to Matthew talk, he briefly turned his head round, and glanced towards the kitchen area. He noticed Ben leaning his back against the kitchen worktop with his hands firmly planted on the edge of the worktop, and registering intently the convivial nature of their conversation. He seemed almost upset by Luke and Matthew's *bonhomie,* which manifested as a serious expression of incredulity directed straight at Luke.

All the retreatants converged in the shrine room, and Aslan gave a talk about the Buddha's discourse on the Honeyball sutra, to the small assembled throng. They then had a tea break, and opened it out into two groups with a period of discussion. At about 1:10pm they all had lunch. Ben and Ian, the cook, were not to be seen. Luke enquired with one of the retreatants, where Ben and Ian had gone. The reply was that Ben was not feeling well, and had had little sleep the night before, and so he wanted to be taken to the train station by Ian in order to go home early. Luke was sure that his departure was related to him and the events that previous night. He wondered whether Ben's possible attempt to kill him that Saturday evening would again, like the Friday night, be futile.

Luke felt a huge wave of relief wash over him at this news, but wished Ben well for the future. He suspected that he would probably never see him again on one of these retreats, and did not think in any way that he was a Buddhist, or even believed in Buddhist principles. He knew Ben was lost with no real meaning, like a lot of others in this world.

From a fairly mild start to the day, the weather had turned into glorious sunshine with big thick fluffy clouds in the blue sky, to give character and depth to the canopy above. After lunch and washing-up duties, Luke went for a pleasurable walk with a young Polish man, named Pawel. He was quite a quiet and thoughtful man, and they discussed his predicament with his job. He had recently been laid off, and was trying to take the company to a tribunal. Luke was trying to gently and tactfully suggest that he should just move on, and find another job without wasting his time with stressful arguments with his former employer. It was a bee in Pawel's bonnet, and he could not let go of the hurt it had caused him. In some way Pawel wanted to retaliate and perhaps settle or even the score. Luke could not help but think that Pawel was not working from a Buddhist context, to try and overcome, or neutralise his anger and hatred, with forgiveness and love - this potentially being a lesson and training for him. Pawel's key Buddhist angle that he would constantly return to was the principle of mindfulness. Although Luke believed that mindfulness was very important in the development of a human, he would also maintain that there were more riches and methods wrapped up in the Buddha's teaching.

While on their walk, Luke asked,

"Isn't the nature around us so beautiful and alive? Don't you find the textures and different shades of green with the leaves so intoxicating, especially due to the warm sunlight enlivening the whole countryside drama?"

"I do agree with you that it's a very special backdrop, and it's good we're appreciating and being mindful of it, rather than it just washing over us," he said with still a reluctance to be entirely expressive in his response. The houses roundabout took on a magnificent quality, as if they perfectly blended with the natural scenery. They were mostly historic period timber-framed buildings, which suitably matched their bucolic context.

That evening after supper they all partook in a 'puja', or devotional worship. Luke had always responded well to these activities, and threw himself wholeheartedly into the affair. As he sat on one side of the room, Pawel was on the other side, directly opposite, and was stubbornly not getting involved with the recital of verses and the chanting of mantras. Luke wondered whether Pawel thought this activity - to arouse faith and confidence - seemed silly and ineffectual. He realised that Pawel was primarily encumbered by the hindrance of doubt and indecision, which is one of five hindrances, which prevent us from accessing higher or super-conscious states of awareness. They can be obstacles not just to meditation but our lives in general, and they can have damaging results, hampering our willingness to grow and develop.

With a considerable weight off his mind, due to the exit of Ben from the retreat, Luke slept soundly that evening, and he had begun to realise that Matthew was genuinely interested in Buddhism and this retreat. Luke had not spoken much to Aslan, but he was aware that they had, earlier in the week, arranged for Luke to take him to a funeral of his uncle down in Solent-on-sea the following day on the Monday. Luke had decided that Aslan would stay the night at his place, before they would both make the trek down to the funeral.

Luke was really looking forward to this excursion with his friend and mentor, Aslan: a well-meaning and authentic person, and also being able to do him this favour of transportation. Luke was aware that Aslan would have struggled trying to get down there in hired transport. Not only had he heard this news a few days before the weekend retreat, but also Luke was aware that he did not receive much money, and this would be an issue for him. If there was any way Luke could help out his dear friend - this would be the opportunity.

Aslan wrapped up the retreat mid-afternoon with a closing ritual around a circle of cut tree trunk slices in the open garden space at the front of the barn. Firstly, there was a recital of the 'Transference of Merit and Self-Surrender' verse, which encouraged the individual to give up all possessions, personality and merit for the benefit of all the infinite beings throughout limitless space. They then chanted the Shakyamuni mantra, a mantra of the historical Buddha, in a distinct sonorous harmony.

They all then said their goodbyes to each other, and Luke and Aslan left the retreat place, in what was a wonderfully sun-drenched afternoon, with Luke feeling both rejuvenated and uplifted on that last day of retreat.

Chapter 25

Both Aslan and Luke agreed that they would take a walk up one of the Malvern Hills close by the retreat place, after they had left the retreat barn. When they arrived at the car parking spot late afternoon, Luke donned some heavy mountain boots, which would every now and then cause him a wince of pain, when walking. They hiked vigorously up the designated path, and passed by a middle-aged couple with their dog and later on a family of four. The path then fizzled out into a much more steep and rugged terrain. The light was beginning to slowly fade, yet Aslan suggested to Luke that they could attempt to climb the steep hill to the top. Luke was nowhere near as wild and adventurous as Aslan, and baulked at this major ascent, especially due to the time of day that it was.

"Let's go back, and drive back to mine. I've got some soup and toast back that we can have," Luke shuddered at the thought that Aslan might be leading him to danger and peril, but immediately dismissed this idea as preposterous.

Aslan mentioned on the way back in the car, saying,

"I feel on the retreat, Dave did my head in, by always trying to crack jokes, which were unnecessary. There is also another thing about him....he likes to interrupt you, when you are talking."

"I know it's a little disconcerting. It's almost as if he doesn't want to learn from his mistakes or undo his habits," agreed Luke. He had the figure of Ben in his mind, but he was reluctant to say too much, except by mentioning to Aslan,

"I thought Ben was a little weird. I didn't get a good vibe

from him at all. He somehow seemed to squirm uncomfortably in my presence."

"That might be, because you are so intense at times," Aslan said, looking in Luke's direction with a wry smile on his face. Luke responded in an amused way saying,

"I know, I probably do come across as intimidating with my beady-eye stare," and with that Luke looked at Aslan, and made an exaggerated expression with his eyes fixing on Aslan in a mock aggressive look. They both immediately dissolved into laughter.

Since Luke had experienced this second very mild episode in the year, he had also begun to regard a very small number of people in the Vandana movement with suspicion again. He was holding this view very lightly, but it still became an intermittent concern for him. Luke however trusted Aslan as a friend not a foe, but he still could not banish a niggling deep-seated doubt that he was taking a bit of a risk with Aslan sleeping in his flat for the night. When Luke reflected on Aslan's life, there was no evidence at all to indicate that he was a charlatan. Instead he was sure that he was the real deal, yet Luke still felt he was embarking on a leap of faith, letting him enter and stay in his inviting abode.

With them both in the flat Luke prepared some soup and toast, while Aslan made a call to a kalyana mitra of his, the Sanskrit word for a spiritual or beautiful friend. This was someone who was meant to primarily be more experienced and initially wiser than oneself. Once the meal was ready they both sat at Luke's dining room table, and savoured the mouthfuls of food with little accompanying discussion – just a pleasant stillness. After the meal they washed up together, and then Luke suggested they watch an old film, about two struggling actors and their adventures residing temporarily in the countryside. Aslan had not seen it, and Luke half suspected that Aslan would enjoy it.

After the film, Luke asked Aslan,

"How was the film for you?"

"It was a little frivolous and silly, I thought," he replied sagely, while looking po-faced at Luke.

"I particularly enjoyed the parts that the uncle spoke. His language was really evocative and poetic, but I agree some of the other parts were a little silly," said Luke weighing up in his own mind the implications of what Aslan had just said to him. They both chatted for a while, before they both decided to go to bed. His sofa adapted to a fold-out bed, which he unfurled for Aslan, and then made up his bed with clean sheets.

Luke had a relatively good night sleep, but he had awoken in the middle of the night, to go to the toilet. He had spent a good subsequent hour moving restlessly in bed. Knowing that this overnight stay was a test of Aslan's authenticity and fidelity, and if Luke came through then it would be definite that Aslan was a true ally and friend.

With an inward relief and joy that he had made the following morning unscathed, he truly felt that he could now count Aslan, as a definite and bona fide Buddhist practitioner.

Eating their breakfast, Luke experienced a profound feeling of joy and eager anticipation at the journey that lay ahead of them. It was almost as if a chink of bright, beaming light was breaking through from a dark cell of his mind.

He drove down to the funeral, on Solent-on-sea, at an agreeably measured speed, which Luke was now accustomed to adopt, as opposed to his erratic driving near the early part of the year. This earlier driving behaviour could well have been a symptom of his lack of medication. The car's steering was unresponsive, and he puzzled over whether the particular car garage had perhaps tampered with his vehicle, during its regular oil inspection service. So many things around him seemed precarious, but were hanging delicately in the balance, due to benevolent forces at work in the universe.

They savoured some hard rock tunes, while also tuning into Radio 4, and relishing a panel of distinguished and eminent guests involved in a heavy weight discussion about an aspect of philosophy.

They arrived with a little time to spare, and they chose to get a coffee in a local supermarket café. It tickled Luke with amusement to see Aslan wearing some trousers, which Luke had lent him, that were quite clearly too big for him, as he was a few inches shorter in height than Luke. They both chuckled to themselves at the comicality of the situation, and that Aslan was not a character to do things conventionally. He was renowned in the movement, for going on solitary retreats for about two to three months in the wilds of the Pyrenees, and just leading a very simple but austere lifestyle, like some famous guru.

Luke was wearing his now trademark attire, that he had worn to London on previous occasions that year – this time with a white shirt. One aspect of his item of clothing, which was additional, was a red silk cravat, patterned with very small dark blue paisley designs dotted all over the red silk fabric. Only very recently he had bought this romantic looking article of clothing, to complete his exuberant look – being inspired by a Dylan Thomas look. Today was the first day he was trying this look out on inquisitive members of the public, and he experienced an equal mixture of trepidation and joy.

Aslan had given him directions to the hotel where the wake would be situated, the previous evening. Once Luke had dropped off Aslan at the funeral, he made his way to the hotel. On arrival at the venue, he noted that it was an old Victorian building with lots of distinctive features and a commanding view over the sea.

The weather was overcast, but this in no way dampened Luke's spirits, as this day would be a precious opportunity to deepen and strengthen his friendship with his wise companion. One's emotional mood depended on a lot of things, but more than ever it relied on human companionship and camaraderie – what Confucius called 'jen' or human-heartedness. This quality was having a sense of solidarity with all beings. Luke felt that this was, by far, the most important factor in one's health and wellbeing.

Luke made his way to the hotel bar overlooking the bay, and ordered himself an Earl Grey tea. The bar and restaurant space had high, elaborate ceilings and had a bank of tall windows plus a large bay window, within which Luke sat, amongst an array of a few more tables.

He sat contentedly reading that day's broadsheet newspaper that he had bought at the supermarket, while gradually taking in larger gulps of tea, as it progressively cooled in temperature.

He engaged briefly with the waitress, who was wearing thick rimmed glasses, in conversation, commenting on the weather and the hotel's idyllic setting. These were two familiar topics about which, Luke felt, he could realistically connect with her. He preferred entering into dialogue with strangers, who operated in a functional role in his life, than being a cool, aloof and detached figure. He was forever curious about the diversity of human beings, but also the similarities we all shared.

Luke experienced a glimmer of the taste of freedom, and formed a resolution that he would definitely undertake the creation of a book over the following year, and immerse himself in the world of being a writer. This would, above all, give him a purpose, and something to meaningfully do with his time off work. He thought that with the remotest of chances, it might even become a bestseller. Anything seemed possible in this day and age. He was therefore willing to live in hope, and not have his dreams smothered with cynicism and crippling self-doubt, engendered primarily by his parents.

While Luke was ensconced in the bar area, he became aware that the people attending Aslan's uncle's funeral were now descending on an adjoining room to the area he was in. Aslan emerged at the entrance to the bar area, and glanced at Luke's seating place. Walking over to him he said,

"You look as though you are thoroughly enjoying yourself sat there. How long have you been waiting here?"

"About the last three quarters of an hour to an hour. I'm

really enjoying the space and peace being sat here, thanks," Luke said.

"If you want to come through and join us, feel free to do so, or else you could carry on sitting here. There is food over in our section.....if nothing else you could get some free grub. It's entirely up to you though?" Aslan commented, with his body language communicating a blend of sombreness and lightness.

"Don't worry, I'll come through in just a moment, once I've put this paper in the car," said Luke eagerly, but not without a little apprehension stirred in the mix, due to being the obligatory and flamboyantly attired stranger in their midst.

On entering the ornate room that had recently been given a contemporary make-over, he went up to Aslan, who had an awareness of people around him, while still chatting to his father, Terry. Luke's initial impression of Aslan was that he was not particularly enthralled with what his father was saying to him.

Aslan had mentioned before how he struggled to effectively and meaningfully communicate with his father. On seeing Luke approaching, Aslan said to his father,

"Dad, I'd like you to meet Luke, who brought me here. He's an architect."

"An architect! That's an interesting profession. I've come across a lot of architects in my time, working as a quantity surveyor," Terry said with his eyes light up and sparkle with interest and genuine enthusiasm. Luke was equally responsive and effusive.

Luke mentioned about his time working as Project Manager and Architect in the Estates Office at the University of Warwick, particularly because it was a good learning experience on construction techniques. Aslan knew what topics his father was keen on, and, for the next half hour, he let both Terry and Luke be captivated by their discussion on the construction industry – without being party to their conversation.

Luke proceeded to mention that he was about to embark on

a book of his life, encapsulating the events of that year. Terry responded saying,

"That sounds like a worthwhile venture, to be doing with your time off work. Do you think you'll return to the world of architecture?"

"I think I might have to when the money runs out, and I guess the likelihood of making the book a financial success will be very slim indeed," Luke replied, concealing a lightly held belief that the chances of a literary success might be a real possibility, even though on the surface it seemed utterly remote – like the chances of winning the lottery.

Luke clocked a young, pretty and voluptuous woman, who was talking to a small group of elderly people at a four person table. She would repeatedly turn her head in his direction, showing an open interest. A little time later, she moved to a centrally positioned long rustic looking oak table with a group of young adolescents and one thirty-something man around her. Luke parked himself on a seat with one chair between him and her. He then took his moment and asked the obvious question,

"How did you know John?" he said tactfully, thinking she would reply with saying she was a relative. He was pleasantly surprised by her response to him,

"I used to know him, when I was working at a bar not far from here, and he used to be a regular. We got to know each other through there, and then later on, once I'd left that bar, I kept in touch and quite regularly went for coffee with him. Sometimes we would even come here, so I'm quite familiar with this setting... How do you know John?" she enquired.

"Funnily enough, I don't know him at all. I'm just acting as a friendly taxi service for my friend Aslan, who was his nephew," this comment by Luke brought a brief expression of laughter to her, and the afterglow of a lovely rich smile.

"Have you come far?" she pursued.

"I've only come from Leamington Spa. It wasn't a difficult

journey – quite straightforward really," he said. She remarked to him saying,

"John would have loved your dress sense, as he would also dress up colourfully. I really appreciated this quality of his," Luke took from this comment that it was an indirect way of saying she liked the way Luke dressed on this mournful day.

The more they spoke, the more he found himself attracted to her personality, her physique and features. At one point he asked her, if she had come on her own, to which she replied that her boyfriend had brought her here, and jerked her head in the direction of the fairly embarrassed looking man sitting opposite her at the table. Luke was curious to think what she saw in him. He also secretly thought that he would love to be the one taking her for coffee in place of Aslan's uncle that had passed away, if he happened to live in that part of the world.

Becoming conscious that her boyfriend was beginning to move in his seat in a pained fashion, as Luke was patently flirting with her, the boyfriend then suggested to her that they should make steps to leave. At this juncture, Luke also thought it right to suggest to Aslan that they make their way onwards from the assembled gathering.

Leaving the hotel and having said their farewells with Luke thinking it would be more appropriate to give the pretty woman a handshake, due to her boyfriend's beady eyes half-heartedly boring into him, Aslan and Luke both made their way along a few different roads, lined with big substantial Victorian houses, then along a coastal path and onto a pebbly beach. On one side of the very small bay were a series of big boulders huddled together. It was as though they were uniting in seeking protection from the elements. The weather was still overcast. Luke climbed on one of the very large rock boulders, and began to look out to sea.

He started contemplating, like he would repeatedly do throughout his life, when he was confronted with large open views, conveying a tiny glimpse of the immense size of this planet. The vista he saw was only the tiniest fraction of the overall vastness of this globe. He was fascinated by whether the difference in size between humans and the globe, was similar to that of the smallest creature in the world, namely the amoeba, a single-celled organism, to that of a fully grown human being.

In the words of his teacher, Leander: man stands half way between an amoeba and the goal of enlightenment. Man has a choice to make a direct conscious individual effort to grow and spiritually develop, or else languish in a collective group dynamic and conditioning, which ultimately is regressive and reactive - not progressive, forward looking, or ultimately creative.

As Luke sat entranced by the view before him, Aslan on the other hand had taken off his shoes and socks, and was clambering over smaller rocks on the other side of the small bay. He was being playful in a wonderfully spontaneous and child-like way. Luke imagined that he was probably relishing the feeling of aliveness that this contact with the icy cold water was bringing.

While Aslan was being adventurous, Luke suddenly felt spontaneously impelled to stand up on his feet on the big boulder and enunciate in a big booming voice,

"I'm an actor!" He said this with an affectation placed on the word, 'actor'.

It later dawned on him the implications of this statement, and wondered whether the viewing public would think that this statement simply confirmed to them that the way he acted was only a charade, and he was thereby very artfully concealing his true intentions. Luke knew that this idea could not be further from the truth, but he was sure that his action would only plant seeds of doubt and suspicion into the minds of the watching public.

After their time in the small rocky bay, they made their way back past the hotel and into the town. Eventually after a good ten to fifteen minute stroll, they got to a very sturdy and well-maintained wide pier that jutted out into the estuary. It had a white two storey building at the end. As they both ambled past anglers, who were mostly on their own, directing their view out to sea with their fishing lines, Luke and Aslan passed a couple of anglers huddled together, talking discreetly, and eyeing them up with keen curiosity. Apart from the anglers, the area around the two-storey building at the end of the pier was almost deserted, except for a young couple walking arm in arm.

Once the couple had departed, Luke and Aslan both messed about by the building, acting playfully like a couple of mischievous school children. Luke took a few photos of Aslan, with his head in the gap from a timber panel that had a painted sailor's body on it, minus the face. The photos later revealed Aslan displaying a delightfully impish grin.

They made their way back to the main road on the shoreline. There were quite a few coffee houses overlooking the expanse of water, and Luke pointed to the one, which had the most life in it, and also looked the smartest.

Entering the coffee establishment, they caused nearly all heads to turn in their direction. They found a suitable spot by the large white timber framed glass windows. The interior was of a tempered down funky design, with the bar counter made out of a brushed stainless steel finish. There were quirky touches: like a low horizontally accented opening between theirs and an adjoining room. Luke had a view of the bar area, while behind him was a traditional looking fireplace. The waitress, who was probably in her early twenties, smiled in their direction, while Luke and Aslan sat at the table, deciding what to choose from the menu. Like a hawk, as soon as they had put down the menus, she swooped down towards their table to take their order.

"Could we have a pot of Earl Grey tea and some scones please," Luke said with a warm honeyed pitch to his voice.

"Sure - anything else?" she enquired.

"No, that will be all, thanks," Luke cheerily responded.

"Your order'll be with you soon," she said with a big grin on her face.

Luke then spoke to Aslan and asked him,

"I really enjoyed listening to your talk about the Honeyball sutta that the Buddha had famously discoursed on. So, as you said, the mind creates stories about its experiences – especially the uncomfortable and pleasant events. The mind then can suffer from a proliferation of narratives, where it can sometimes spiral outwards and get out of hand, being all-consuming for the individual."

"And yes, as I mentioned to all of you in the group, to prevent the mind from billowing outwards with increasing momentum, you have to bring awareness to your mind, and realise that you need to stop habitually reacting, and instead respond afterwards to any given situation creatively. The key is then, once either the painful or pleasant event has taken place, to try and stop the thoughts from mushrooming, without however blocking, or denying your experience. The most successful method is to let go of the negative stories, while nevertheless engaged in the process of experiencing and observing the difficult or pleasant emotionally loaded thinking. It's not a good idea to forcefully suppress your negative emotions, as that just leads to bottling them up - and ultimately repression. The way I see it, it's like witnessing clouds coming and going in the sky, and yet not fixing your attention on them. As you and I know, it's much harder than it sounds, and it requires a great deal of patience, time and possibly aptitude as well," Aslan remarked, like some great sage master of old.

"Although it's a skill, I think some people have a much greater aptitude than others, and I feel that I'm particularly able to transform unskilful emotions. Although I guess I probably haven't had some overwhelming negative or positive experiences to challenge me recently," Luke responded.

"We're always presented with situations that can cause a mental proliferation of sorts, but, as you rightly say, there are degrees of experience. Do you actually believe that you have more of an aptitude than others?" Aslan asked inquisitively, but with a straight-forwardness.

"Well yes, I really do believe that I've got a greater propensity than most, and it comes firstly from an innate ability, a definite perseverance in practising patience, also from the fact that I've been working on myself for the last twenty-one years, as a practising Buddhist, and lastly it comes from my own particular understanding about the law of conditionality or dependent origination," Luke uttered forcefully and wholeheartedly.

"You might be right, and I'm sure you know your wonderful mind better than anyone else does," Aslan replied warmly and affectionately.

After settling the bill, they made tracks back to the car, and Luke took Aslan back to his community in Birmingham.

At the community building in Birmingham, Luke went briefly inside to go to the toilet. He came back out, and embraced Aslan with a big, friendly hug. Reaching into his rucksack, Aslan produced an object wrapped in paper napkins to give to Luke. Delicately un-wrapping the paper, he revealed a large scone that he had kept from their visit to the coffee house. He had concealed it - unbeknown to Luke, while Luke had gone to the toilet in the coffee house. Luke thought this was a lovely touch from Aslan, as a mark of gratitude for Luke's generosity. Although, it was a very simple material item, it was the surprise sentiment that Luke was really taken by. He had not seen this gesture coming, and was a little moved by his friend's thoughtfulness.

Luke drove back home, experiencing a warm fuzzy feeling stemming from the depth and intensity of their blossoming friendship. For the remainder of the week, he savoured the journey he had embarked on, and now he had no doubt in his mind of Aslan's wholesome intentions. He felt he could now rest easy with this unmistakable knowledge about his wise companion.

Chapter 26

It was Saturday 25th October, and Luke had resolved to venture into London again, but this time he would try a different location to explore, rather than Angel, where he had been before. He remembered how with a University friend, he used to frequent the area around Brick Lane, with its fashionable bars, independent coffee houses and quirky shops. His choice of location was very much determined with how familiar he was with the area, which provided him a degree of comfort and certainty.

Setting off quite early from Leamington to London Marylebone, he arrived at around ten o'clock, and proceeded to Liverpool Lime Street Station.

Again like the occasion before, when he took Aslan to the funeral and wake in Solent-on-sea, he was dressed in his signature attire. This did not come easy, but kept him alive and awake to his moment to moment experience.

Luke ascended the escalator at the entrance to Liverpool Lime Street Station, onto the outside paved milling area. He stopped for a moment, panning his head round in a panoramic movement - witnessing the bustling scene with a colourful array of people and a multitude of vehicles moving constantly along the road. He was conscious that he was very visible to the public, and began to stride purposefully towards the crossing. Taking a trip through the new architecture of Spitalfields Market, he stopped in a coffee house, full of sharp lines of stainless steel, glass and mirrors, that seemed to loudly announce its trendy appeal. He chose a bottle of water for his purchase, as this would be safe ground for him.

Although, he had still not quite adjusted to a more relaxed and positive approach, with the continued threat to his life.

The weather was gloriously sunny again, and this particular coffee establishment had outdoor furniture for customers to sit at. Luke parked himself on one of the outdoor seats, with his back to the store and a view out onto the other seats, the large extended pavement, the road and the backdrop of the tall traditional buildings in front of him.

As he sat slowly taking small mouthfuls of still water from the bottle, he observed a couple of odd looking gentlemen. It was not the fact that they looked odd individually, but the two of them together was, to Luke's mind, a little bizarre. The man with his back to Luke, was probably in his mid-thirties, and he was wearing a suit, a smart shirt and tie - pretty much what Luke expected from being near the city of London. The other person wore a black T-shirt with a logo of a heavy-metal band on the front, and he sported some mirrored glasses, so Luke had no way of telling, who he was actually looking at. His hair was peroxide blond, and was fashioned in a punkish hairdo. He was older than the other gentleman, by a good ten years – if Luke was to hazard a guess.

While Luke continued to glug the water down in fitful motions, it seemed to him that this rock-and-roll looking bloke was taking a very keen interest in Luke. Luke could not be certain, but his face was very much angled directly at Luke's head. Eventually, he placed his mirrored glasses on the top of his head, and Luke then became aware of his gaze meeting Luke's with a distinct inquisitiveness. Luke felt a twinge of anxiety, wondering why this bloke was inordinately fascinated with him. He knew that progressively, over time, the amygdala, which is the part of the brain where the fear receptor resides, was probably diminishing in size, while he was becoming more used to the idea of his life's constant surveillance, and forces trying to attack and silence him. He would continue to meet unsettling experiences with greater calmness and patience, but every now and then his emotions would falter, and he would experience feelings of fear and dread. Luke knew that as long as he kept up his meditation practice, and kept leading his life without obvious constraints, then the extent of the amygdala would progressively reduce in his mind.

Luke left the coffee establishment, and sauntered along the market stalls inside the huge modern building of Spitalfields atrium area. One stall caught his eye, with a sweet young woman with a punkish fluorescent red hairdo, who was trying to sell some of her arty photographs. They predominantly featured areas of London with scenes of streets, people and skies, but of a theatrical flourish with marks of bold colour set against black-and-white backdrops.

Luke spotted the pictures he really liked, and said to her,

"I love the way you've captured the bright red balloon floating away from the little girl, while the girl and the backdrop of the Houses of parliament and bridge leading to it have all been caught in a black and white print." She appeared very grateful, and returned his compliments with a slightly embarrassed but nonetheless warm smile, and replied to Luke by saying,

'Thank you that's sweet of you to say.' He discussed a few of the other pictures, and what specific qualities moved him. As he said his farewells to her, he moved away slowly, like a stalking black panther, by the other stalls, and decided he would get a coffee near Brick lane.

Just before getting to Brick lane itself, he spied a narrow-frontage coffee house, and decided to try it out. He saw that there were a couple of tables that were occupied in the heart of the place. He plumped for ordering an Americano, while being at the front of the store, and then paid for the drink. Luke was then told that the cup of coffee would be brought over to him, when it was ready.

He sat on one of the banquette seats at a two person table at the back of the deep store, and his view of the coffee staff was shielded by a dividing wall between their area and his. Even though there were few customers in the store, his coffee took, what felt like, an age before it was brought over. The person who delivered it was a big bearded bloke with ginger hair, and he flourished a laddish grin at Luke. He laid down a jug of tap water and a glass along with the coffee.

Luke proceeded to taste the coffee. It was utterly revolting, and seemed to stick, like glue, to his mouth. Whatever they had put in the coffee was not what he had ordered. Even so, he polished off all of its contents. Just before he made his exit, and without turning to look at them; they remarked,

"You've not wasted any time with drinking your coffee. You've just downed it in a flash," they then dissolved into raucous laughter. Luke just responded with,

"Yes, it was quick wasn't it," but still not looking in their direction, he made a quick and abrupt getaway. He thought that he would never visit that specific coffee house ever again, and experienced a negative vibe towards the store and all the staff.

Luke quickly glanced at his watch, and observed that it was time for lunch. He had made a plan to go for a pizza at a well-known pizza place. Again this was somewhere he was familiar with from his past excursions into the area around Brick lane and near Shoreditch. While walking to the pizza restaurant, he noticed how he felt light-headed, and how he was not walking in a straight line, but taking an uneven path in the direction of the restaurant. His immediate thought was, 'They've done it! They've successfully managed to poison me.' This was tempered with a quieter but more sympathetic, soothing voice saying, 'Don't worry, you'll be okay. Time will be the healer.' He then thought that if the poison at the coffee house does not affect him, then the poison at the Pizza restaurant might do the trick, as a double-whammy. He truly felt that he was putting his life in the hands of the gods, yet he was continuing to develop unbridled trust and confidence towards those gentle and benign but spiritually powerful beings.

Stepping through the totally glass doorway of the restaurant, which was situated on the corner; it had glass windows on both sides of the corner. The restaurant was pretty full with groups of business people in smart suits, along with quite a few groups of young girls and some couples possibly finding a spot of lunchtime romance. A man in his late forties asked in an Italian accent,

"Table for one sir?"

"Yes, please," Luke said with a subtle fear mingled in with the clarity of his voice. He was directed to a seat at the far corner next to the till and entrance to the kitchen, where the door to the kitchen was discreetly hidden away.

The staff, a mixture of two waiters and a couple of waitresses, seemed generally to give him a cold reception, but he was not perturbed by this, and continued to be as charming and polite to all of them as possible. They were only being given orders by the authorities, and they had been influenced negatively towards Luke with unhelpful propaganda.

After ordering and consuming a pizza fiorentina, and washing it down with a large bottle of sparkling mineral water; he spotted a couple of waiters standing by the entrance glass door, and talking quietly between themselves. Every now and then they looked in his direction with their expressions being serious. Perhaps they were feeling the guilt and shame of their actions, or they could not quite believe what was happening, Luke speculated.

Luke noticed that he was not feeling as woozy, as earlier, and he wondered whether with the time and the space, the poison in his system was being nullified. Settling the bill, he then left the restaurant.

The weather again was sunny with a few thick clouds scudding across the bright blue sky. Heading towards the big piazza, just by the entrance to the new Spitalfield's development, he chose to get an americano again from a mainstream coffee shop to take away with him.

After his purchase, he took his coffee to a stone slab at the edge of the piazza, where other people were sat. Luke parked himself next to a woman, who was in her late twenties. She was pretty, but with a girl-next-door type attractiveness. Seeing as Luke had barely talked to people in the last couple of days, except for purely functional reasons, he decided to strike up a conversation with this woman, sat to the left of him.

"It's lovely the weather we're having this year," Luke said feeling this was the easiest topic to strike up a conversation with. It is funny how, especially in this country, weather nearly always seems like the ideal ice-breaker, to start up any initial dialogue with strangers.

"I wouldn't know, as I'm not from here," she responded with a very pleasant smile.

"Oh, where are you from then?" Luke detected the unmistakable thick German accent in her voice, but did not want to appear presumptuous.

"I'm from Austria, and I've come to visit a friend of mine, who works in London." she said being visibly buoyed by the random engagement in communication.

"I thought you might be German speaking, from the accent. Are you over here on your own then?"

"Yes. Why are you here, if you don't mind me asking?"

"I've given up my job, as I've some inheritance money to fall back on. I've decided that I want to write a book about the events, which have taken place this year, because they have been dramatic to say the least. I also love exploring London, which will definitely feed into my writing material." Luke said.

"What a bold move of yours! I would love to do the same, and quit my job. It's nice to meet someone, who has taken that leap of faith, and actually carried it through," she paused for a second, and then continued, "What have the dramatic events in your life been then, apart from leaving your job?"

He paused for a second, deliberating on whether he should take the plunge and reveal an enticing snapshot of his book that would also expose uncomfortable truths that Luke still found difficult to admit to the public.

"Well…it's about a person, who believes there's a conspiracy around his life and that he is under constant TV surveillance, as a kind of Big Brother figure. The authorities believe he is a threat to the established world order, and are trying any way they can to eliminate him. The other aspect to him is that he has bi-polar, which is a mental disorder."

"Yeah, I know of it," she remarked confidently.

"So the question to the reader is: whatever he is thinking about the threat to his life, is it a symptom of his bi-polar disorder, or is there in fact truth to everything he is experiencing. I will try and show that there is mounting evidence to support his claim."

"That sounds really interesting – maybe even a bestseller,"

"Well I can still continue to live in hope. The dream's still alive for me!"

"Do you know what you are going to call the book then?" Luke had a vague idea, but was reluctant to share it with her, as it had not been fully formed in his mind.

They continued chatting about what she was going to see, while in London, and she became ever more animated in her speech. Luke could sense with her wide eyes, and intense focus on what Luke was speaking about that she was very interested in what he seemed to stand for. After about twenty minutes indulging in uplifting conversation, she said,

"As I mentioned to you, I've been meaning to tick a few of the sight-seeing destinations off on my map. I also need to be back for my friend early this evening, as we're going out later."

"Well, have a lovely time this evening, and try not to get overwhelmed by visiting too many sites. The fewer the better I would say. Quality, rather than quantity - I'd think is the best strategy."

"Not to worry, I'm only intending to see a maximum of two sites, and if I feel tired, after the first place, I'll go and get a coffee somewhere," she replied with a radiant healthy glow enveloping her, like some warm, ghostly wash.

"That's the spirit!"

She jumped up from the seat by the side of him in an exuberant and joyous manner, and turned her whole body to Luke's, shook hands, and said,

"It was really lovely to meet you. You've definitely given me food for thought, and even inspiration for the future course of my life."

"I wish you every success in your life, and by the way - enjoy the rest of your stay here in London, and your night out tonight," said Luke - mixing the profound with the trivia. With that she thanked him, and walked briskly away from where he was sitting, like some confident schoolgirl, who knew that term-time was almost over. For a moment, Luke delighted in the wonderfully arbitrary nature to their brief exchange.

Luke remained in that spot a good ten minutes after she had left, basking in the sunlight, and then was emotionally stirred to venture to the heart of Brick lane itself. He imagined that, as it was a Saturday, he would meet a lively throng of assorted people amusing themselves over drinks, while sat in bars, or perambulating through the street.

One place he wanted to visit was a popular bar, which he knew well from previous times with an architectural student friend. It had an outdoor area that on weekends in good weather would be invariably packed. On arriving, he was not wrong in his assumption, and found it teeming with people. This aroused a degree of anxiety in him, being so flamboyantly dressed, and he opted for the safer confines of the inside of the building – being slightly shaken by the sheer numbers.

Inside there were far fewer people to observe, and he could also find a single seat arrangement more easily.

He ordered a lager shandy from the bar, knowing this was his favourite alcoholic tipple. It was not the sweetness he necessarily enjoyed, but the quantity of alcohol was less and would not be sufficient to cloud his judgement. Yet still it would be enough to slightly quell his frayed nerves, being so outwardly visible, as he was inside the bar.

Once he had been served, Luke parked himself on the raised platform, adjacent to some old industrial looking steel framed windows. With open shoulders and an open stance he looked around the joint, and appreciated the interesting comic book style cartoons painted on the opposite walls to the windows. They depicted both male and female figures for the respective toilet areas. The bar had a grungy feel about it, but it was still well-maintained and looked after. Things inside the space were generally clean and ordered, but in a free and relaxed way.

There was a large party of girls and a couple of guys at a large table. It appeared that this was them just starting their day's entertainment and revelry. They were talking quite quietly with the occasional raising of their voices and sporadic, raucous laughter.

When Luke glanced in their direction, while they were sat to the side, and a little behind Luke's chair, he saw one of them immediately look away from him, and she fixed her attention back to the group. On the periodic occasions that Luke turned to them, he felt as if they were surreptitiously observing him, when he was not looking their way. He just had a hunch that this was the reality. It caused him to feel a little on edge, but the effects of the alcohol were ever so slightly mellowing his demeanour, until just before they were beginning to depart, he had finally become comfortable in their presence.

Luke was becoming aware that the bar area was starting to fill up with Saturday revellers. There was periodic riotous laughter in the bar area. When Luke felt that his ego was being wounded, through what he presumed was their hilarity directed at him, he pondered that they were all entitled to their laughter and amusement about him, and if nothing else, Luke was not getting physically injured. Fundamentally, he saw this as a learning experience of him being buffeted by the worldly winds or factors of praise and blame and fame and disgrace. There were also the worldly winds, of gain and loss, and pain and pleasure, but these characteristics were not as strident in this particular arena.

After sitting awhile, having consumed two drinks with the second being the same as before, he had the sudden and surging desire to dance to the visceral and grungy music that was being played in the space. He would therefore be making an even bigger spectacle of himself than he was already making. Although, the urge in him was very powerful, he thought about the mitigating factors, in that, it was about half-three in the afternoon, and there was not even a dance floor to be had in that space. Although he was brave, even he could not venture into such choppy sea waters as these. He backed down, and mulled over that his decision was probably for the best. It might have been a particularly foolhardy act that even he would find embarrassing.

Luke left the bar, and sauntered leisurely further down the main part of Brick lane. He noticed a quirky, Moroccan looking tea shop with its folding/sliding doors opened wide, to allow an enticing Middle-Eastern looking interior, to be made apparent. Liking what he was seeing, he went inside.

Ordering a green tea, it came to him in a large ornately decorated metallic pot, with accompanying refined crockery. Lounging as he was, on low comfortable seating, he enjoyed listening to tracks from the biggest band of the 60's. The choice of music, which was the psychedelic end of the band's musical spectrum, was one of the other store's attributes that had drawn him in, when he had momentarily stopped outside.

Directly opposite Luke in the space, a middle aged father was sitting with his two young children. He had a full head of hair and donned black thick-rimmed glasses. Looking like the intellectual, bookish type, he was wearing a dark brown, corduroy sports jacket. His expression was one of world-weariness, and he did not seem to be particularly engaged with what his children were asking him. His interest was more focussed on Luke, but in appropriate and discreet intervals. Luke felt a pang of compassion for him and his predicament. Luke felt that this life with children was thrust upon him by conventional mores and customs, and if he could do it differently next time, he probably would. He wondered if this gentleman felt a yearning desire to have the life Luke was leading – one more of the nature of freedom and authentic happiness.

Slowly but surely, Luke was becoming accustomed to the notion that nothing would kill him off, however hard people tried his life would be implicitly guarded by the gods. Throughout his time in the coffee house, the notion of poison in his tea was at the very fringes of his consciousness, and was not making any discernible dent in his faith and trust. After taking a good hour of slowly drinking the large pot of green tea, he paid and then walked swiftly but gracefully back to the station, and then on home.

Ensconced in one of the two person seats in the train carriage, bound for its end destination at Snow Hill in Birmingham, he churned over the day's events in his mind. He mused that on the whole, it had been an enlivening experience - one which was waking him up to a bigger reality around him. A reality that felt fresh and full of vigour and excitement.

Chapter 27

It was a wet Friday morning on 14th November, and Luke had managed to book himself on a last-minute retreat in a former hotel, by a loch, north of Stirling. The night before, he had prepared his clothes and other miscellaneous items into a large faded brown leather travelling bag. He collected his vibrant blue waterproof coat, put on his sturdy waterproof shoes, and then, with his gear, proceeded to lock the house door. Making some final mental checks, he took the series of steps up from his flat to the pavement above.

As he opened his black metal gate, he spied a man, who seemed to fill the confines of the driver's seat of a new white small German-engineered car, parked a few vehicles away from where Luke was standing. His engine was on, and he seemed to be waiting for something expectantly.

Luke had parked on another road adjacent to the one he lived on, and made his way to its parking spot. Opening the boot of his car, he took longer than expected to sort out and arrange the contents inside. Just as Luke reached for the boot door to close it, he was aware that the same white vehicle was passing his car, at quite a slow speed.

Once it had passed him, it sped up gradually to the end of the road. Instead of turning either left or right, it continued on to the opposite dead-end road, and started to do a three point turn, to come back in his direction. It then stopped by the side of the road, a fair distance away, and waited ominously.

Luke thought this instance was very suspicious. He wondered

if Luke had been that bit quicker in closing his boot, and taking the couple of paces to his driver's door that this would have been the perfect opportunity for this lone figure to squeeze the side of his car to Luke's vehicle, while Luke was about to get in. This would then squash Luke's body, and create severe physical injury. Luke would probably double over in agony and fall to the ground, and then this would give the spy a chance to run over his body, and convincingly seal his terminal end. Luke felt that the chances of this being the reality were not remote, due to so many other events happening that year to him.

As he made the long journey up to the retreat place, he started mulling over the series of events that had occurred to him in the past two to three months.

The first episode that dealt Luke a sudden emotional blow, transpired in the early part of October. For a few days the temperature had plummeted, and was close to low single figures. After he had meditated that morning, as per usual, his routine would be to open two of his windows – both one to the bedroom, and then the transom window to his living room. This was deliberately so he could get a good, cross-flow, fresh air circulation through his flat. He had meditated quite early that morning, and at about 7:55am, he was reaching for the transom window, when something unusual instantly struck him with a mild dread. There was a bank of windows to a very wide dormer window at the roof of the terraced house, directly opposite. What was alarming was the middle window was wide open, and what definitely appeared to Luke like the thin barrel of a sniper rifle was being aimed straight at him.

Although Luke experienced a sudden but brief pang of fear, he still opened the transom, and, as calmly as he could muster, carried on his duties without being too shaken by the incidence. This was where he pondered that a sniper would, at the moment Luke was opening his window, have the perfect opportunity available to him to present a direct hit at Luke's head or heart.

As nothing happened, Luke could only conclude that this was just one more area to convince him of extra-terrestrial help, using their disabling magic to safeguard his passage through the world. Luke tried to doubt the veracity of this assumption, but he thought what was also interesting was that it was particularly cold that day, and why would someone living in that flat have the window so wide open, when it looked a particularly cold and un-insulated space.

Another experience cropped up in his mind. This time he had gone to the Buddhist centre in Birmingham, and on returning home at about 10:45pm, he had parked his car a long way up one of the adjacent streets. As he walked past some of the warmly glowing closed curtained rooms, on his left hand side, he spied a house that had the curtains wide open and the owner's TV screen was on full display. What he then noticed, which later became extraordinary and peculiar, was that the TV image showed a figure standing by some windows with a hedgerow in the background, and what seemed like the identical stance and backdrop that Luke was standing in. He could not make out the appearance of the man, but it was definitely a male figure. At the time, he did not take much notice of it, so he did not bother about the details of the clothes the figure was wearing, compared to his. He initially assumed that it was some kind of detective programme that the householders were watching, but later the near identical match of his position and surroundings with those television images gave him a shred of evidence that his life was definitely on show across the country and possibly the world.

He curiously observed that whenever he subsequently walked past that house, the curtains were drawn shut, or at times at least partially drawn, so as not to allow any onlooker visual access to their TV screen.

There was another specific incidence that happened to Luke near the beginning of this month in November, when the nights had been drawing in earlier. It was a Saturday, and Luke was about to settle down on the sofa, and watch a film from a selection he got from a DVD rental place. Before reclining on the sofa, he had made a resolution to wash up his dishes. He found this mild exertion in labour a worthwhile undertaking, before his reward of a carefully selected movie.

While standing and leaning over the sink, and going through a methodical system of washing up, he heard the sound of a low flying helicopter passing overhead. It then rotated and hovered just in front of his kitchen window, a good thirty to forty metres from where he was standing - directly opposite his flat. It had its front angled away from his kitchen window, so that the side of the helicopter was at 45 degrees to the rear of his flat. Luke could not make out any figure inside the machine, but he again imagined that there was probably a trained marksman resting his weapon on a fixed contraption, and was desperately trying to fire a bullet into Luke's head.

This time Luke had a bit more faith in otherworldly figures and their spells that they could cast, so relatively calmly continued on with the small remainder of the cutlery, which he was drying. By the time Luke finished the washing-up and drying, the helicopter was still hovering in the exact location, as before. It was only when he calmly settled down on the sofa, and pressed play on his remote that the noise gradually disappeared, leaving behind a wonderful, glistening trail of peace that pervaded the flat.

There seemed to Luke to be such overwhelming evidence to support his general hypotheses. He truly believed that there were a lot of people hoping for his removal from this planet, due to their much deluded thinking and ideology, but there was however quite a huge section of society in the world, who thoroughly endorsed the actions he lived his life by, and who believed that he was completely genuine.

As he got past Birmingham, he turned his mind to the retreat he was embarking on. He knew there would be something waiting in store for him. GCHQ would have immediately clocked that he had booked himself on this Scottish retreat, and would have sent out their most lethal double-0 agent to be a retreatant himself. Luke thought that this person would have had previous meditation experience, and he believed that the secret service world knew the effectiveness that mindfulness and meditation could bring to their staff's productivity and lives, and ultimately to make their secret agents more effective killing machines – acting methodically and with precision.

While these dark thoughts swilled around in his mind, it caused the palms of his hands to become sweaty, as he alternated between gripping the steering wheel tightly, and opening his palms to allow them to breathe. His body temperature was also becoming warmer. The weather that day was generally overcast, and on occasions it was accompanied by drizzle. It almost felt more satisfying to Luke, when the rain really poured down in torrents, than a lukewarm and feeble rainfall. This might have been dependent on being snugly cocooned in his car, for this sentiment to be aroused.

Luke got to the motorway services near Kendall, where in the past he had stopped off many a time with his father, while being taken to Dundee University. He remembered those times at his *alma mater* with fondness, where he had spent a good deal of his twenties in that part of the world. In the first year at University, he had really discovered himself and slowly nurtured a trajectory that he was going to take throughout the rest of his life. This was one of combining his architecture with his practice of Buddhism, and developing what later became a relatively stable marriage of the two. Although this year in 2014, he had become disillusioned with this specific path of working in architectural firms, as he knew it took away from him the space and time that he could devote to meditation and Buddhist study.

As he stood waiting to be served at the restaurant buffet counter, he acknowledged that he had come a very long way. He had made considerable personal and spiritual progress, and he was starting to find a path that really worked for him, both in meditation and Buddhism, but also in his writing endeavours. He could feel the unbridled passion surging within him with the possibilities that this could bring.

Luke sat down at the edge of a very busy and lively space, with big oak beams cutting across the space, and therefore loosely defining the large open-plan area. Tucking heartily into his macaroni cheese and chips with accompanying baked beans, he savoured the stodgy nature of the meal.

Between occasional mouthfuls, he would stop fixating on his plate of food, and would instead view the assorted clientele, who were collectively chatting and consuming their food. One young guy with blond hair, who was with his wife and child, was taking particular interest in him. Luke met his gaze, and this prompted a smirk and a devilish grin on the man's face. Luke could feel a sharp jolt in his gut. His ego was feeling affronted. Instead of reacting, either by trying to outstare him, or looking away embarrassed, and not meet his glare again - he pursued the tack of looking at him in intervals, while noticing his own emotional response to the situation, and applying wisdom and understanding. This man found Luke amusing - so let it be. Luke was amusing in a foolish way, and he had done many things in his life that would be considered embarrassing and humiliating. So had so many other people, but unlike Luke's life, they had gone mostly unnoticed, and they could be brushed underneath the carpet. We are all fools, but the ones that are wise know that they are fools. Ryokan, a famous Zen monk, who was renowned for being a very wise man, described himself as a 'Daigu', which literally means a 'Great Fool'. Luke could see this statement of Ryokan's, as being paradoxical to people. On the one hand, why was he saying that he was a great fool, if he was meant to be a wise individual? Was it not self-evident that a foolish person could not be wise as well? The way Luke understood it was that Ryokan saw all his foolish tendencies very clearly, due to being extremely aware of his own spiritual devil within him, and the devil's hordes of demons, tempting, seducing, belittling him or whatever evil or foolish action they would throw at him. Ryokan really saw that this would always be in play until one gained enlightenment, or complete release and freedom from the reactive mind. In this respect, Ryokan was very wise to see himself as the great fool.

Luke tried to let go of the issue he was having with this certain individual and just continued, as calmly as he could muster, with eating his lunch. After buying some chewing gum, he left the motorway services, and continued on with his journey to North of Stirling, where the retreat lodge was situated.

Chapter 28

With a great deal of caution, Luke navigated the narrow, windy road leading up to the retreat lodge. To the left of him extended the beautiful loch with a mountainous and wooded backdrop and various houses dotted here and there, amongst the idyllic setting. The weather was overcast, but with no droplets of rain in evidence.

As he approached in his car to the gate of the retreat lodge, he observed a non-descript, bespectacled man of relatively tall build getting out of his vehicle, and trying with a few attempts to keep the gate firmly open. The gentleman had a curious expression on his face. It was almost indicating why could this small thing, like having a gate properly open, not work first time round, and what on earth, am I doing coming on a retreat like this? He briefly looked at Luke, and it seemed like there was an attitude of condescension in his demeanour and expression – yet one which was, at the same time, comparatively restrained.The insidious thought crept into Luke's mind, to suggest that this man – it seemed now wrong to call him 'gentleman', as this word seemed too refined for his look - might well be the secret services deadly weapon in person removal.

His father had told him, when he had been working for the M.O.D that when interrogating spies, in a Whitehall bunker, they struck Jeremy as having no discernible features. They were definitely not the classic Bond character, of good looks, and exuding a debonair charm. They appeared to Luke's father to be just very plain and somewhat boring looking. Luke noticed, as he parked his car and was unloading his belongings, that the lone figure, stationed in the opposite side of the car park, was making a phone call and sitting very serenely inside the comfort of his modest car. He made Luke think that he was like some kind of large deadly venomous viper. One that was cool and calculating, and which would move very slowly and deliberately, waiting for the opportune moment to strike out with a killer blow to the neck, sinking fangs deep into the flesh – and thereby unleashing a deadly poison into the victim's bloodstream.

The retreat lodge was a white house, and had quite a large expanse of garden area in the front part of the grounds. The building definitely had a cottagey feel. As Luke entered the vestibule, and took his shoes off, he was greeted by a young woman, who he had seen from a previous Buddhist festival, a couple of years back.

A vision of her in that previous gathering came back to him. It had been good weather then, and she had been parading around in a revealing T-shirt, whilst wearing bunny ears. The contrast this time could not be greater. She was wearing a patterned greyish jumper and standard fare jeans, and her hairstyle looked far more restrained and modest than her appearance before. He wondered whether this was her growing up, but becoming altogether more conventional and more staid. Luke could think of better things than being cooped up in this retreat place for a whole year. He enjoyed his freedom that was afforded to him - living in Leamington Spa, and there was so much more room for manoeuvre being resident there.While he chatted to the woman, it felt to Luke like there was a thick, dark thunder cloud hanging menacingly over the pit of his stomach. He could not help but be reminded of the ominous nature of the man, he had seen on his arrival.

After sorting out the administrative procedures with the woman, whose bunny ears had now become a past obsolescence; Luke took his large travelling bag upstairs to his room, and dumped his bag on the floor adjacent to the lower bunk, which was on the left hand side of the room. He quickly made his bed, so there would be no ambiguity, as to which bed he had chosen. As soon as he had prepared the final touches to his bed, he walked back along the corridor and then downstairs to the living room. His mouth was starting to feel parched, so he went to get some tea from the dining room area. The long, fairly narrow living room was connected to the dining room, in an open-plan arrangement. Walking through the living room area, you could get to the dining room, which covered a wider area.

The solitary man, who he had seen on arrival, was sitting at one of the dining room chairs, and was looking in his direction. Luke averted his gaze, as he walked past. Immediately, as Luke motioned past him, he emitted a barely stifled expression of mirth. Luke could feel his ego inwardly tensing up with a mixture of fear and indignation. He wondered if the man was thinking that his mission would be undeniably straightforward, and that it therefore seemed to him to be amusing. Or was his hardly contained hilarity, due to all the embarrassing things Luke had done in his life that had been caught on film, to be discussed by everyone at length and ad nauseam. It could however have been another reason, but Luke was not so convinced by any third option.

After supper all the retreatants gathered together in the shrine room, which was in a small rustic outbuilding with timber flooring, which could comfortably contain the eighteen people, who had booked on the retreat. The theme was entitled 'Body Earth Breath', which appealed to Luke's sensibilities, suggesting a grounded-ness with one's body and mother earth, to be all-encompassed by the breath. This intimated to him that a large slice of the activities would involve meditation practice.

As they all sat in an oval arrangement with warm, subdued lighting radiating out from four big candles in the centre of the space, they, one-by-one, went round sharing with the assembled group their names and reasons for being part of the retreat. Over the years Luke had become more at ease with large groups, and he would now rarely get flustered. While he was waiting his turn, he could not help but try and formulate the key points of his justification for being part of this themed retreat. Once his turn had been, where he expressed his fondness for the title, which really piqued his interest; he waited to hear what the lone figure had to say.

It slowly moved round to the serene but suspicious looking man, and he slowly and deliberately spoke, almost as if he was imbuing the principles of mindfulness wholeheartedly. His words were,

"Hi, my name is Mark. I've never done anything like this before, but I thought there is always a first time for everything." This was all he had to say. It was very concise and to the point, and one could say sparing in its disclosure.

Luke discovered the following day, while he sat diagonally opposite him at lunch that he lived just outside of Norwich, on a farm. He had come a great deal of distance, for something, which, Luke felt, did not in any way appeal to him, but as he stated - he was prepared to give it a go. This just confirmed to Luke that there was some Machiavellian plot that had been concocted by the authorities, and Mark was their main protagonist.

That Friday evening, Luke brushed his teeth, and was the first to be in bed in his room. He had still not met his roommate, as their paths had not crossed inside the space. Luke's head was screened by his grey towel hanging over the rungs of the ladder to the top bunk. This gave him a discreet view of whoever entered, without them easily noticing his open inquisitive eyes. The side light of the other person sleeping in his room was on, and Luke had turned his side light off, to wait like some anxious hare in the undergrowth of the duvet.

About ten minutes had passed when the door to the room, which was situated down a tight passage next to the bathroom, opened. The person walked very methodically down the passageway, and then stopped in between the two bunk beds by Luke's head, and paused for what felt like a good half-a-minute. Luke's heart started to immediately pump faster. He had glimpsed with a quick peak that it was the lone man. A fight or flight mechanism was trying to kick in, but Luke just stayed with this uncomfortable experience, and reassured himself that he would not suffer. Slowly but surely, the doubt started to take hold and worm its way into his mind. How could he survive a whole week of this retreat, with the potential assassin sleeping at such close quarters? It was a tall order, even for the gods to prevent from happening.

For the entire duration of the night, Luke was having an inward tussle with the doubting on the one hand, and the confidence and trust on the other. This caused him to have a near sleepless night worrying about the implications, but also desperately trying to soothe his mind with quieter but sweet, whispering, consoling words of comfort.

The following morning, after getting up at about 6:30am, and having a quick shower; he went to make tea before the early morning meditation. There would be about an hour-and-a-half of meditation before breakfast. As Luke had a steady and quite lengthy, daily meditation practice, he was genuinely looking forward to this quiet and peaceful time for his mind.

What troubled him, during the hour-and-a-half sit, which was broken up into two sits, was it was primarily a guided meditation - more for beginners than intermediates or advanced practitioners. The talking by the retreat leader just got in the way of the clarity of his meditation. Luke was curious to know how he would get on with the body movement, in the latter part of the morning. He seriously doubted whether this retreat's theme was really for him. Had he made a foolish mistake by choosing this retreat? It was also particularly wet and cold that day, which compounded his bleak mood.

From about 10:30am to 1pm, they all congregated in the shrine room for explorations into the body and its sensations. Luke threw himself into the exercises that were given. One of them was to act out an activity that you really enjoyed doing - perhaps something creative. After each person performed an imaginary activity, everyone else would repeat that same action in a process of mirroring. One of the guys, a sweet natured man, with a genuinely friendly smile and demeanour, acted out a little abashedly - him brushing his teeth. Luke acted out himself playing the piano, both gently and vigorously, which he, a little smugly, thought was more in keeping with something creative. The minute Luke thought this he also believed he was being foolish for judging the sweet man harshly.

Mark, on the other hand, acted out himself kneading dough. What gripped Luke quite forcibly was Mark had his shirt sleeves rolled up, and Luke was aware of the very powerful strength in his arms and hands, while he performed the actions. His hands in particular were very large and muscular. They typified a brute strength that could easily be deployed, to potentially suffocate Luke with a pillow, while he slept. Again the idea occurred to him: how long could Luke maintain his survival, with the help of the gods? There were so many conditions and factors in play working against him. Surely, there would be a time when the gods would slip up, and there would be an opening for the intelligence services to claim victory.

After having had lunch Luke went out on a solitary walk, still with it being cold and wet outside. His walk was bracing due to the light but steady rain continually pelting his face. He felt thoroughly invigorated on his return. After dropping off his coat in his bedroom, he then settled himself on a sofa in the lounge area, next to an older woman.

Luke got talking to her. She was dressed in an average looking way, but she was very well spoken with a cut-glass English accent. Her name was Daphne. After some introductions and pleasantries, Luke asked her,

"What do you do for a living?"

"Well, I've actually turned my hand to writing books, and I've just completed an illustrative book on horses, both in the cavalry and in dressage. I drew the horses in all sorts of poses, and I must've created about two hundred images of them for the book.

I've long had a fascination with them, and in my younger years I used to ride horses a lot."

"What medium did you use to create the images of the horses?"

"Well, it was a number of different mediums. I did them in charcoal, pencil, watercolour, and also acrylic," she replied with a very upbeat and positive spirit. Before Luke could interject, she proceeded to say,

"I was very lucky to have been given a small advance for the book. It was a delight to receive, even though it was only a few thousand pounds."

"As advances go that isn't bad at all, I'd say," replied Luke.

"Mind you, it was hard work and I had to complete it all within the space of a three month window. By the end of it, I was completely shattered, but the good news is that I actually did it within the timescale," she said with obvious joy and healthy pride welling up from inside her.

"How do you find living on your own? You did say that you live by yourself didn't you?" Luke asked her, seeing the vague similarities with his own life, and experiencing a kindred spirit in her.

"Sometimes it can be tough, and lonely. I don't always have people to come and see how I am. Although, while I'm occupied with work, I'm generally fine. It's when it dries up that I sometimes get despondent. I love tending to my garden, which nearly always lifts my mood, but the hard part is motivating myself to actually get started on it in the first place. Although, once I'm doing it, the positive energy levels flow through me. How do you find living on your own then?" she delicately enquired.

"I'm writing a book myself, and as long as I have that as a project, more often than not I'll be buoyant and content. There are some days when I literally feel that I'd rather be in bed doing nothing, than doing something. It's on those days that the internal battle can be quite immense. There are some days, when I manage to shrug off the boredom, and occupy my time with writing, while on other days, the inertia can be too strong, and I succumb to slumber," Luke said with a resignation in his tone, as he inwardly contemplated the reality of his predicament.

By all accounts, Luke could see and feel that she lived by pretty modest and humble principles, and she was a very grateful woman. She expressed that she was not a Buddhist, but was very keen on the body movement angle of the retreat, having done a lot of dancing in her time. He imagined her to have been a very glamorous woman in her heyday, but her charm and vivaciousness had not been lost, and still sought to exert its influence on those people she met.

After their entrancing conversation, where he mentioned more of his book, and its subject matter; Luke took himself off to his room for a quick nap.

That afternoon at about 4:30pm, all the retreatants assembled again in the shrine room. They all did more acting and body exercises with half of the group performing, while the other half acting as witnesses. This would then be swapped around. The afternoon seemed to drag for Luke, and he was noticing his response being one of pointlessness around the movements. There seemed to be no Buddhist teaching being expounded, or time for quiet meditation, and he was starting to think that this retreat was just a waste of his precious time.He knew that it was his own fault, for not carefully checking out the details of the week's programme. He should have enquired more with the retreat administrators, before plunging headlong into payment; although sometimes Luke went on gut instincts and intuition not on purely rational analysis – and this time, at least, it did not pay off.

That late evening, Mark had taken himself off to bed early. When Luke entered the room, Mark had his side light switched on. He had his eyes closed, and was resting fully clothed on top of the duvet of his bed, with both hands tucked under his head and lying on his side. Luke noticed that he had a box of aspirin on his bedside table and less than half-a-glass full of water.

Getting undressed and into his pyjamas, he gradually wondered if Mark was going to try something out tonight. Could the headache he had, be a way of the gods disabling him for now, and give Luke the respite he desperately needed.

After brushing his teeth he slipped into bed, and waited. Luke's eyes were still concealed by his towel, draped over the bed's ladder rungs, but they were wide open, and he remained poised and alert. With about ten minutes gone by, Mark raised himself from his side, and slowly went to the bathroom. On his return, he lingered to the side of Luke's head board, like he had done on the first night. This time, the duration seemed to be that little bit longer and the potential looming threat hung menacingly in the confines of the room.

Luke felt decidedly worried, and lay rigid in his bed. All the while, over these two nights, he had not spoken to Luke in the bedroom. Luke was admittedly unwilling to speak to him either – the feeling was definitely mutual.

Mark undressed, and then got into bed, and switched off his light. They were then plunged into darkness with just the very faintest illumination from one solitary light outside. Luke carried on waiting, and ruminated obsessively. For most of the night, Luke got very little sleep with a lurking fear coursing through his body, which manifested as a restless tossing and turning under his duvet, accompanied by an incessant inner dialogue.

Gradually, over the course of the night, his mind eased off into a comparative stillness. Only in the last remaining hour or so, did he finally fall asleep. Mark, on the other hand, remained totally silent. Could this have been the same situation, as the previous retreat, when the character Ben made very little movement, but confessed to not getting any sleep – probably biding his time for the right evil intentioned moment to strike with a killer blow or suffocating move?

The following morning, Luke engaged Mark in a brief, "Good Morning," and he asked him how he had slept that evening. His reply was what Luke half-expected him to say, which was,

"I slept very well, thanks – considering I had a blistering headache." Luke was sure the gods had a part to play in Mark's deep sleep and pulsating headache that previous evening. This occurrence had not happened by chance. Luke also thought about how much longer he could bear this close proximity to an assassin – and started to seriously think about an impromptu exit that day.

That Sunday morning after breakfast, they all gathered together back in the shrine room for more movement exercises. It was only about ten minutes into the programme, when Luke made the conscious decision to make a sharp and noticeably abrupt exit from the outbuilding. He went to sit in the quiet room, which doubled as a library, inside the main house. It had a wonderful view over the loch with the waters shimmering, due to the accompanying sunlight breaking through the big, greyish clouds, and everything around him looking fresh and alive. The hardy trees seemed to sparkle and glitter with a magical quality. Slumped in an armchair, he reflected on the previous two days. He was definite about leaving this retreat that day, and nothing would veer him away from this hardened resolution.

After a good hour had passed, he heard the patter of steps making their way for toilet breaks or liquid refreshments. The main retreat leader, Akahana, a mancunian woman, opened the door to the room, and came and sat next to Luke. She sat in an opposing armchair, with both of the armchairs tilted inwards at forty-five degrees to the bay window.

"How are you? Are you not enjoying it then?" she eased in the question gently. She came across as a warm and kind woman, with a lot of bubbly but at the same time settled energy. Luke could tell that in particular her yoga practice gave her this body-embedded attribute.

"No, I'm really finding it difficult to persevere with. I know what you're probably thinking. Why did I book myself onto this retreat, when I knew there would be a lot of attention placed on the body and its movements? I guess it was just my impulsive streak coming out," Luke replied sincerely. After a brief exchange with Akahana trying to offer prudent advice on the merits of staying, and Luke trying to persuade her that it was more than just natural resistance, and he had very rarely experienced it this strongly, she concluded by saying,

"Don't you think you should really just keep giving it a go? Don't you think that this is always the resistance that comes up for everyone, and you probably need to break through this psychological barrier?" she said, trying her best to appeal to Luke's reason and understanding. Luke was reluctant to tell her the other reason why he was keen to leave, due to Mark's foreboding presence in the bedroom, and what Luke thought he might be capable of.

"No, I think I'm now pretty resolute. I can hear what you are saying, but I think my heart is telling me to actually listen to my resistance, and acknowledge it. I've also been sleeping badly, what with one thing and another. Don't get me wrong I feel alright now, but I know my lack of sleep will catch up with me," he said with gentle defiance.

"Well, it's up to you. If you do leave – for the sake of the group dynamic – it would be best for you to leave directly after lunch. Also could you make an announcement, during lunch, of your intentions to leave this retreat? This will allow for a clean break in your parting," she said with gentle and appropriate authority. Luke thanked Akahana for her time, and confirmed to her that he would definitely make an announcement during the lunch period.

He started to feel a little jittery, due to the upcoming little speech, he would have to make. He knew that there were some people, among the participants, who would not take kindly to his decision, while others who would genuinely sympathise. He realised again that these were the worldly winds of praise and blame, buffeting him in this upcoming ordeal, with the latter of the two being, of course, a little difficult to accept.

After Akahana had left, and he collected his thoughts on what he should say, he decided to retreat to his bedroom. Luke was lying on his bed for about ten minutes, when the bedroom door opened. He was surprised and a little perturbed by this occurrence, as everyone, except him, should have been in the shrine room.

Mark entered the space, and he had brought with him two dining room chairs. Mark fumbled a little to decide how the two chairs should be arranged in the space, and then positioned them parallel to the two bunk beds – with them facing each other. As Luke continued to lounge on his bed, Mark sat down on one of the chairs, and started talking to Luke by saying,

"I hear you're leaving us today,"

"Yes, that's right. I'm not getting anything out of the body movement exercises, and the mornings don't give me the chance to do a proper meditation."

"I'm sorry I couldn't get more of a chance to speak to you, as we're roommates. I'm not really sure why I came onto this retreat myself. It's so far away from where I live in Norfolk. I'm not sure, like you, I quite see any point in the movement exercises, but I guess I will continue to see it through to the end of the retreat. It'll be a shame though not to have someone to confide in about the retreat, but such is the notion of change and impermanence – being a very Buddhist concept. I used to be part of this movement in Norfolk a long time ago, in the 70's, and I was fairly instrumental in shaping it in Norwich, but then I lost interest in the movement, and retreated back to my farm."

As he was opening himself up to Luke, Luke pondered on the intelligence of the man. He made a lot of sense, and spoke volubly and with a measure of worldly knowledge. Mark's admission that he had been part of Vandana in Norfolk in the 70's, where there had been sexual scandals just reinforced Luke's belief that he was a spy, working for the British government. Luke wondered whether he had played a pivotal role in the nefarious proceedings at the Norfolk retreat place, considering he described his role there as being 'fairly instrumental' - to possibly undermine the movement's standing.

The thoughts that Mark was sharing with Luke touched darker aspects of his psyche, and they seemed to Luke to be quite revealing of his deeper motivations. He then said to Luke,

"Come and sit down in the opposite chair to me." Luke felt uneasy by this request, and his breathing started to accelerate - becoming shallower and more audible. Was this some kind of manipulative game that they taught at MI5 and MI6 to their special agents? Once Luke had sat down opposite Mark, whose back was facing the window, Mark said to Luke,

"Let's sit here for a moment, and close our eyes." Initially, Luke was hesitant in shutting his eyes, but rather than appearing nervous, he gave himself to the moment, and a little quiveringly closed his eyelids. Luke tried desperately to control his breathing pattern, to hopefully appear more confident than he actually was. Luke presumed that the appearance of calmness in him would hopefully suppress whatever malicious motives Mark might be harbouring.

Five minutes had elapsed, before Luke opened his eyes to see Mark looking intently at him. Mark extended a large, powerful hand out to him. Luke did the same, and grabbed his hand to shake it, in a strong forceful action. They then both stood up, and Mark embraced him, with Luke reluctantly reciprocating, but nonetheless experiencing a chink of light emerging from his mind. Luke seriously believed that he would now come through this ordeal unaffected, while still feeling deeply suspicious about Mark's underlying motives for this brief and peculiar set-up. Mark then uttered to Luke,

"I'm sure I'll see you again, and that our paths will cross in the not too distant future."

"Yes, I'm sure we will," Luke said - secretly hoping that he would never see him in this life again.

"It would be good to get your e-mail address, so we could stay in contact," Mark said. Luke could not be honest and reveal that he did not want anything to do with him, but politely yet involuntarily and insincerely replied,

"Yes, we could do that." Luke then left it at that. The sun continued to break through more grey clouds with wonderful crepuscular rays, which magically echoed the splinter of light emanating from his heart.

Luke made an announcement at lunch, and was surprised to find that he was more confident than he at first expected himself to be. As he had already imagined, there were some who took his decision well, and appreciated the bold move he was making, while others engaged with him as little as possible, and gave him the cold shoulder. Daphne pronounced to the group, directly after Luke's speech saying,

"Good on you Luke! It was great to get to know you. I wish you all the best!" She was smiling radiantly at Luke, having been ebullient in her utterance. Luke was touched by her heartfelt sentiments of well-wishing. After saying his farewells, which always were a protracted business for Luke, he went to the retreat's administrative quarters, and paid for the weekend on a pro rata basis.

Finally, as his car trundled along the windy, narrow lane, with the loch to his right hand side, he could properly say goodbye to another close shave to attempts on his life. Luke knew that they would still keep on coming, but one way or another - he had faith that he would come through these challenges and ordeals unscathed.

Chapter 29

Once Luke had got back from the retreat, he spent the remainder of the two weeks getting a structure in his life, with writing most days in the week, but allowing a great deal of space around his condensed, vigorous writing activity. His parents had booked a night's stay and an evening meal at a historic and captivating hotel in the Northamptonshire countryside for Saturday 29th November. The reason they had done this, was they were celebrating Luke's 40th birthday, which was on the Thursday 27th November. There would only be his parents, sister, her husband Robert and Alexander, Luke's nephew; joining the muted celebrations. Luke's brother, Tom was living in Australia, so was too far away, to make a visit - especially for the occasion.

Before Luke had his main episode that year, he had initial plans to have a much larger event to take place at his parent's home, set up in a marquee. At the time, he felt he and his parents would spare no expense in indulging his guests with fine food and a reputable DJ for the night. Luke had even contacted a band that he had witnessed at a friend's 40th, as he thoroughly enjoyed their playlist and acoustic set. Fortunately, as things transpired, this large 40th birthday bash did not materialise, and this sedate but nonetheless sumptuous affair was organised instead.

Luke had arrived before the rest of the family, and went straight to reception with his overnight bag, where he met a well-spoken, pretty young woman in her early twenties, who Luke was convinced, after listening to her talk, had had a public school or boarding school education, due to her posh accent, and at times, elaborate use of language. She asked Luke,

"How can I help, sir?"

"I've booked into a room for the night. The name's Trevelyan, Luke Trevelyan," said Luke with a full body in his voice, like that of a fine, vintage claret.

"I like the name Trevelyan. It makes me think of a character in one of those British gangster films, like the hero," she said sweetly and self-assuredly, and then proceeded to ask in a non-sequitur fashion,

"I can offer you a choice of three rooms, which your parents have booked. If you like I could take you up to the rooms, and show you all three of them, and then you can decide."

"That would be marvellous, if you could do that," Luke replied. He was not at any point disappointed by the degree of courtesy and efficiency that she displayed – honed from her solid upbringing and education. She gave a synopsis of all three rooms, before taking him up to them. Luke had been to the hotel before - never to stay the night - but just for evening meals, and he had been made aware of Elizabeth the first's sojourn in this historic building. He then asked her,

"Are any one of the bedrooms that you are taking me to, the one that Elizabeth 1 stayed in?"

"No. That one's a bridal suite for a couple, who have their wedding day today. Sorry, if you were keen to take that one," she responded.

"Don't worry. I am not in the slightest bit fussed - just curious that's all."

The first room seemed to be too dark and moody for his subtle and refined tastes. There was a lot of dark heavy mahogany, which gave it a lugubrious feel. The second room was lighter and more airy with natural light coming in from two sides of the room, but it still had a four poster bed with dark heavy wood and assembled furniture of a weighty disposition. Before he was to make up his mind, he was shown the third room. This one was called the

Jane Seymour room. All the bedrooms in the hotel appeared to have names, or definitely those rooms of a grander nature. This particular room felt right. The furnishings were unfussy and light. There was no four poster bed, and it had a lovely view over the rolling countryside. "This is the one I'll go for. It's lighter and less heavy than any of the other two," Luke said with conviction.

"This is the one, I would also have gone for, if I was choosing between them" she agreed, with what felt to Luke like a sincerity in her voice. "Here are the keys for this room. I hope you have a lovely stay. If you have any problems, while in this room, just dial 0 and that will take you through to reception, and I'm sure we will be able to help you."

"Thank you. It's definitely the best room out of the three," said Luke.

"I know I like it the most as well. I think the room has an air of majesty and pomp, but not in an overly done way," she uttered effusively. With that she left, and let Luke sort himself out in his room.

Luke needed the toilet to do a number two. Once he finished, he had two attempts in flushing the toilet, and on the second attempt, he was successful. He got a text from his sister, saying she had got held up in traffic, and she would be arriving at what she reckoned would be 4:30pm. She asked Luke, if he would like to join her in the hotel's spa building, although she could not be definite of her arrival time, due to heavy traffic. Luke told her he would wait, but then after a few minutes communicating with a volley of texts; he changed his mind and walked down to the spa on his own. Unfortunately, he did not respond back to his sister that he had made this surprise U-turn decision.

On entering the spa building Luke felt awkward as to how it operated. He also felt a little intimidated by the few, attractive looking clientele, assembled in their white dressing gowns. He asked at reception with a shade of hesitancy and unfamiliarity, where the changing rooms to the swimming pool were situated. The young black-haired woman, who was covered in discreet make-up and had her hair tied back in a pony-tail, gave him helpful directions – where he sensed she was sympathetic to his slightly ungainly plight. Luke felt under the spotlight, and a bit out of place in these unfamiliar upmarket surroundings – partly because he was on his own, which made him stand out, like some kind of solitary neon light set amidst a sumptuous, historic mansion – and partly due to not knowing the appropriate etiquette and form.

Luke placed his clothes in one of the allocated lockers. The interior of the changing room was of a very high quality specification. He made his way through a narrow passage, and then entered in upon the swimming pool area.

There was a middle-aged burly guy in the pool with a naturally blended shaved head, who was staring at him as Luke approached the stainless steel ladder in the pool. Luke slowly descended rung by rung down into the deep-end of the pool.

Luke was not intent to make this a staring contest, and looked away as their eyes on occasion met. By his demeanour and general physique, Luke wondered if this person would be the individual, who would carry out the evil-intentioned crime against him that night. Had he come with an accomplice Luke thought to himself, or would he be acting as a solitary assassin? Or would there instead be a less obvious candidate residing tonight in the hotel? Luke propelled himself through the water, predominantly swimming breast-stroke in a vigorous fashion, interspersed with a bit of front crawl. He noticed a group of girls in their thirties, who, he imagined, were part of the wedding ceremony. They had joined the swimming pool area, but had then quickly retreated to the steam room – to primarily chat more privately. Had their sight of Luke sparked feverish interest that they felt they needed to vocalise – hence the shelter of the steam room being the perfect gossip refuge?

After a good quarter of an hour of doing vigorous exercise in the pool, he observed the shaved headed man go outside to the

Jacuzzi, where other people were mingling in the warm giant tub. Luke waited a few minutes before following him there.

As Luke lowered himself gently into the whirling, foam-induced water of the outdoor Jacuzzi, the shaved headed man was chatting to a very beautiful blond haired woman. They were talking quietly and laughing discreetly at sporadic intervals. She had given Luke a warm smile at the beginning, while he was gradually lowering himself into the bubbly water, but then she chose not to look his way, from then on in. Could this be the man's partner-in-crime? He wondered if only for the sake of this covert operation that they were acting as a couple?

They struck Luke as being an incongruous match. She probably appreciated the individual's ruggedness and manliness. He, on the other hand, would undoubtedly have been swept away by her sheer beauty and his physical attraction towards her. Whatever could be said about them, Luke found the pair to be deeply suspicious, especially the man's earlier confrontational stare in the pool. He did not buy that they were together, and was convinced that they must indeed be MI5 operatives.

While in the Jacuzzi, he alternated between resting his head on the top edge of the Jacuzzi and gazing upwards at the circling rooks and the great white billowing clouds moving effortlessly and silently across the fading blue sky – while every now and then continuing to pay special interest in this odd looking couple. Not at any time could he make out what they were saying, as their voices were just out of Luke's earshot.

After fifteen minutes of feeling especially awkward and a little lonesome, he walked back to the changing rooms. Finding a hot power shower invigorating and enlivening, he then put on his clothes again, and made his way back to his bedroom.

On entering his bedroom, he made a bee-line directly for the bathroom toilet, to take a pee. Suddenly a deep convulsive fear gripped him. Someone had been in his bathroom, and had planted a number two, amongst a wash of discoloured urine. He knew he had tried to flush the toilet twice, but he was sure he had seen his urine and faeces be flushed away on his second attempt. He was convinced that his earlier remnants had been replaced by clear water. To see not only faeces in the loo, but also urine in the mix, but without any loo paper in the bowl convinced Luke that they had already begun to ominously send a direct message to him. This suggested that the assassin or assassins would be back later.

What was interesting to note was the couple, who he saw at the spa building, had been around him most of the time that he was out of his bedroom. They were probably genuine after all, and whoever was staying here, intent on killing Luke, was not apparent to him. As his dad had mentioned before, the spies were never the ones you expected them to be. They would just be the people, who would melt away into a hazy, mysterious backdrop. Luke steadied and collected himself. He could not mention this to his parents, or his sister, who he had a close relationship with, as they would just consider his conviction to be fabrications of a lunatic. He probably could not even mention this to his closest Buddhist friends. They would view him with caution and mistrust. This made Luke feel alone and vulnerable. What magic could the gods exercise for his death not to occur tonight? If the assassin and their accomplice were given a key, it would be very difficult for them to be stopped. Serious doubt started seeping into his slightly fragile mind. He just needed to try and let go, and relax into the moment.

Having dressed for the evening, in his signature attire, he lounged in the chair in his bedroom with the latest issue of a popular women's magazine. Luke read a piece on meditation and mindfulness, and how its interest with the public had exploded in the last couple of years. The article was saying how everyone seemed to be talking about meditation and yoga at some point in the last couple of years, with a specific searchlight directed on mindfulness. Luke was a little concerned how big businesses were jumping on the bandwagon, to promote greater productivity in the workplace. It somehow did not seem like it was aligning itself with the Buddha's original message of kindly awareness and ethical actions and behaviour. On the other hand, this interest could be seen as a genuinely good development in society's further engagement with Buddhism and its fundamental principles – Buddhism by stealth.

Luke's sister had still not arrived with her husband, Robert and Alex, Luke's nephew. After reading a few more exciting articles in the woman's magazine, which he found much more entertaining than any of the men's magazines, he made his way downstairs to the great hall, which had a very high, lofty and ornate ceiling, almost competing with the fine ceilings of some inspirational chapels. The ceiling was barrel-vaulted with historic beams and the walls were made of stone. It was a hall built in Tudor times, and it also had a large number of paintings with people of nobility from the medieval ages predominantly. Luke ordered a fizzy soft drink at the bar, and made his way back to the great hall, to wait for his sister to, at some point, walk by. There were only three older women in the corner of the large space, speaking in soft, quiet tones. Occasionally, they would steal a look in Luke's direction - averting their gaze, when Luke looked inquisitively back at them. It had just turned five o'clock, and Luke was sat just by the main route through the space, so he could easily clock any passer-by, especially from the reception end, where his sister Rebecca would be arriving.

After drinking the cold, refreshing, sweet liquid for about ten minutes; Rebecca arrived at reception, and caught a glimpse of her brother seated. She came over, holding Alex, who was just over 18 months old, and she said eagerly, and with a big grin on her face,

"Are you waiting for me, so we can go to the spa together?"

"I'm really sorry Rebecca, but I've already been. I should've really let you know – I'm sorry. It was also starting to get dark," Luke apologised.

"That's a real shame. I was really looking forward to having quality time with you in the spa building. I've even been building up to this, while stuck in traffic in the car," she replied with a mixture of wistfulness and annoyance.

"I'm really sorry Rebecca. I was starting to get restless, and then I acted on impulse. I'm really sorry - I know I should've let you know. You've still got Robert you can go with," Luke stated to Rebecca.

"Well, technically he's not allowed to go, as he's not staying the night here. He's taking Alex back home with him, after the meal tonight. I think it's a little unfair of you," she said with rising indignation in her voice.

"Look, let's leave it there. I probably should've waited, but you were taking a long time, and I was becoming more and more restless. Next time we can do it," Luke was starting to get irritable himself. He had not been feeling well with all the events that had been happening in his life that year and especially in the last couple of months, but at the same time he could not share his experiences with anyone. This made him feel especially frustrated and isolated, like some kind of forlorn stray dog, yet one with a great deal of strength and courage.

His sister let it lie, but Luke observed her picking up her bag quite abruptly and vigorously, and letting out a sigh.

"Well, I'll see you at dinner then?" she said with a petulant tone and turned her head towards her husband, Robert, who was approaching them both. He greeted Luke with a firm handshake and then Rebecca and Robert both headed for their room, with Alex now transferred into Robert's strong, protective arms. Luke could see that as a pair they were perfectly suited to each other, and Robert was a thoughtful and courteous individual – not without a humorously playful streak.

It was 7:25pm, and Luke was just preparing to go downstairs. His parents had said that everyone should meet at 7:30pm in the great hall for a glass of champagne to toast Luke's 40th birthday. While they all gathered round one of the central seating islands with a glass of champagne in their hands - Jeremy made a toast to Luke. The upholstered furniture was of upright armchairs and body enveloping large sofas with a bold use of eccentric colours. The surrounding windows to the space were tall and narrow, with a very high and deep bay window on one side, overlooking the grounds and the countryside beyond. Admittedly, at this time of year, it was too dark to see anything outside the windows, although the courtyard on the other side of the hall was elegantly lit with washes of warm yellowish light, from discreetly positioned lamps.

After drinks in the main hall, they were all ushered into one of the many dining spaces by the maître d'. Luke felt especially uncomfortable and anxious, due to not being able to share with his parents the earlier bathroom spectacle. He also believed another attempt on his life would be made, with the cooks trying to poison his food at dinner under the auspices of the government authorities. The atmosphere in the dining space that they were seated at, felt like a heavy weight on Luke's shoulders. It was, as if a dense, pungent smog had enveloped his aura. Although his parents or sister did not comment, Luke could sense that they were tangibly aware of his heavy and solemn mood. Having prepared a speech earlier in the week, he was deliberating when would be the opportune time to present it. There was not a single point during the meal, where it felt right to give the speech.

Luke ordered a starter of goat's cheese on a bed of rocket salad with dressing, and then a fillet of sole for the main course. His father had asked for two bottles of a vintage claret, and this was balanced with a couple of large bottles of sparkling mineral water.

Through the first course, Luke would ponder whether the chefs had mixed the dressing for the salad with a liquid poison. He also questioned what looked like black leaves slipped within the filleted fish for his main course, and wondered if that could potentially be a wafer-thin poisonous substance. Luke, however, did not refuse to eat any of it, and gobbled it all up obediently. If he happened to die, then it had been a good life for him, but another softer voice, like on previous occasions, reassured him that he would definitely live.

He was sure that his role on this planet and in the universe was much too important for him to die so suddenly. He vacillated in mood between thinking that the gods were able to perform magic feats over vast inter-galactic distances, and then thinking with the mind of a cynic that magic was ultimately an illusion.

After the evening meal they were all sat down in the great hall with their coffees having just arrived. Luke decided to give his speech with a mild degree of nerves, as he believed he was going to be overheard by the other guests, with his loud, booming voice. He took out the piece of paper from his top pocket of his waistcoat - unfurled it - and then proceeded to speak,

"I would like to just say a few words to all of you here, as a token of my appreciation. I am so appreciative of how wonderfully you have brought me up. This has been primarily down to the wise counsel and guidance you imparted to me. What with mum's strong family ethics, and Dad maintaining an untiring patience and perseverance in helping me to realise my full potential in most aspects of my life. He has been primarily a mentor, guiding me through those tricky paths of work life, and helping me to become a more rounded individual. Overall, what I love about my parents is their fostering in me a broad interest in all areas of life's rich tapestry. Then there is Rebecca, my big siss, no my darling siss. Since University, she has grown to become a very good, close and loyal friend. I really enjoy her company, and also, in the last year or so, becoming more acquainted with my little nephew, Alex, who is such a delight and joy to behold. Praise would not be complete, if I did not mention Robert. I am very fortunate to have a great brother-in-law, who is a really able and caring father. His enthusiasm and gift for cooking is exceptional, and allows Rebecca to relax a bit more. It is a way of shifting those traditional gender roles towards a more equal partnership. I might have said this before, but I am so glad to have you on board in the family circle. It is a shame that Sophie and Tom cannot be here to celebrate my birthday, but I am sure they are here in spirit, without actually being present in physical form. I do hope that they still love Australia, but it would be nice to see them return at some stage in the not too distant future. Without further ado, it leaves me to ask you to raise your cups and toast to the Trevelyans and the Stuarts." Both his parents and his sister were touched by the seemingly simple but refined sentiments. Just after 10:30pm, they all went to their rooms, except for Robert, who took Alex back home with him.

For the first part of the night, Luke could not sleep, and he moved restlessly in his Queen-sized bed, although from about four onwards he managed to sleep for the remaining part of the night. There would be occasions, between one and two in the morning, when he would hear someone's feet outside his room, and Luke would be on tenterhooks. Then a door would open, and he would be lying totally still with bated breath, but would immediately realise that it was not his. For a good hour in the middle of the night, he got out of bed and read the woman's magazine again, to hopefully pick up any fresh insights into a woman's mind. He normally suffered from not being able to sleep properly in new beds, but this particular night was more extreme than most, being in strange and foreboding surroundings. The following morning, the curtains were brightly glowing in his bedroom. Luke needed to get out in the fresh air to clear his head, and breathe large intakes of pure oxygen before breakfast. After immersing himself in a hot power shower, and going through the relevant ablutions, he dressed with his blue suede waistcoat, and purple trousers, but this time he donned a grey fashionable T-shirt from a well-known brand. He felt confident in this look, and believed that it was an ensemble that he could see some rock star wearing. To all intents and purposes, he might already be someone famous or infamous, depending on one's point of view.

There was hardly anyone up and about, except for one receptionist standing dutifully behind the counter - a different one to yesterday afternoon. She had frizzled blond hair and was very charming towards Luke. She beamed a lovely smile, and said 'hello, how are you?' with an Eastern European accent. He responded with, "I'm well, thanks," in an equally engaging manner, and proceeded to ask her how she was. He found this very short exchange immensely satisfying and savoured briefly the warm feeling it engendered.

While wandering around the grounds of the hall, he wondered if he could tell which window corresponded to his parent's room, and for that matter, which window was the room that Elizabeth 1st had stayed in. This sense of history and links to royalty tickled his fascination. Before he became the Buddha, he was a prince, named Siddhartha Gautama, destined to either become a universal monarch or a great sage. Thankfully, for all our sakes, he chose the latter route, and taught the way to Enlightenment, as a path to liberation and freedom from the reactive mind.

Luke dwelt on the various similarities between his life and Siddhartha's. Siddhartha was known to be extremely friendly with everyone he met, and was commonly termed, by people, as the 'Happy One', once he became the Buddha. This was definitely a characteristic that Luke shared with the Buddha - although an understandably paler imitation. He could still at times find himself getting wound up by certain people, where patience needed to be nurtured and gently practised. Luke knew that the art of 'letting go' was the fundamental principle to be adopted, by a truth-faring practitioner, which the Buddha and all his disciples were. Luke was also blessed with strength, good health, handsome features, and enough wealth, which Siddhartha enjoyed in a more extreme and pronounced way, before he renounced worldly ties. They also both shared an idealistic streak, in their pursuit of the goal of nirvana. There were, on the whole, a lot more similarities than differences to their respective lives.

Once Luke had inhaled large quantities of pure, fresh air, and reflected on yesterday's evening's events, while taking in the landscape and especially the trees around him, he went back to his room. After sitting quietly reflecting in his bedroom, he made his way to the bedroom his parents were staying in, and knocked on their door.

"Come in!" his mother Louise said in a loud strident voice.

"Hi Mum. Morning," Luke said seriously. His dad was in the bathroom.

"What's wrong with you Luke? You were really serious and solemn last night at the table," enquired his mother.

"It's nothing really, just that I feel I'm being spied upon," replied Luke sincerely, but unwilling to give too much away.

"Not this again. You aren't being spied upon. This is just a problem with your mind, and the thoughts you're fabricating. Can't you see the truth of your situation?" Louise said almost pleading with him to delve deep into the chasm of his saner mind. Luke was tired of the knockbacks from his parents, who he knew would not understand his predicament, as they were so immersed in their ordinary worldly existence, to see the truth of the matter.

"You're probably right," he acquiesced for the sake of keeping a semblance of peace and order.

"We know we're right. Trust us. We only have your best interests at heart. We do want you to get another job, even though you've given up two very good offices," said Louise.

"Well actually, I really want to pursue writing a book, and I don't want to just rush into any old job again. I have got sufficient funds available to me to live for a good year and a half, and I'd like to use it wisely. I just want to do creative writing, as I believe that's what my heart wants to do!" said Luke, speaking with passion and a raised volume.

"Don't you think this is another one of your pipe dreams or fantasies?" said Louise slightly mockingly, but with a pained expression on her face.

"No, I really want to give it a go, and I've already managed to complete eight thousand words to the start of my book. I'm already finding that I'm getting into the swing of it," retorted Luke.

"Well, if that's what you want to do then I cannot do anything about your decision," Louise said with a beleaguered resignation.

"Thank you for respecting my decision, mum. I will see you down there for breakfast. How long will you be?"

"Probably about ten minutes or so.....See you down there," Louise mumbled the remaining few words, as Luke left their bedroom, and he shut the door a little louder than he had intended.

At breakfast, Luke could have sworn that he overheard the waiter, who was on duty the previous evening, saying to his fellow colleague,

"Didn't he have the fish last night?" Luke inferred by this statement that although they had tried to poison him, it had been magically intercepted by the gods, and transformed into a harmless substance - hence why Luke felt well that morning, and not on death's door. Luke made arrangements to leave directly after breakfast, and he experienced the obvious lifting of a heavy burden from his athletic frame. The weather was glorious sunshine, which also helped with the relief of his tangible oppression.

Although Luke was very grateful for the expense his parents went to in booking him into this wonderful hotel, he hoped he did not have to return for some time to come. On his solitary car journey home, he left it quiet and peaceful inside, and reflected over the previous day's and morning's events. He could not be hundred percent certain if the chefs had tried to poison him, or that there was someone trying to kill him in his bedroom on his birthday celebrations. One thing he could be sure of was someone had entered his bathroom, while he was at the spa building, and had defecated and urinated in his loo, as a probable signal that they would be back later. This specific detail led him to believe that everything else he surmised - was ineluctably true and correct.

Chapter 30

It was Friday 12th December, and Luke had arranged to pick up Pawel, the Polish man, who he had been on retreat with a couple of months back. This was going to be his final retreat of the year. Luke had started to get to know Pawel over the last few months. He showed Luke around his rented house, which he shared with three others, before they set off on their journey.

During their car journey, Pawel continued to emphasise the idea of mindfulness to Luke. It still seemed to be the only concept he wanted to acquaint himself with. Luke tried to argue or reason with him that although the key to the spiritual life was mindfulness, there were still many more riches to be gained from a deeper exploration of Buddhism. Luke also felt that Pawel's approach to the concept of mindfulness was a little one-sided. He got the impression that Pawel seemed to be only touching the surface of what mindfulness entailed, and felt that his understanding was a little too dry and barren around the subject. Pawel just listened and at times murmured, while Luke made his case. He tried to understand, where Pawel was coming from, but he considered Pawel's view of Buddhism, too narrow and circumscribed. All Luke was trying to do was open Pawel's eyes a little, to the greater and more wondrous truths of the Dharma, or the Buddha's teachings.

Luke let go of the subject, when they were getting very close to the venue. They both concentrated with how to get to the retreat place, with Pawel helping with the navigation through the use of GPS on his mobile phone, and with Luke looking out for signposts to the village. Again, like a lot of that year, it had been a sunny day, but by the time they arrived the light had descended into darkness, interspersed with bright dots of warm light scattered amongst the jet-black silhouetted backdrop.

When they both got out of the car, Luke noticed a palpable stillness in the countryside they were in.

"Pawel, can you feel how quiet and peaceful it is around here? Isn't it just wonderful, don't you think?" said Luke convivially, while looking both around him at the twinkling lights from homes in the distance and at Pawel's soft glowing face.

"Yes, I feel it as well. It feels good, definitely," Pawel replied with a slight hint of emotion in his voice, which he normally did not show to people. Luke looked up to see some prominent bright stars in the night sky.

They both made their way to the small registration building, where Hedvig, an order member, and an older woman called Orla greeted them,

"Welcome to the retreat. It's good to see you both," Hedvig said with effusiveness.

"Hi Hedvig, thanks for the welcome," Luke replied.

"Likewise," Pawel pitched in.

"You'll all have a room to yourself – you'll be pleased to know. Do you require bed linen, or have you brought some yourself?" Hedvig enquired.

"No, I'll be fine. I've brought along my own bed linen. What room number am I in?" asked Luke.

"You're in Room 9 on the first floor, just by the stair door," said Hedvig without looking at the roster.

"That's very perceptive of you. You must have a good spatial awareness and memory," Luke said with a measure of surprise and astonishment.

"It goes with the Buddhist territory," he replied with what Luke caught was a hint of smugness in his facial expression. Why not feel a little proud, knowing the whereabouts of rooms - Luke pondered? It is an art, knowing and remembering the details of one's environment - both immediate and distant.

Luke set about immediately making up his bed, while in his bedroom. Quite a few familiar faces from the Buddhist centre were here on retreat. Daire was here on the retreat. He would enjoy chatting to him, and perhaps spending a little quality time together. There was of course Hedvig, and also Varick, who was a very warm and conscientious practitioner of Buddhism, and a good friend.

That evening, after supper, they all congregated in the long and narrow lounge area, which was a large space just under a series of large oak beam trussed rafters. There were seventeen people on the retreat in total. Once they were all settled in their armchairs or sofas with a soft ambient light cradling them, Hedvig began to speak loudly, but with a tinge of nervousness to his raised voice,

"It feels as if one's going to half expect one of the oil magnates to walk in now to our gathering." Hedvig was looking for a response of laughter, but was only met by silence, interrupted by smirks from a couple of the younger women amongst them. It was odd why Hedvig should feel at all nervous, as he knew most of the people in the room, and he had been leading retreats now for many years. Luke saw that he did not come across as natural, but instead rather stilted and awkward. Somehow, Luke felt that he tried too hard to be popular and ingratiate himself with men and women – especially the females. Luke wondered if the reason he appeared awkward, was perhaps not being authentic and true to himself.

Once they all had reported into the circle, they left for the shrine room for a meditation and a dedication ceremony that always happened at the start of any retreat. That night, Luke slept surprisingly well, and felt thoroughly refreshed the following morning. The theme of the retreat was an intensive meditation retreat with no study or guidance at all – only interspersed with soul-enriching periods of silence.

That following day on the Saturday after a full day of

meditating, walking in the countryside, forging new friendships, while developing existing ones, and eating tasty vegetarian meals; they all rounded off the evening with a seven-fold puja. Luke then took himself off to bed with a light and buoyant heart.

That night, he was awoken to the sound of rotating blades of a helicopter that somehow sounded as if it was landing not far from the retreat place. It was 3:30am in the morning when he glanced at his watch, just after he had awoken, and his ears had pricked up with immense curiosity at the noise. He wondered if it was perhaps landing in their field, as quite a lot of land belonged to this retreat headquarters. The site used to be owned by an oil company, who had owned a large swathe of land as well as the cluster of new and old buildings that were fairly tightly grouped together in this contained sprawling complex. Luke thought it extremely unusual for a helicopter to be landing so early in the morning, and especially in the hitherto peaceful and quiet countryside that they were in. Could this potentially be a crack team of SAS commandos desperately trying to noiselessly storm Luke's sleeping quarters, and kill off, in their eyes, this most wanted of men? Unlike on other previous occasions, Luke felt more robust and confident in this specific trial and ordeal. Each new threatening experience would in some way deepen his confidence and trust in cosmic forces seeking out his safe passage through the world, although, with recent events in the last couple of months, he did still feel burdened by restlessness and a modicum of fear.

Awake - Luke calmly rested in his bed. The noise of the helicopter reverberated for what seemed like a good hour. He imagined that the Gods had magically warped the distance from his sleeping quarters to where the helicopter was stationed. The hit squad would think that they had not very far to run, before they arrived at their target destination, but in reality their range had been increased a thousand-fold, by the God's magical spell.

The last thing that Luke remembered before falling asleep was the continued sound of the helicopter blades rotating in the distance. The next thing Luke knew was that he had awoken just before 6:30am. He collected his sponge bag and towel, and went to the bathroom for a quick shower. When he returned back to his room with the curtain blind pulled down and the light on in his room; he was rifling through his suitcase, deciding on the most appropriate article of clothing to wear that day, when Daire opened his bedroom door. He did not just open it a little, realising he had got the wrong door, but pushed it wide open. Luke was naked and was crouching down on his haunches. Daire's eyes clapped onto Luke's for a good two to three seconds, and then with an abashed face, he stepped back, mumbled a quiet 'sorry', and closed the door evenly shut. Luke immediately thought that this must undoubtedly be an honest mistake on the part of his friend, and he let the incidence wash over him.

At the first early morning meditation on the Sunday, Luke observed none of the resident Buddhists had come to the morning sit. This was unlike the Saturday morning, when all of them were present in the shrine room. Luke pondered on whether this absence could be due to their complicity in last night's helicopter operation. Were some of the Vandana order members perhaps trying to help the authorities, with their mutual aim of removing Luke from this planet?

Later on that morning after a couple of sessions of rigorous meditation, Luke took himself away from the shrine room. Feeling light-headed, due to the intensive nature of the meditation, Hedvig advised him to lie down and bring his focus into his feet and the lower part of his body, to compensate for the giddiness he was experiencing. Luke was glad that he had never gone to the retreat place in North Wales, where one would do intensive periods of meditation. From this little incidence, he was sure that he could not sustain that amount of meditation practice over a week long period. Due to various biological and psychological circumstances, Luke believed that some people were just not gifted in sustained periods of meditation, and they would therefore have to work on themselves in other ways, or meditate for moderate periods at a time.

As Luke lay on his bed, trying to get over his trippy head, he still heard, from time to time, helicopters flying overhead, with their roars receding into the distance. Lying on the bed, he thought this could again be an ideal opportunity for someone to take his life, but he nonetheless maintained a dignified calm throughout.

On that Sunday in the early afternoon, they all gathered outside in a courtyard space, and they had arranged themselves in a circle. Orla asked the assembled throng to collectively recite the verse, entitled 'Transference of merit and self-surrender', in call and response. She then suggested that after that they all repeatedly chant in unison the beautiful phrase, 'Sabbe Satta Sukhi Hontu', which translates as, 'May all beings be happy', until after a few minutes, it would naturally peter out.

Luke observed that when they were saying their farewells, a few of the people appeared to Luke, to be a little hostile to him. One tall woman in her thirties, named Justine, had a very unconvincing smile about her, and she weakly embraced him. She left him feeling cold and a shade suspicious that she might doubt his honesty and authenticity.

*****

It was Wednesday 17th December 2014, a few days after the retreat. He had arrived at the Buddhist Centre in Birmingham for his last Buddhist study group of the year. While sat by one of the many tables in the main café area, he was engrossed in conversation with a mild-mannered German man, called Kurt, discussing how his PhD, in a particular aspect of Psychology, was going. Kurt was relating, how he had had to produce a lengthy document in record time, and this had taken its toll on his stress levels. Firstly, due to the tight time constraints, but also because it was a very important document that would be assessed by senior academics in his field.

After about fifteen minutes rapt in intriguing dialogue with Kurt; Ciaran, an order member, who normally led Luke's particular group, emerged from the corridor adjacent to the café area, and as he came up the three steps to the elevated seating area, Luke said, 'Hello' to him. This fairly amicable gesture was completely ignored by Ciaran. Instead, he chose to talk directly with Kurt in a friendly manner.

Ciaran was a softly spoken man in his seventies, and he appeared as a gentle and humble man, but in Luke's opinion, appearances can be deceptive, and he would now and then show a more harsh and critical side to his personality. Luke could not be sure, but he believed from the various experiences he had encountered over the years he knew him that he was not entirely genuine and sincere – albeit to Luke. He was a particularly intellectual person, and in some ways Luke wondered if this fierce rational intelligence sometimes got in the way of a more heartfelt warmth.

Ciaran parked himself opposite Luke, and very rarely looked in his direction. He wore a very severe expression on his face. The weather happened to have been sunny that winter's day, and Luke asked Ciaran in a kindly way,

"Did you sit out on your terrace this afternoon at all?"

"Terrazza please – not terrace! And no I didn't sit out at all, but just remained indoors." Ciaran said this with venom in his voice, but one that Luke distinctly registered. Luke felt Ciaran just wanted to be obstreperous with him, and whatever Luke had said, he would have responded with a harsh comment.

That Wednesday, Ciaran was not leading the group, but he had just come to say hello. So for the next couple of hours Luke's group would have a different study leader. After the evening, on Luke's drive home, he mulled things over in the car. Could Ciaran's unexpected hostility towards Luke be in any way connected with the events of that previous weekend retreat? It was a possibility. He had very rarely been so inimical in the past to Luke, and it was not as though he responded to

Kurt, like he had reacted to him. Therefore, it did not seem like this was his general mood that day, and by all accounts, it was very uncharacteristic of his normally habitual mild-mannered demeanour. Still, Luke was prepared to give him the benefit of the doubt, and not jump to rash conclusions.

The following morning after Luke had showered, he came out of the bathroom, with a towel draped over his waist, and he checked his phone for messages or calls. There had been a missed call from Ciaran. He had left a voicemail message. Luke thought he might be feeling he should be apologising for the previous evening's events. Instead he said in the message, 'Hello Alastair. It's a lovely day today. I'm thinking I would like to go for a walk. It would be nice if you could join me on this fine wintry day. We could perhaps go to the woods. It would be good if you could get back to me, thanks,' In the message, his tone wavered and sounded false. This made Luke exceedingly wary and distinctly anxious. Ciaran had never before taken the trouble to get to know Luke outside the context of the Buddhist centre. Why was he doing it now, and so soon after yesterday's antagonism towards Luke? His first thought was whether in collaboration with MI5, they would engineer an ostensibly innocent stroll, which would result in secret service agents trying to take a hit on Luke's life, yet again.

A mushrooming story was building in Luke's mind about some members of the order, and his perception of their possible duplicitousness towards him. Had what he experienced, near the beginning of the year, been fallacious due to his mental episode? Or had it in fact resounded with a smattering of truth. Again he continued to reflect on all sorts of characters he had met on retreats, in Birmingham, and in other centres he had gone to, both in England and in Scotland. This time, he definitely was well, and was thinking with a heightened clarity of mind. He was sure the episode at the start of the year had, on the one hand, been filled with a degree of lucidity, but it had also been tainted with a degree of confusion.

He spent the whole of that Thursday and most of Friday reflecting. On the Friday evening he joined an evening's puja with a very small number participating, namely five. He appreciated this small, intimate gathering for his ever so slightly delicate mental state.

Throughout the evening, he mentioned nothing of his intent to leave the movement to anyone. There was a woman at the puja, named Sandra, who Luke had total faith in. She had expressed to him some views that a lot in the movement would have found outlandish, but to Luke's more open mind, were in synchronicity to his own very personal takes on reality. Luke discreetly got her number before she left, and said he would contact her very soon to discuss something that he could not divulge at this present juncture. She had a very open and warm energy to her, but as Luke found out later, she was very sensitive to the way some order members behaved towards her. This would generally be quite painful emotionally for her.

After the evening's puja, Varick, who had been leading the evening's devotional ceremony, would often talk to people with sensitivity. He displayed a genuine quality of kindness, normally manifesting as calm and interested facial expressions and mannerisms. He spoke to Luke softly and slowly saying,

"A taste of freedom."

"Definitely, you're right. You know Varick, I really value you as a good friend that I can trust, and I hope we will continue to have contact with each other," Luke responded. They then both hugged each other warmly and fondly. Inwardly Luke thought that this was a wonderfully appreciative way to part from this movement, so unlike his more poisonous e-mail, near the beginning of the year. He made sure that that evening no-one would know that he was leaving the movement, and pretended to be fully engaged with it all.

The following morning on the Saturday he wrote an e-mail to the ordination team in Norfolk and also Daire, and said,

Dear All

Following certain events that happened last weekend in Herefordshire, and what I learned through my episode near the beginning of the year, plus how one particular order member acted towards me, leaving a very peculiar voice message on my phone this Thursday morning, I have decided not to be part of Vandana anymore, in any shape or form. Before you ask if I am experiencing another episode, I would say I have never felt better health wise, mentally as well as physically. I have come to this conclusion from the evidence around me, and as mentioned before from last weekend. I do not want to go into the reasons - suffice to say - I have been applying the principles of reason, experience and intuition to my experiential findings.

The other notable difference between this and last time, when I announced my resignation from the order, is that I feel a lot of love and appreciation for you all, and not the previous ill-will. A lot of you have been very accomplished teachers, and you have taught me so much useful and helpful material. A lot of you have also been very friendly towards me, and this I have also very much valued.

I will be, from today, withdrawing all contact from the movement, and I wish you all well with whatever you do with your lives. However, it would be futile to try and persuade me to come back to the movement, as I have now made a firm resolve.

With metta,

Luke

Once Luke had sent the e-mail, he went to London on a day's cultural excursion, which he had been planning for a good month. Originally, he had arranged to go with Daire, but Daire had declined less than a week before. This would definitely not prevent him from going, and also he was not sure if he could ever trust Daire again.

Luke had a great day out in London, but one symbolic, and,

one might say, quite mythical event happened, while he was walking to the Tate Modern, just underneath the Oxo Tower Wharf building. As he walked under the arcade, a Far Eastern Buddhist monk, in dark brown robes, appeared from behind the columns and outer wall. With a distinct glow and brightness in his eyes, and a beaming smile, he wanted Luke to have a shining gold card and a bracelet with beads attached to it. The card read 'Lifetime Peace' on one side, and on the reverse it said, 'Work smoothly'. It also had a picture of a Bodhisattva or Buddha-to-be emblazoned on it. He then asked Luke for donations, in return for the gift the monk had given him.

As Luke displayed his cash, which was tightly packed inside a slim metal case - the monk gesticulated, and pointed to his pound notes, expressing, what seemed to Luke, like an urgent plea to part with all his cash.

"Donations, donations," the monk would keep repeating in a jolly and exuberant way. Luke was a little reluctant in donating the rest of his cash to him, although admittedly, he could still use his credit card to pay for a meal at the Tate Modern. Luke did feel a little uncomfortable in letting go of all his physical money, but felt this incidence acted as a spiritual test - so he went ahead and separated himself from all his remaining pound notes. What seemed magical was how he had left the Vandana movement the previous evening, and now on the first day emerging into a new dawn, he had met a truly spiritually developed being, who was unequivocally Buddhist. What happened that specific Saturday morning was a wonderful exchange of positive energy, which made Luke feel totally inspired and exhilarated from his chance encounter. The universe was definitely looking out for his continued welfare, and he knew he would never be alone in this new horizon he was stepping into.

Chapter 31

It was New Year's Eve, nearing midnight - on his own in his warm flat - but without feeling any sense of loneliness. He had spent the Christmas with his parents and then at his sister's house with her family. It was the first time he had ever spent New Year on his own, and for once he really appreciated this solitary arrangement. In his right hand he held a glass of red wine, at the ready, to usher in a New Year and a new beginning. On the whole, Luke was feeling upbeat and buoyant.

Slumped on his sofa, he had been reflecting on the friendships and relationships he had formed over the past twenty-one or so years, of being with the Vandana movement. He did believe that most of them were really trying to practise and forge a spiritual path in their lives. However, a lot of them were stuck with their particular views, based primarily on one person's perception of reality – namely the founder, Leander. Although, Luke agreed with a lot of the principles that Leander espoused, there were more things happening around them in the world and the universe, which had significance and meaning, but did not fall under the radar of the founder's vision. Luke felt that quite a lot of them from the movement did not display a real open-mindedness that comes with genuine spirituality.

However, the overriding reason for his sudden withdrawal from the movement was not how he thought they came across to him in their practice, which he could not substantiate, but the basic worry he had that a certain number of them might want him dead. He believed that this was due to their much mistaken belief, influenced by the authorities, that Luke was some kind of Beelzebub figure – to be completely distrusted. Admittedly, Luke was on a few occasions told he looked like the devil or some demonic presence, but in his case, looks were totally deceptive. If they only knew that his heart was filled with more kindness and love, than so many others would care to give him credit for. If anything his more habitual response to people that he met and spoke to - would be to smile and connect. Like anyone, he had his moments of ill-will, but they would - with a conscious balanced effort conjoined with wisdom and understanding - dissipate into one of stillness and calm.

Could he really be certain though that specific members of the movement wanted him dead? Had he mistakenly interpreted the series of events that took place on his most recent retreat, and the follow-up incidents thereafter? He had been told by his sister Rebecca that sometimes in the middle of the night in her place in the countryside, she would hear sounds of a helicopter flying close by. Could the incidence with the helicopter have been some kind of training exercise for the military, like what his sister had encountered? Had Daire genuinely mistaken his bedroom door for the staircase door? Was Ciaran just in a foul mood, when he came to pop in before the study group on that Wednesday? Had he let his inner unskilful emotions be vented on Luke, as he happened to feel more ill-will towards Luke than the rest of them? The following morning's voicemail message from Ciaran could have been a way of him trying to apologise and remedy the embarrassing display of ill-will on the previous evening. It was possible, and he could not rule it out. What was clear to Luke, though, was he had lost trust towards these two order members, and was reluctant to pursue any meaningful relationships with them in the future.

Over this last year, his world had been wrenched apart, but with that possibilities had opened up to him. He had now been given an opportunity to thoroughly embrace a destiny - one which he was unsure how it would unfold. It was definitely not the malevolent notion of world domination that some might have perceived was his inclination, but instead it would be trying to instigate more harmony and peace in ever wider and wider ripples of influence, on this precious, beleaguered planet of ours.

Ultimately, could it be that his view of this last year's events was seriously flawed, due to a wild and distorted imagination, come about from his bi-polar condition, or was there indeed some truth in nearly everything that happened that year? He could not prove to himself or anyone else that what he believed was, wholly, the objective truth.

As the pips on the radio announced the arrival of the New Year, he raised his glass, and at the stroke of midnight, he inwardly toasted himself with a light and jubilant heart, saying the words: good fortune for the New Year ahead, you being of kindness.

THE END

Acknowledgements

This book emerged initially from a few words of praise from two people, whose opinions I valued and respected. This was as a result of saying some words of appreciation that I expressed to a good friend, who was going off on a four-month long retreat in the wilds of Spain. The two older gentlemen's words of encouragement really sowed the seeds of confidence that I could actually embark on a much bigger challenge of completing my own book. Then, that same year in 2014, the thought came to me that what happened to me in that year were momentous events, and could lead to an exciting read for anyone interested in knowing more about a mental condition, and Luke's parallel spiritual path and journey.

This is where I would like to thank Samacitta Muller for helping with editing and refining the text in the first four chapters of my book. I believe she helped enliven and just sharpen the text, where it was most crucial. Unfortunately she had to attend to an un-well mother, so could not continue with the work on the book. Above all, she brought a freshness and joy to our exchanges.

There is also Sarah Bayliss, a warm and kind woman, who I had met at a Buddhist class. She commented that I probably should not pitch it as a thriller, but instead as a more human interest/ spiritual genre. I was a little reluctant at first to change the genre, but once Paul Rose, a good friend, had read it, and concurred with her statement that he felt in no way tense or frightened in the delivery of the script; I decided to pitch it differently, as a sort of coming-of-age spiritual book. Thank you to Paul and Sarah for giving me these helpful comments on the book, and what really worked for them.

Then there is Adam Ryan, who helped with editing and proof reading my whole manuscript near the end of my book journey. He gave some very welcome feedback at the initial stages, with then latterly a very thorough and meticulous examination of the text, which I very much welcomed. Unfortunately, his work commitments were onerous, and he had to attend to them, so he was only able to give me very helpful written feedback on the first seven chapters of my book.

At the very end of the editing process, I asked Sue Kenney, a woman who I had just got to know at the Buddhist group in Leamington Spa, whether she would like to give me a critique of my manuscript. I think it was the good vibe I got from her that persuaded me to enlist her support. With a very limited timescale upon her, she really rose to the challenge, and gave me some invaluable advice, which has made the text that bit richer. Also I must thank her for saying to me that I should probably go ahead, after a few changes, and just submit it. "Just go for it," were her words.

Finally, I want to thank my parents for being so loving and supportive throughout my time writing, and coming to the view that it was doing me a world of good, yet unconvinced by the financial rewards that might come my way. I suppose in that way it is down to you as an audience to help me along the way in my process of becoming a full-time writer, by buying and supporting this venture. I have poured my heart and soul into this work, and I hope you will all appreciate the interesting journey Luke Trevelyan embarked on during the year 2014.